# Transforming *the* POWERS

# Transforming *the* POWERS

## PEACE, JUSTICE, AND THE DOMINATION SYSTEM

EDITED BY
RAY GINGERICH AND TED GRIMSRUD

Fortress Press
MINNEAPOLIS

Cover design: Brad Norr Design
Book design: James Korsmo

Library of Congress Cataloging-in-Publication Data

Transforming the powers : peace, justice, and the domination system / Ray Gingerich and Ted Grimsrud, editors.
    p. cm.
  "Selected writings of Walter Wink": P.
  Includes bibliographical references (p.      ) and index.
  ISBN 0-8006-3817-4 (alk. paper)
  1. Powers (Christian theology)—Biblical teaching. 2. Power (Christian theology)
—Biblical teaching. 3. Bible. N.T.—Criticism, interpretation, etc. 4. Wink, Walter. Powers. 5. Wink, Walter. I. Gingerich, Ray. II. Grimsrud, Ted, 1954–

  BS2545.P663T73 2006
  261.7—dc22

                                                                              2005037895

The paper used in this publication meets the minimum requirements of American National Standard for Information Sciences — Permanence of Paper for Printed Library Materials, ANSI Z329.48-1984.

Manufactured in the U.S.A.

10    09    08    07    06    1    2    3    4    5    6    7    8    9    10

# Contents

## Part Three. Engaging the Powers

# Contributors

RAY GINGERICH is Professor Emeritus of Theology and Ethics at Eastern Mennonite University, Harrisonburg, Virginia.

TED GRIMSRUD is Associate Professor of Theology and Peace Studies at Eastern Mennonite University, Harrisonburg, Virginia.

DANIEL LIECHTY is Associate Professor of Social Work at Illinois State University, Bloomington/Normal, Illinois.

NANCEY MURPHY is Professor of Christian Philosophy at Fuller Theological Seminary, Pasadena, California.

GLEN STASSEN is Lewis B. Smedes Professor of Christian Ethics at Fuller Theological Seminary, Pasadena, California.

WILLARD M. SWARTLEY is Professor Emeritus of New Testament at Associated Mennonite Biblical Seminary, Elkhart, Indiana.

WALTER WINK is Professor of Biblical Interpretation at Auburn Theological Seminary, New York, New York.

# Contents

# Foreword

## Walter Wink

This book is part of a much larger and growing conversation regarding the biblical language of the "Principalities and Powers" and what that strange language might mean for our own world. Gradually, that language is finding its way into theological, psychological, and sociological discussion. The chapters that follow make good on the promise of fresh insights sparked by "the Powers," and they will in turn foster additional reflections.

The beginnings of that conversation antedate my own writings, in the work of Heinrich Schlier, Hendrikus Berkhof, G. B. Caird, William Stringfellow, and John Howard Yoder, among others. Then there are my writings: first, a trilogy, The Powers, made up of *Naming the Powers: The Language of Power in the New Testament* (Fortress Press, 1984); *Unmasking the Powers: The Invisible Forces That Determine Human Existence* (Fortress Press, 1986); and *Engaging the Powers: Discernment and Resistance in a World of Domination* (Fortress Press, 1992). Next came a number of other books that deal with the Powers, listed in the bibliography at the end of this volume. These writings have in turn stimulated a number of articles and books by authors who have found the language of "Principalities and Powers" fertile and suggestive.

We can safely say that this relatively new discipline has already proven itself; yet, as these chapters show, we are only at the beginning of exploring this rich vein. I am grateful that these authors have been willing to set aside the time and energy to join in the exploration, for it is not just an academic concern. It is one that has already contributed to "Naming, Unmasking, and Engaging" the Powers.

# Introduction

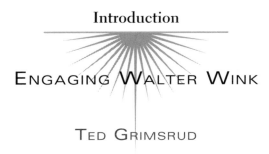

# ENGAGING WALTER WINK

## TED GRIMSRUD

As Walter Wink has shown us, the New Testament offers crucial insights into the nature of the Powers. The Powers are simultaneously (1) a necessary part of the good creation, providing the ligaments of human social existence, the structure and even languages that we require to function; (2) part of creation as fallen, with a tendency to seek to usurp God's centrality and pervert God's purposes for the good of the whole; and (3) part of creation as the object of God's redeeming work, seeking to heal and transform brokenness into wholeness.

Wink is that rare cross-disciplinary scholar and committed activist who informs and inspires. Trained as a New Testament specialist—his first publications in the late 1960s makes still-cited contributions to the study of John the Baptist[1]—Wink began reaching a wider audience with his provocative *The Bible in Human Transformation*,[2] in which he broadened his concerns to psychological and ethical ramifications of how we read the Bible. *Transforming Bible Study*[3] emerged from Wink's work as professor of Biblical Interpretation at Auburn Theological Seminary in New York—work that pays special attention to the study of the Bible among laypeople.

But Wink is perhaps best known for his "Powers trilogy," published by Fortress Press, beginning with *Naming the Powers: The Language of Power in the New Testament* in 1984. As Wink recounts in that book's preface, it originated as a book review, critiquing another book on the Principalities and Powers in the New Testament, with which Wink disagreed. He had already been working on the theme of the Powers for a number of years, originally stimulated by the pioneering work of the eminent Episcopalian lawyer and lay theologian William Stringfellow.

*Naming the Powers* was eventually followed by two additional books, *Unmasking the Powers: The Invisible Forces That Determine Human Existence* (1986) and the magisterial *Engaging the Powers: Discernment and Resistance in a World of Domination* (1992), and several shorter works fleshing out the trilogy's core insights.

1

In these books, Wink argues that the language of "Principalities and Powers" in the New Testament, and similar terms, refers to the realities of all human social dynamics—our institutions, belief systems, traditions, and the like. All of these dynamics, what he calls "manifestations of power," have an inner and an outer aspect. "Every Power tends to have a visible pole, an outer form—be it a church, a nation, an economy—and an invisible pole, an inner spirit or driving force that animates, legitimates, and regulates its physical manifestation in the world. Neither pole is the cause of the other. Both come into existence together and cease to exist together."[4]

> To put the thesis of these three volumes in its simplest form: The Powers are good. The Powers are fallen. The Powers must be redeemed. These three statements must be held together, for each, by itself, is not only untrue but downright mischievous. We cannot affirm governments or universities or businesses to be good unless at the same time we recognize that they are fallen. We cannot face their malignant intractability and oppressiveness unless we remember that they are simultaneously a part of God's good creation. And reflection on their creation and fall will appear only to legitimate these Powers and blast hope for change unless we assert at the same time that these Powers can and must be redeemed.[5]

Wink sees the Powers motif as pervasive in the New Testament. We must not be bound by simply looking for the terms "Principalities and Powers," though they are plentiful in Paul's writings. There are many other terms that speak to power and hence speak to our theme. Wink lists a number of examples. "Rulers and great men (Mt. 20:25); those who supposedly rule and great men (Mk. 10:42); Kings and those in authority (Lk. 22:25); Chief priests and rulers (Lk. 24:20); authorities and Pharisees (Jn. 7:48); rulers and elders (Acts 4:8); kings and rulers (Acts 4:26); angels and principalities (Rom. 8:38); power and name (Acts 4:7); power and wisdom (1 Cor. 1:24); power and authority (Lk. 9:1; Rev. 17:13); authority and commission (Acts 26:12); authority and power (Lk. 4:36)."[6]

We must recognize that in each of these cases, and in all the others where the New Testament writers refer to various expressions of power, political and spiritual alike, both the inner and outer aspects in some sense are in mind. All expressions of power have both. In Wink's view, this awareness is essential for us today if we are to be able to accurately understand the world we live in and fulfill God's calling that we be agents for healing in this world. "Any attempt to transform a social system without addressing both its spirituality and its outer forms is doomed to failure."[7] Awareness of how crucial the application of the Powers analysis is to the Christian mission leads to Wink's deep concern with addressing the questions of worldviews. The worldview that people in Western culture live with inhibits our ability to be properly attentive to the inner/outer aspect of social life. "Only by confronting the spirituality of an institution *and* its concretions can the total entity be transformed, and that requires a kind of spiritual discernment and praxis that the materialistic ethos in which we live knows nothing about."[8]

So, with his Powers trilogy and related writings, Wink has undertaken several interrelated tasks. He first describes in detail the New Testament teaching on the Powers, with close exegesis and examination of specific key words and New Testament passages. Then he looks at the broader meaning of the language of power in the biblical world and in our own, addressing the key question of the place of worldviews in understanding that language and "the invisible forces that determine human existence." And, finally, he provides a perceptive cultural analysis of contemporary North America, focusing on the role of violence in our culture. Wink applies what we have learned through these exegetical and worldview discussions in his critique of the "myth of redemptive violence" and in his profound proposals for how to combat that myth and help create "God's domination-free order" that Jesus inaugurated.

The language of power in the New Testament includes numerous words (e.g., *archōn, archē, exousia, dynamis, kyriotēs, thronos, onoma*), variously translated as "power," "authority," "dominion," "throne," "name." This language is dynamic, unsystematic, impressionistic.[9] The key underlying understanding, in Wink's view, may be summarized by recognizing that the spiritual Powers are not separate heavenly or ethereal realities but rather the inner aspect of material or tangible manifestations of power:

> I suggest that the "angels of nature" are the patterning of physical things—rocks, trees, plants, the whole God-glorifying, dancing, visible universe; that the "principalities and powers" are the inner or spiritual essence, or gestalt, of an institution or system; that the "demons" are the psychic or spiritual power emanated by organizations or individuals or subaspects of individuals whose energies are bent on overpowering others; that "gods" are the very real archetype or ideological structures that determine or govern reality and its mirror, the human brain; that the mysterious "elements of the universe" are the invariances (formerly called "laws") which, though often idolized by humans, conserve the self-consistency of each level of reality in its harmonious interrelationships with every other level and the Whole; and that "Satan" is the actual power that congeals around collective idolatry, injustice, or inhumanity, a power that increases or decreases according to the degree of collective refusal to choose higher values.[10]

Wink's exegetical work in *Naming the Powers* focuses primarily on writings in the Pauline constellation, largely because Paul and his close followers use "Principalities and Powers" language most overtly. However, the underlying assumptions and theology reflected in Paul's writings have parallels in other New

Testament writings. This is most obvious with the book of Revelation's symbol-ism. However, as well, "the synoptic Gospels use the terminology of power almost as frequently as Paul," only they speak more overtly of human or structural power rather than using spiritual terminology.[11] Given that in the New Testament, "spir-itual" and "human" are not separate categories, though, the differences in termi-nology do not reflect theological differences.

The biblical worldview, in Wink's understanding, allowed its writers to com-prehend the spiritual nature of human systems and structures. The language of demons, angels, spirits, principalities, and so on, gave biblical writers a way to rec-ognize that social life has both seen and unseen elements, and that both need to be genuinely taken into account in order to understand the dynamics that shape our lives. That worldview fell by the way with the development of the modern consciousness, and it cannot simply be reappropriated. The biblical worldview, Wink believes, "is in many ways beyond being salvaged, limited as it was by the science, philosophy, and religion of its age."[12] However, the materialistic, mod-ern worldview has proven itself inadequate in taking account of the complexity of social reality since it cannot recognize the possibility that the Powers actually exist. Among other things, as Wink makes clear, when we fail to respect the real-ity of the Powers, we become the most vulnerable to their manipulations—for example, when we are blind to the pervasiveness of the myth of redemptive vio-lence in North American society.

What is needed is recognition that we have the power and responsibility to adjust our worldview to better take actual reality into account. To resist destruc-tive myths we must acknowledge that myths do have power and that reality does involve more than materialism allows for. Wink challenges us to adjust our worldview in order to appropriate the profound insights of New Testament Pow-ers thought:

> A reassessment of these Powers—angels, demons, gods, elements, the devil—allows us to reclaim, name, and comprehend types of experiences that materi-alism renders mute and inexpressible. We have the experiences but miss their meaning. Unable to name our experiences of these intermediate powers of existence, we are simply constrained by them compulsively. They are never more powerful than when they are unconscious. Their capacities to bless us are thwarted, their capacities to possess us augmented. Unmasking these Pow-ers can mean for us initiation into a dimension of reality "not known, because not looked for," in T. S. Eliot's words. . . . The goal of such unmasking is to enable people to see how they have been determined, and to free them to choose, insofar as they have genuine choice, what they will be determined by in the future.[13]

Wink's third book of the Powers trilogy, *Engaging the Powers*, both completes the series and transcends it. Here he reiterates his discoveries about the Powers in the New Testament and provides a quite perceptive, if preliminary, account of possibilities emerging in our postmodern world for a worldview that will help us do justice to the multilayered reality of which we are part. The bulk of the book, then, powerfully applies the Powers and worldview insights to a powerful proposal for peace and justice activism.

Rarely, if ever before, has a contemporary biblical scholar done so much to show the profound relevance of biblical teaching for social life in our current world. This relevance, in Wink's portrayal, lies not so much in particular teachings as in worldview-shaping and consciousness-raising. Along with his cultural criticism, theological analysis, and powerful articulation of the need for thoroughgoing nonviolence, Wink concludes his amazing book with some perceptive reflections on spirituality and hope for the person committed to being an agent for peace in our violent world (obviously drawn from his own wide-ranging experiences).

Like Reinhold Niebuhr's *Moral Man and Immoral Society*, Martin Buber's *I and Thou*, and John Howard Yoder's *The Politics of Jesus*, Wink's *Engaging the Powers* is a classic with a depth of meaning one never fully plumbs even after repeated readings. Among other extraordinarily important insights that he offers, these are several that I believe have the potential to shape Christian thought for years to come:

1. He delineates the revolution going on in our contemporary world concerning our worldview (a discussion expanded in chapter 2 below). He helps us understand what worldviews are, how much they shape our perceptions of the world around us, and how important it is that we seek to revise our modern worldview if we hope to be able to integrate biblical insights into human well-being. Only the "integral worldview" will enable us to remain modern people while also recognizing the interconnections of all things and the spirituality that infuses all of creation.

2. He coins the useful term "Domination System" to help us understand our present context. Only with the aid of the analysis of the role of the Principalities and Powers in human culture may we make sense of why it is that our structures are so destructive of human well-being. The Domination System operates according to the myth of redemptive violence and entraps us all in the amazingly self-destructive dynamic of violence responding to violence, and on and on.

3. Along with providing necessary insight into why we are so dominated by the forces of violence, Wink's Powers analysis also offers a crucial angle that provides an essential sense of hope and empowerment. As we break free from the illusions of the Domination System, we may be freed to recognize the

biblical confessions that not only are the Powers corruptible ("fallen"), but they are initially the good creations of God and, most essentially, they are redeemable. So Wink's analysis, sobering as it is, counsels not despair but hope and empowerment. The Powers can—indeed, must—successfully be resisted.

4. Wink then gives us a biblically based vision of a domination-free order based on the life and teaching of Jesus (a vision since developed in scholarly detail in his more recent book, *The Human Being: Jesus and the Enigma of the Son of the Man*). Here Wink demonstrates how antithetical violence is to the vision Jesus gives us of genuinely authentic human living. As if his biblical, theological, cultural, and psychological insights are not profound enough, Wink also displays some genuine tough-mindedness and honesty in discussing some of the main tensions of and potential problems with nonviolence.

Wink helps us understand both the depths of our culture's commitment, to its very core, to the way of violence (and why this is happening) and the depths of the gospel's presentation of a viable alternative to that way of violence. Anyone who might suspect that Wink's preoccupation with the Powers has primarily esoteric significance surely would have to admit that he makes an irrefutable case for the practical relevance of the analysis he has constructed.

Wink's work certainly deserves our deepest gratitude. Few if any other Christian thinkers in recent memory have done so much for assisting people of faith to apply their convictions to real life. And few if any have done so much to help us have courage and hope concerning the relevance of the gospel.

However, even more than deserving our gratitude, Wink's work deserves our ongoing attention. He has helped unlock a world of theological and ethical resources from the biblical tradition that are needed in our world today. But the work has only begun. The best display of our gratitude for Wink's accomplishment is to converse deeply with it, to challenge his insights, and to seek to continually test them and apply them in ever-broader spheres of life.

---

This volume seeks both to offer tribute to Wink and to contribute to the ongoing task that he has laid out for us. Walter Wink has joined in this next step by offering two more contributions for our reflection. Collected here are papers that were presented at a conference on Wink's thought held at Eastern Mennonite University in March 2001. We have supplemented conference presentations with an additional chapter by Wink.

Wink's keynote address for this conference, "The New Worldview: Spirit at the Core of Everything," begins part 1, "Worldviews and the Powers." Here Wink reprises the introduction to *Engaging the Powers* but greatly expands and updates his analysis of the emerging worldview that promises to help us better understand and apply New Testament Powers theology.

Nancey Murphy's chapter, "Social Science, Ethics, and the Powers," and Daniel Liechty's, "Principalities and Powers: A Social-Scientific Perspective," both consider Wink's thought in relation to social science as practiced in North American culture. Murphy points out that the social sciences are *about* the Powers that govern society: economic, political, social, and legal. However, the sciences themselves are also Powers that shape the culture they purport to study. Since the social sciences have been divorced from the Christian tradition in the modern academy, their analyses are inevitably distorted, as they understand *fallen* social realities as "normal," hence legitimating them. To gain accurate knowledge of the actual world, according to Murphy, we must utilize something like Wink's Powers framework that will enable us to understand the social world as fallen and redeemable. To the extent that the social sciences maintain a neutral stance toward the social Powers they describe, they inevitably *mislead* us about the true nature of social reality. A stance committed to the insights and values of the gospel provides a potentially much better perspective. For example, the discipline of economics justifies egoism when it proposes selfishness as the key to human motivation with the assumption that this is morally acceptable. Or political science after Hobbes also posits human selfishness as "natural" and thereby legitimates a state of "perpetual war" as acceptable for human societies.

Murphy argues that Wink helps us see how social systems such as capitalism and the military-industrial complex have "interiorities" that are in rebellion against God. Social-scientific analyses of these spiritual powers are not neutral descriptions; because of their assumptions they are actually countertheologies. Only by recognizing that fact are Christians going to be freed to bring a genuine word of challenge and healing.

Daniel Liechty presents a more sanguine portrayal of social-scientific contributions to understandings of the world. Drawing most deeply from the work of social theorist Ernest Becker, Liechty offers a basically descriptive portrayal of how social scientists recognize that much of what occurs in human society is motivated by unseen forces and factors of which we are only vaguely aware and over which we have almost no control. Liechty sees this awareness as complementing Wink's analysis of the "invisible forces that determine human existence" (the subtitle of Wink's *Unmasking the Powers*).

For Becker, in Liechty's account, the most powerful of these "unseen forces" is the "generative death anxiety" that arises from human beings' self-awareness that each of us will inevitably die. This anxiety leads to "immortality projects" in order to "deny death." At some point, we risk treating these immortality symbols as if they really do have the power to bestow immortality upon us. An example all too common in North America may be seen in wealth accumulation to an extent far beyond what is needed for mere material security. Liechty argues that nearly all human-caused evil stems from embarking upon these immortality projects. We tend to see anything that hinders our immortality projects (or that we perceive might do so) as evil. As we fight against such "evil," we invariably bring more evil into the world. The Powers have us in their thrall, to use Winkian imagery.

Consequently, Liechty argues, and as Wink would point out, the spiral of evil and violence grows, and we are unable to point to any one person or group of people who made conscious decisions about creating the violent chaos that characterizes our world. Liechty, drawing directly on Wink and on his own Anabaptist tradition, argues that the only way effectively to resist this spiral of evil and violence is to embrace nonviolence. Such an embrace offers potential, at least, for resisting genuine evil in ways that do not add to the evil.

The fourth chapter, Ted Grimsrud's "A Pacifist Critique of the Modern Worldview," attempts to complement and expand Wink's analysis of problems with the modern worldview. Following from Wink's insight that the fallen Powers in our world *conceal*—distorting and hiding from us the true nature of reality and thus keeping us from accurately perceiving that which binds us and that which liberates us—Grimsrud argues that the best antidote to such concealment may be found in the commitment to nonviolence. Such a commitment provides the core criteria for discernment in the face of our culture's worldview that itself serves to alienate us from truth and life.

Grimsrud draws on the work of James Scott and Richard Tarnas to develop a critique of the modern view. Scott uses the metaphor of Europe's disastrous "scientifically managed" approach to forestry in the past century to characterize central elements of the modern worldview. In "scientifically managed" forestry, as in many other areas, we see attempts to dismember exceptionally complex and poorly understood sets of relations and processes in order to isolate a single element of instrumental value. Grimsrud argues that such tearing apart of things for the sake of "knowledge" itself constitutes a violent act—and, following Scott's story, cites the depressing consequences of modern forestry practices as evidence.

Using the term "high modernism," Grimsrud describes key characteristics as commitment to consistent forward movement (progress), absolute truths, and rational planning of ideal social orders under standardized conditions of knowledge and production. A key consequence of high modernism has been a separation between human consciousness and the other-than-human world and the consequent redefinition of nature that opened the gates to massive disregard for other forms of life and, inevitably, massive disregard for human life. Affirming the basic insights of Wink's analysis of the emerging integral worldview, Grimsrud concludes with an alternative to the modern worldview, what he calls a "pacifist way of knowing," based on respecting the interconnection of all life and affirming the "eloquent reality" of life in this world.

A chapter from Wink, "Providence and the Powers," begins part 2, "Understanding the Powers." Here Wink applies the Powers analysis to an extraordinarily vexing—and perennial—issue, the problem of evil. In reflecting on the theme of the providence of God, how it is that God is indirectly involved in the various good (and bad) things that happen, seemingly without clear moral cause and effect, Wink asserts that we must not treat providence in isolation from the Powers. When we separate these two themes, we inevitably end up turning providence into privileged treatment granted by God to the few—thereby making the recipients of hard times morally responsible for their own suffering. However, bad things do happen to good people—and good things happen to bad people. A God directly responsible for those realities is not one Wink finds worthy of worship.

All notions of providence as a kind of divine favor are incompatible with the New Testament understanding of God's providence. Wink points out that Jesus' God played no favorites. The early Christians *expected* to be assaulted by the Powers. It would have been unthinkable of them to ask, "Why do bad things happen to good people?" They believed that truly good people are people who confront the Powers and suffer consequences as a result. History is full of examples of "things working together" for the sake of evil as well as good. Wink cites the rise of Adolf Hitler as an example of "all things working together" for *Hitler's* good. This is to say that providence is not simply a gracious intervention. Wink asserts that it can also serve the malevolent goals of the Powers. Providence is merely one of the spiritual facts built by God into creation, to be used for life or for death, however we choose. After these reflections on providence, Wink concludes with a strong affirmation of human responsibility. When evil Powers are strong and those who should be in the vanguard of spiritual opposition are silent, God is no more able to vanquish evil than the body is able to reject cancer cells when the immune system is suppressed.

Nancey Murphy's second chapter, "Traditions, Practices, and the Powers," addresses epistemological issues. She refers to the common criticism of modern epistemology as having an overly individualistic orientation, drawing on the thought of Alasdair MacIntyre, whom she believes provides the best resources in our time for thinking about rationality and knowledge. However, even MacIntyre is overly optimistic in his account of social practices, even as he perceptively makes the case for their importance for epistemology.

In Murphy's view, MacIntyre's narrative-based approach to testing truth claims provides a much-needed alternative to relativism and absolutism. He points out that knowledge comes from social practices that aim at truth. His overly optimistic approach to these issues, though, emerges when one contrasts his approach with Michel Foucault's, who emphasizes (to a large degree, correctly, in Murphy's view) that social practices aim for social control. In light of Foucault's argument, MacIntyre is seen as ignoring the distorting elements of the socially embodied intellect.

Murphy at this point brings in the Powers analysis of Wink, along with a parallel analysis from theologian James McClendon. Wink and McClendon help us see that the social forces that shape our knowing (the Powers) are indeed corrupted (à la Foucault) but at the same time are necessary for human well-being and are transformable. Applying the Powers analysis to thinking about the social embeddedness of learning leads Murphy to argue for the centrality of non-violence and other social practices characteristic of the Radical Reformation for what she calls "Christian epistemic practices"—that is, contrary to MacIntyre, we need to recognize the *fallenness* of the Powers, the need to be suspicious of the social practices that shape our knowing and the awareness that those practices need to be transformed. Contrary to Foucault, we may believe that such transformation is a possibility. Along with Wink and McClendon, Murphy affirms the practice of nonviolence as central to how this transformation might happen.

In part 2, chapter 7, Willard Swartley's "Jesus Christ: Victor over Evil," provides a comprehensive introduction to the Powers theology in the New Testament and the early church—and the ways that theology shaped the practices of the first Christians. Swartley understands his summary to be largely compatible with Wink's analysis, though he does portray the Powers more clearly as being aligned with evil forces than does Wink's more nuanced argument. Swartley, who does not engage Wink's worldview analysis at the level of hermeneutics, directly applies first-century understandings of the conflict between God and evil to the present. He sees the conflict between God and the demonic realm as the Bible's central motif. God is portrayed in the Bible as, at the same time, Peacemaker and Divine Warrior. The forces of evil, which Swartley understands as personal beings (much more than does Wink), manifest themselves both politically and spiritually.

Jesus' entire ministry centered on the struggle with evil powers, as evidenced by the centrality of exorcism and healing among Jesus' mighty deeds. Ultimately, though, Jesus' victory over the Powers was won through his faithful obedience in accepting his death through crucifixion and in trusting in God's faithfulness; the trust was vindicated in God's raising Jesus from the dead. This is to say, Jesus' way to victory was through nonviolence. The basic message of Paul's proclamation focused on Jesus' victory through cross and resurrection. Swartley reads Paul as emphasizing that God's salvation in Jesus Christ is the only power that delivers us from the Powers of darkness. By the power of this gospel alone can humans be delivered from the bondages of sin, evil, devil, and demons.

The message of Jesus and Paul shaped the lives of the next several generations of Christians. Swartley presents the early Christians as believing that it was not their task to defeat the Powers of evil themselves, but rather simply to manifest, through their common life as a contrast society to their surrounding violent world, the victory Jesus had already won. In particular, Swartley discusses the early church's practices of exorcism, nonviolence, charity, and transformative worship as central ways these people lived out the already-achieved victory of Jesus over the Powers of evil.

Completing part 2, Ray Gingerich's "The Economics and Politics of Violence" challenges us to engage the Powers of economic oppression (covert violence) and warfare (overt violence) in transformative ways in line with the politics of Jesus. Gingerich looks at a fascinating historical moment, the Peasants' War in Western Europe during the sixteenth century, as a case study of the Powers running amok and at least somewhat successfully redeemed through costly Christian witness. The Peasants' War was fought between the princes of Germany and Austria, strongly supported by Martin Luther, and the peasants, led by Thomas Müntzer. A group of peasants issued an edict, the Twelve Articles, that articulated a theology for social transformation. However, at this point, they understood that the transformation might be achieved through military action. Their violent revolt was smashed, and out of the rubble a paradigm shift emerged wherein many of those who had supported the war turned to a combination of gospel-centered nonviolence and economic sharing.

Gingerich, broadening Wink's analysis of the Powers by drawing on Clifford Geertz and Thomas Kuhn, uses this case study to illustrate the religious elements of both trust in warfare and the economics of nascent capitalism that allow for terrible oppression. These are "Powers running amok." However, as sad a story as the Peasants' War might be, its aftermath provides hope that the Powers may successfully be resisted when nonviolence and communal solidarity are combined.

In part 3, "Engaging the Powers," Glen Stassen seeks to broaden and deepen Wink's insights concerning the "third way of Jesus," in his chapter, "Jesus' Way of Transforming Initiatives and Just Peacemaking Theory." Stassen strongly affirms Wink's insights about Jesus' offering a creative alternative to either "fight or flight." He agrees with Wink's reading of Matt 5:38ff. — asserting that Jesus indeed had in mind creative and society-changing action. Stassen goes further, though, in suggesting that the "turn the other cheek" text reflects a deeper structure in Jesus' Sermon on the Mount. Stassen argues that from Matt 5:21 through Matt 7:12 Jesus' teaching is structured as fourteen sets of threefold teachings. Each set begins with a statement of conventional piety (e.g., "take an eye for an eye"), followed by the diagnosis of a vicious cycle the traditional teaching establishes (e.g., "to retaliate by evil means"). Concluding each set, Jesus offers a transforming initiative that seeks to create an entirely new, peaceable situation (e.g., "turn the other cheek" — understood as Wink does as an act of creative resistance to oppression).

The transformative initiatives that Jesus proposes seek to change human beings' ways of relating, hoping to give his followers alternatives to giving in or fighting back and hoping thereby also to change the ways our enemies relate to us. The goal is to transform hostility and conflict into justice and peacemaking. Stassen then summarizes work he has been involved in with an ecumenical group of Christian ethicists to develop a just peacemaking theory that would bring together pacifists and those from within the just-war tradition to build on their common convictions. He outlines ten just peacemaking practices that reflect, to a large extent, the general thrust of Jesus' transforming initiatives. Stassen writes with hope of the profound relevance of these transforming initiatives to our political world today, giving numerous examples of their fruitfulness.

Willard Swartley's second chapter, "Resistance and Nonresistance: When and How?" picks up on Wink's critique of "pacifism" (or "nonresistance") for being too passive. Swartley defends the more traditional Mennonite stance of nonresistance (with nuances) but argues that a better term for what he understands to be the biblical view would be "nonretaliation." For Swartley, the New Testament concerns itself much more with "nonretaliation" than with nonviolent resistance. He focuses especially on writings in the Pauline tradition, most of all the letter to the Ephesians and the call for Christians to partake in spiritual warfare as an alternative to military violence. Christians are called upon to overcome evil with good—that is, we are called not only not to resist evil using evil means (nonresistance), but to fight against evil using appropriate means.

When the writings in the Pauline tradition focus on spiritual warfare (see, most clearly, Ephesians 6), they carry on the message of Jesus in his confrontation with demonic powers. The New Testament, then, does call Christians to confront evil—but insists that such confrontation take appropriate forms. Spiritual warfare centers on prayer, on servanthood, on forgiveness; hence, it is more concerned with remaining free from coercion than with any exertion of human self-will.

Swartley does mention justice as an appropriate concern for Christian nonretaliation, but he asserts that this must be "God's justice," not human justice. The Mennonite nonresistance tradition, though embracing much that is consistent with the New Testament emphasis, needs to be broadened to be more attentive to justice concerns. However, he believes that justice-seeking, activist, nonviolent resistance tends not to take seriously enough the New Testament call upon disciples to avoid coercive activities.

In the last chapter, "The Kind of Justice Jesus Cares About," Glen Stassen seeks to complement Wink's work by fleshing out an area that Wink has not paid close attention to—thinking self-consciously about justice in an unjust world. Stassen sides with Wink in debates with other biblical scholars in asserting that Jesus did give his followers a social ethic that included an activist nonviolence that has direct relevance for political life in our current world. However, he believes that Wink's argument would be greatly strengthened with more attention paid to the theme of justice. Stassen outlines how Jesus did care about justice—the same kind of justice that characterized the witness of many Old Testament prophets. This "covenant justice" concerned itself with challenging four particular types of injustice: exclusion of outcasts, deprivation of the powerless, domination by the power elite, and the use of violence. All four themes are apparent both in the prophetic witness in the Old Testament and in Jesus' teaching and practice. Echoing John Howard Yoder, Stassen also outlines how Jesus' approach to social life in his own community produced meaningful analogies to social life in our contemporary world—centering on this concern for justice.

Because justice as conceived by Stassen ultimately concerns social well-being for all people in our society, he believes that Christians must find ways to communicate their values to people outside the Christian tradition, while at the same time remaining committed to Jesus as their normative source of beliefs and practices. One important element of doing justice in this way includes finding public theorists who have done some of the heavy lifting in articulating an understanding of social justice that would be, in general, compatible with Christian values but also accessible to all in our culture. Stassen finds the Jewish political philosopher Michael Walzer to be an important resource for Christian approaches to justice and concludes his chapter by outlining some of what Walzer has to offer us.

# Part One

# Worldviews and the Powers

# Chapter 1

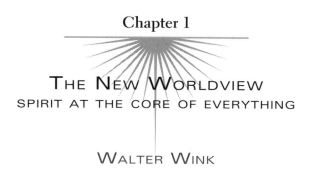

## THE NEW WORLDVIEW
### SPIRIT AT THE CORE OF EVERYTHING

## WALTER WINK

For some time now I have wanted to expand the discussion of "worldviews" with which I began both *Engaging the Powers* and *The Powers That Be*, because understanding worldviews is one key to liberating people from unconscious control by the Powers. Our worldviews determine to a large extent what we can believe about life, faith, and the very cosmos. If we are unaware of which worldviews claim our allegiance, they will continue to determine our behavior in ways to which we are simply blind. At a far deeper level than ideologies or myths, worldviews tend to dictate what we are able to believe. They are the presuppositions by which we think, the very foundations of thought itself. Consequently, people who have difficulty believing in prayer, or spiritual healing, or the life of the spirit, or God, are, in my experience, suffering far more from a worldview problem than from a theological problem.

### WHAT ARE WORLDVIEWS?

Worldviews are the fundamental presuppositions about reality, the elementary bases of thought for an entire epoch. A worldview dictates the way whole societies perceive the world. It is neutral, in the sense that it provides only the presuppositions with which to think, not the thoughts themselves.

Worldviews provide a picture of the nature of things: where is heaven, where is earth, what is visible and what invisible, what is real and what unreal? As I am using the term, worldviews are not philosophies, or theologies, or even myths or tales about the origin of things. We might think of them rather as the foundation of the house of our minds. On that foundation we erect the walls and roof, which are the myths we live by, the symbolic understandings of our world. The furnishings—the stuff to sit on and lie down on and eat with—are our theologies and personal philosophies. People notice the sofa and rugs (our theologies), they comment on the structure (the key myths), but no one notices the foundation

17

(our worldview). It is covered, hidden from view. In the very act of opposing another person's thought, we usually share the same worldview. Thus, during the Cold War, the Russians and the Americans shared a similar worldview, but with no comprehension that we were so alike.

Worldviews are the background against or context in which faith exists. Hence, a worldview can *prevent* certain kinds of faith. The basic tenets of a worldview are not argued to but argued from.[1] A worldview is always presupposed, being transcendent to daily life and even to philosophical rationality. It tends to be global, a pre-understanding by which whole societies live. Worldviews are antecedent even to our reflections and discussions of them.[2] Here are five worldviews that have impacted Western societies:

1. *The Traditional Worldview.* This is the worldview reflected in the Bible and, for that matter, in just about all ancient societies. In this conception, everything earthly has its heavenly counterpart, and everything heavenly has its earthly counterpart. Every event is thus a combination of both dimensions of reality. Everything has a visible and an invisible aspect. If war begins on earth, then there must be, at the same time, war in heaven between the angels of the nations in the heavenly council. Likewise, events initiated in heaven are mirrored on earth. This is a symbolic way of saying that every material reality has a spiritual dimension, and every spiritual reality has its physical consequences. There can be no event or entity that does not consist, simultaneously, of the visible and the invisible.

There is a beautiful example of the Traditional Worldview in the book of Revelation:

> When the Lamb opened the seventh seal, there was silence in heaven for about half an hour. And I saw the seven angels who stand before God, and seven trumpets were given to them.

> Another angel with a golden censer came and stood at the altar; he was given a great quantity of incense to offer with the prayers of all the saints on the golden altar that is before the throne. And the smoke of the incense, with the prayers of the saints, rose before God from the hand of the angel. Then the angel took the censer and filled it with fire from the altar and threw it on the earth; and there were peals of thunder, rumblings, flashes of lightning, and an earthquake

> Now the seven angels who had the seven trumpets made ready to blow them. (Rev 8:1-5)

This is a magnificent picture of the indispensability of prayer within the Traditional Worldview. Normally, events "come down" on us from the mighty systems and structures, corporations, and nation-states that determine so much of social reality. People experience this overwhelming power simply as fate. But John indicates that when believers pray on earth the power of fate is broken. The Powers force us by their sheer size and power to do their bidding. But rather than things "coming down," these prayers rise from the earth and change what subsequently happens. The angel at the altar of incense mingles the prayers of the saints with coals of fire and hurls them upon the earth. Now something is going to happen in history that would not have happened had they not prayed. In short, *history belongs to the intercessors, who believe the future into being.*

This Traditional Worldview was held not only by the ancient Hebrews and Jews, but also by the Greeks, Romans, Egyptians, Babylonians, Indians, and Chinese, and it is still held by large numbers of people today. There is nothing uniquely biblical about this worldview. It just happened to have been the view current at the time the Bible was written. That mean there is no reason the Bible cannot be interpreted within the framework of other worldviews as well.[3]

The problem for us in the modern world is that we know the world turns. There is no "up" in the world any longer. That may seem a small matter; most of us are able to accommodate the fiction of "up" in order to interpret Scripture and tradition. But the fact is that many of us can no longer let down the full weight of faith on a spatial metaphor that we no longer believe is true.

**2. The Dualistic Worldview.** Perhaps this should more accurately be called the Gnostic Worldview. In the second century C.E., this new worldview emerged to radically challenge the Judeo-Christian notion that the creation is basically good. In this worldview, creation *was* the fall. Spirit is good; matter is evil. This world is a prison into which spirits have fallen from the good heaven. Having become trapped in bodies, these spirits became subject to the deformed and ignorant Powers that rule the world of matter. Consequently, sex, the body, and earthly life in general, were often considered evil. The religious task was to rescue one's spirit from the flesh and the Powers and regain that spiritual realm from which one had fallen.

This worldview is historically associated with religions like Gnosticism and Manichaeism, the Orphic mysteries, and the sexual attitudes we associate, however unfairly, with Puritanism. (After all, the Puritans did populate New England!) It continues to be a powerful factor today in spiritualism, sexual hang-ups, asceticism, eating disorders, negative self-images, and the rejection of one's body. The UFO (unidentified flying objects) phenomenon may reflect this longing to escape our planet for a better world. This longing was literally depicted by the Heaven's Gate cult, which committed mass suicide in hope of flying up, bodiless, to a spacecraft hiding behind the Hale Bopp comet that would take them "home." The members not only pledged celibacy, but some of the men, their leader included, had been castrated in pursuit of their ideal of androgyny. The body was, they believed, a disposable container to be shed when they returned to the world from which they came.[4]

But the Dualistic Worldview is also reflected in those forms of Christian faith that use asceticism to mortify the flesh, or that place all the emphasis on getting to heaven when one leaves this "vale of tears."

**3. *The Materialist Worldview.*** This view is, in many ways, the antithesis of the world rejection of dualism. The Materialist Worldview claims that there is no heaven, no spiritual world, no God, no soul—nothing other than what can be known through the five senses and reason. The spiritual world is an illusion. There is no higher self; we are mere complexes of matter, and when we die we cease to exist except as the chemicals and atoms that once constituted us. Matter is ultimate and eternal; we are ephemeral.

There is a popular materialism associated with consumerism, self-gratification, and an absence of spiritual values. And there is a philosophical materialism that sees the universe as devoid of spirit. Popular materialism is huckstered by the media; by the unashamed espousal of greed; by the worship of the dollar in its temple, the mall; by the belief that owning things satisfies; and by the substitution of fads for values.

Philosophical materialism is far more insidious. It is characterized by David Ray Griffin as "sensationist, mechanistic, materialistic, deterministic, reductionistic, relativistic, nihilistic . . . which rules out not only supernaturalistic religious belief but also any significantly religious interpretation of reality whatsoever."[5] Here are three representative statements by evangelists for philosophical materialism. The physicist Steven Weinberg states, "The more the universe seems comprehensible, the more it seems pointless."[6] The biologist Jacques Monod comments, "Humanity lives on the boundary of an alien world. A world that is deaf to his music, just as indifferent to his hopes as it is to his suffering or his crimes."[7] And zoologist Richard Dawkins reports, almost with glee, that the central purpose of evolution is the survival of DNA, not of the beings that are DNA's temporary expression. "The universe we observe," he writes, "has precisely the properties we should expect if there is, at bottom, no design, no purpose, no evil and no good, nothing but blind, pitiless indifference."[8]

Since the universe is itself meaningless, we must create our own meanings. But, of course, these meanings are meaningless. They cannot be regarded as true because we made them up. Truth is coherence with reality. It is the very foundation of science, without which scientists would falsify data at will. If the universe is indifferent to our crimes, why not be criminals? If the world is pitilessly indifferent, why not commit suicide? If all is pointless, what is the point of belaboring the dreary point? If there is no evil, why should we strive to be good?

These scientists are simply living off the capital of Greek and Christian civilization. Their "scientism" is not science at all, but simply bad philosophy.[9] The irony is that the new physics has now gone all the way through materialism and out the other side, into a world in which matter no longer exists, but only energy-events, patterned energy, spirit-matter. Meanwhile, some scientists seem to be going the opposite direction, back toward a reductionist science that many physicists abandoned with the discovery of relativity and quantum mechanics.

**4. *The Supernaturalist Worldview.*** In reaction to materialism, theologians appended to a supernatural realm. Acknowledging that this higher realm could not be known by the senses, they conceded earthly reality to modern science and preserved a "spiritual" realm immune to confirmation or refutation. The materialists were only too glad to concede to the theologians the "heavenly" realm since they did not believe it existed anyway. This meant splitting reality in two and hermetically sealing off theology from the discoveries of science.

An extreme example of this split is a friend who was a doctoral student in geology at Columbia University. As a religious fundamentalist, he believed on Sundays that the universe was created in 4004 B.C.E., but during the rest of the week he accepted the theory that it was created around fifteen billion years ago. But that is only an extreme form of the split accepted by the vast majority of twentieth-century theologians. In a world inundated with scientific data and discoveries, most theologians simply are not interested in science.

Terrified that the ground under their feet was eroding, theologians proposed the slogan that many students learned in seminary: "Science tells us how the world was created; theology tells us why." This is basically a schizoid view of reality. This how and why distinction is spurious; as Bruce Bradshaw points out, science and religion ask different kinds of why questions. To the extent that they address different why questions, science and religion are not dichotomous or competitive. Instead, science serves religion by focusing on the intermediate why questions. The answers to these intermediate questions shed light on the ultimate why questions.[10]

The price paid for this uneasy truce with science was the loss of a sense of the whole and the unity of heavenly and earthly aspects of existence. Science and religion cannot be separated. The heavens and the earth reveal the glory of God, and it is the divine vocation of scientists to uncover the majesty of God.

**5. *An Integral Worldview.*** This new worldview is emerging from a number of streams of thought: the new physics; the reflections of Sigmund Freud and Carl Jung on the unconscious; the ecstatic vision of paleontologist/priest Teilhard de Chardin; the thought of process philosophers Alfred North Whitehead, Charles Hartshorne, John B. Cobb Jr., and David Ray Griffin; Paul Tillich's "ground of being"; liberation and feminist theology; the writings of maverick theologians Morton Kelsey, Thomas Berry, and Matthew Fox; the reflections of ethicists William Stringfellow and Jacques Ellul; the writings of scientists Brian Swimme, Ian Barbour, John Polkinghorne, Arthur Peacock, and Fritjof Capra; black religion; Celtic spirituality; the engaged Buddhism of Thich Nhat Hanh and Joanna Macy; many Native American religions; and mystics of every period and persuasion. This integral view of reality sees everything as having an outer and an inner aspect. In Revelation 1–3, for example, "angels" are the spirituality or the ethos or the corporate personality of a church. Those of us who go from church to church recognize how different the spirituality of different congregations is. Sometimes one immediately senses something terribly pathological. At other churches one receives a palpable impression of warmth, acceptance, and love. And this is true of every corporate entity, whether it be a family, school, office, factory, or city—all of these have a corporate culture or spirit or personality at the core of their reality. This spirit does not exist apart from its physical manifestations in the form of its building, personnel, trucks, computers, territory, demographics, and so on. It is the *unity* of outer and inner that characterizes our experience of the integral worldview.

This new worldview takes into account all the aspects of the Traditional Worldview, but combines them in a different way. Both worldviews use spatial imagery. The traditional idea of heaven as "up" is a natural, almost unavoidable way of indicating transcendence. But that's all it is, a metaphor. For if the world turns, there is no longer an "up" anywhere in the universe, just as on a map north is no more actually "up" than south is actually "down."

Few of us in the West who have been deeply touched by modern science can actually think that God, the angels, and departed spirits are somewhere in the sky, as most ancients literally did. The Integral Worldview reconceives that spatial metaphor not as up but as within, not only within people but also within institutions and organizations, within corporations, even within states (see, for example, the angels of nations in Daniel 10).

In the Integral Worldview, soul permeates the universe. God is not just within us but within everything. The universe is suffused with the divine. This is not pantheism, where everything is God, but panentheism (*pan*, everything; *en*, in; *theos*, God), where everything is in God and God is in everything. Spirit is at the heart of everything, even down to the smallest particle of spirit-matter. Hence, all creatures are potential revealers of God. This Integral Worldview is no more essentially "religious" than the Traditional Worldview, but I believe it makes the biblical data more intelligible for people today than any other available worldview, the Traditional Worldview included.

This Integral Worldview is also evident in the Native American representation of Sky Father and Earth Mother and in the Buddhist yin/yang figure. It is given modern representation by the Moebius strip, which can be demonstrated by taking a belt, forming a loop, and then rotating one end of the belt 180 degrees onto its back side. If you follow the loop with your finger, it will seem to be now on the inside, now on the outside, and inside again, and out, and so on, illustrating the intrinsic oscillation of inner and outer. This is a fascinating metaphor for the Integral Worldview, which sees all of life as an oscillation between visible and invisible, spirit and body, inwardness and activity, contemplation and social engagement. So the goal is not to have some people practicing mysticism, while others engage in social action. Rather, we wish to bring those two aspects together, both in the lives of individuals and in their communities.

In the worldview of the new physics, everything is related. All the matter in the universe derives from the Big Bang. We are all one matter. Our bodies are mostly water, and every drop of water in our bodies has been in every spring, every river, every lake, and every ocean during the last four and a half billion years on earth. We are all one water.[11] Each breath we breathe contains a quadrillion ($10^{15}$) atoms, writes Guy Murchie, and more than a million of these atoms have been breathed personally sometime by each and every person on Earth.[12] We are all one breath. But we also breathe the dust of all those beings who have been vaporized in our warfare, our death camps, and our gulags. We are all one body, for good or ill. Likewise, attraction is characteristic of almost everything, from gravity to love. We are all one embrace. If any creature should feel at home in our universe, it is a human being.

If everything is related, then the self is coextensive with the universe. "Hence this life of yours which you are living is not merely a piece of the entire existence, but is, in a certain sense, the whole," writes Erwin Schrödinger, the discoverer of wave mechanics.[13] We have a heat shield around the body, and an electromagnetic field as well, that can be detected by incredibly precise instruments. Theoretically, these fields (and no doubt others) extend out infinitely, in the sense that there is no point at which they can be said to have ceased to exist, though they become so minuscule that they no longer register on experimental instruments. If, then, we are coextensive with all things, we also interpenetrate each other. We are all one.

Yet the materialists would have us believe that we are alien to what is. Quite the contrary, everything interpenetrates everything else. Sperm and ovum unite, becoming related. We are already related to our mother in her womb. We enter life with relationships of every kind. Babies cannot even survive without touch. We are not isolated billiard balls knocking up against each other as if we were essentially separate and alone. Rather, we are a hive of six billion humans, always already related. We must be taught to be alienated, to hate, to kill. This to me is the profound sadness and waste of the existentialists, with their painful angst at having to create meaning in a meaningless universe. Sartre said hell is other people. But try living without them. Other people are hell only when they are deprived of genuine relatedness, attraction, and love.

One of the greatest blows to materialism came with the discovery that matter does not exist; only patterned energy, or spirit-matter, exists. We in the West may have tried to dodge the implications of this discovery, but Joseph Stalin understood perfectly. If matter is not ultimate, there can be no materialism. And with that concession, dialectical materialism, the foundation of atheistic communism, would be shattered. Stalin called in Beria, the head of the secret police. Stalin proposed killing all the physicists. Beria objected; they were needed to create an atom bomb. Fine, said Stalin. "Leave them in peace. We can always shoot them later."[14]

That we are related to everything is no longer a hypothesis. In what physicist Henry Stapp has called one of the most profound discoveries in all of science, John Bell posited the following theorem: "A change in the spin of one particle in a two-particle system will affect its twin simultaneously, even if the two have been widely separated." Put more simply, when paired particles are sent in opposite directions at the speed of light, even to the limits of the universe, and the spin of one is changed, the other particle's spin also changes, *simultaneously*.

That was in 1964. Bell had no idea what the implications of his theorem were. But in 1972, John Clauser was able to fashion an experiment that proved Bell right. Now the theorem was no longer a hypothesis but a fact of the universe. But how could such a thing be possible? How did the second particle know that its partner's spin had changed? How could a message be transmitted from one to the other, since that would require speeds far in excess of the speed of light? And to suggest that anything could exceed the speed of light would be to cancel the very foundations of relativity theory, which seemed inconceivable.

Finally, it dawned: there is no distance. There is no separation but rather mutual interaction through a field. Everything is already related. This means that the universe is a single, multiform energy-event characterized by nonlocality. Physicist Max Planck had already grasped the implication: each individual particle of the system exists simultaneously in every part of the system; hence, no particle can be explained *except in reference to the entire cosmos*. Everything is related.

In terms of the Integral Worldview, the spiral carries us from the outer edge, or local reality—the reality of everyday life—to radical inwardness, or nonlocal reality—the nonseparability that characterizes the world of quantum reality. Mystics have long known this deeper dimension of reality. It is what John's gospel calls "eternal life" (John 17:3), or what Jesus called "the kingdom of God within" (Luke 17:21).

## IMPLICATIONS

Now we are in a position to test the capacity of the Integral Worldview to do justice to key theological themes.

1. **Creation.** In the Supernaturalist Worldview, it was impossible to affirm that God was the actual creator of the world. Rather, that worldview maintained a fiction in which science told how the world really was created, and theology told an "as if" story that wasn't really true. The result was a split worldview that created split worldviewers. In the Integral Worldview, however, God's role in creation may be seen as literally true. God really is the creator, and science is the means of discovering how God did it. This is not creationism, which is simply a literalistic throwback to the Traditional Worldview. Nor does it condone materialist distortions of biology. Rather, the Integral Worldview insists that if God is real,

then God will have to be included in our experience of the nature of things. This holistic way of perceiving reality regards the new scientific story of creation as *approximately true in a metaphoric sense.* Did God create the world? Definitely, though we are still trying to figure out how.

Several years back, I was lecturing in Annapolis and made some uncomplimentary comments about scientists being caught up in the Materialistic Worldview. At the break, seven or eight physicists confronted me. "You don't know what you're talking about," they insisted. "We physicists talk about God more than any other department, including the religion department!" The new physics has opened a whole new way of perceiving, and relating to, reality. It will be decades before we take the full measure of its accomplishment.

**2. Prayer.** Since everything is related, then, we have no need for actual physical contact in order to impact each other. Now that Bell's Theorem has proven that there is no distance in nonlocal space, prayer and spiritual healing can be understood as just the kinds of communication that we would expect from a world in which there is no distance.

If there is no distance, then our prayers can be as effective halfway around the world as they can be in the hospital room, since nonlocal influence doesn't diminish with distance. Unlike local events, nonlocal interactions link up one location with another without crossing space, without decay and without delay.[15] If prayer doesn't have to go anywhere, then it may simultaneously be present everywhere, enveloping the praying party, the party prayed for, and the total field of reality, which we might call God. Instead of being a superstitious throwback to an irrational past, prayer can be seen as the highest kind of rationality.

It might help to contrast the understanding of prayer in the Supernatural Worldview with that in the Integral Worldview. In the Supernatural Worldview, one might pray for *spiritual* healing. But because the Supernatural Worldview allows no real contact between the realm of science and that of theology, or between body and spirit, spiritual healing and prayer would be inappropriate, even foolish. And so another slick adage is born: God may not cure us (physically), but God can heal us (spiritually). That adage is no doubt true in some cases, but it can also be a cop-out when it is used as a way to avoid prayer for actual physical healing.

When I lecture to clergy on divine healing, I routinely ask for a show of hands of how many had a course on prayer in seminary. Only a few hands go up. When I ask if any had even a single lecture on divine healing, the response is almost invariably zero. Yet Jesus spent most of his ministry, according to Mark, doing healings and exorcisms and praying.

In the Integral Worldview, however, prayer is given the place of honor in the life of the spirit. Since we are all already related to each other, we are immediate to each other. We don't have to get related; we already are related. We don't have to pump ourselves up in order to release a charge of healing energy. The other persons don't even have to know we are praying for them. Because we are already related, and we are one body in God, God's healing power is already there, or here (but there is no distance), and our prayer is simply a matter of opening the situation to God. In the light of all these considerations, David Ray Griffin can pronounce that "the idea of 'nonlocal' influence seems philosophically unproblematic and empirically verified, both in physics and in parapsychology."[16]

And because ours is not a schizoid reality, but only one world, scientific research into prayer and spiritual healing is both appropriate and urgently needed. In *Healing Words*, Larry Dossey examined over a hundred empirical studies of prayer, many of them double-blind, some of them done on cultures of bacteria or on animals so as to eliminate the human factor or the placebo effect. One hundred years ago, the Nobel prize–winning scientist Alexis Carrel commented that, in the future, scientists would take love into the laboratory and find more power there than in the atom. His prophecy is being enacted before our eyes.

**3. *Everyone is a mystic.*** In the Integral Worldview, everyone will be a mystic. Not in an intentional sense, perhaps, but at least in an unconscious way. As this new worldview penetrates society, people will simply recognize the reality of the spiritual world. They may not believe in God. They may not perceive themselves to be religious or belong to any kind of church. They may not engage in any practices, disciplines, spiritual readings, or even prayers. But they will have absorbed by osmosis the Integral Worldview and they will be willy-nilly spiritual. This has already begun to happen. For this we may take as our models those Native Americans who can hardly utter a sentence without reference to the Great Spirit.

However, one of the great deceptions of the spiritual world is that the spiritual realm is wholly good. We will need to recover a sense of the depth of evil, and of the idolatries perpetrated by the Powers That Be, lest we be blindsided by them. For there are people of every religious persuasion who are praying *against* the well-being of others. And so we will need to take more seriously the need to protect ourselves from the darkness in the psyche, including the collective darkness. So, too, we will recognize that the atheism of our time is a tragic form of collective soul-suicide, induced by the Materialistic Worldview and propagated by an intelligentsia largely blinded by Promethean pride.

Because the mystical experience will so often reunite people to nature, nature itself will be reenchanted, capable of providing theophanies of God.[17] And because we are all related, nonviolence will become the norm of social action and political life. As Fritjof Capra notes, subatomic particles are not "things" but interconnections among things. "In quantum theory we never end up with any 'things'; we always deal with interconnections."[18] Competition yields to cooperation as the dynamism of natural selection. "Fit into the community and become a fully functioning participant or else you will be left out for good," write Brian Swimme and Thomas Berry. "If you are to stay, we must become related, and not just externally related. We must become kin, internally related. . . . [For] rooted in the core of anything alive is the communal reality. At the heart of the individual is everyone else. . . . The universe is a communion of subjects rather than a collection of objects."[19]

**4. Everlasting life.** I have always had a difficult time swallowing the notion of everlasting life. I can understand it as the timeless dimension of the present. I can appreciate Whitehead's idea that nothing of creative value is lost. I am able to allow for a kind of eternal memory that, as it were, preserves in God something essential about every person who ever lived. But I have never been able to get excited about the idea of personal immortality (or, for that matter, the resurrection of the dead). I trust God to take care of all that and am sure that God will not disappoint (assuming that I will be a part of that transformation!).

But I also have to acknowledge that it is the Materialistic Worldview that has made this issue difficult for me. The lack of empirical proof of an afterlife is an embarrassment. In the Integral Worldview, however, eternal life is a natural corollary of the infinitely inward-spiraling center at the heart of all things. The fact that consciousness is nonlocal means that the mind cannot be limited to the brain and to the present, only to perish when we die.

The Gospel of John asserts something similar: "And this is eternal life, that they may know you, the only true God, and Jesus Christ whom you have sent" (17:3). Eternal life begins the moment we encounter the living God and God's revealer. In the more neutral terms of Bell's Theorem, when we recognize nonlocal reality, in that moment the world becomes reenchanted for us.

Quantum physics cannot, and never will be able to, prove the existence of God or eternal life. But just as theologians can use metaphors from science in order to make the Integral Worldview intelligible, so also scientists can use metaphors from theology or poetry. After all, "God," too, is a metaphor, in the sense that all language fails in the presence of the final and absolute Mystery—the God beyond all Gods—the God beyond even our God. These metaphors and images drawn from science are transient and quickly replaced by others. Nevertheless, they are invaluable because they help us to hold science and faith together in a single reality. It is our task to leap nimbly from one image to the next, abandoning what is no longer useful.

For example, we can speak of God metaphorically as a "strange attractor," as the astronomer John Hitchcock has done, because the expression "strange attractor" is already used metaphorically in physics. Or we can conceive of photons clapping their hands with joy, or see the "weirdness" of the universe and the incredibly rising improbability of ever more complex forms as the finger of God.

The Integral Worldview will, of course, be subject to misuse. Societal acceptance of this new way of looking at the world will not usher in utopia. People will still find ways to pervert higher values. There will be superficial spiritualities, selfish prayers, and the manipulation of spirit for material gain. Some will seek spiritual power over others. There will be shallow, cafeteria-style religiosity, franchised insights; egomaniacs huckstering their own amalgam of snake remedies; nostrums, and cure-alls; and automatic writers claiming a direct line to ancient prophets. But none of that is new. We will simply have to live with it.

What an exciting challenge: to be able to help shape that new Integral Worldview along lines that honor life, the environment, and the very universe itself, a view that sees the whole teeming world as capable of providing, in some sense, a revelation of God.

# Chapter 2

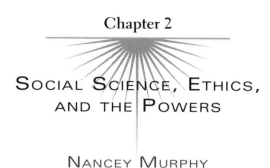

## SOCIAL SCIENCE, ETHICS, AND THE POWERS

### NANCEY MURPHY

In "Traditions, Practices, and the Powers,"[1] I consider the problem of knowledge—in particular, the question of whether the pursuit of power inevitably distorts the pursuit of truth. I took a middle position, arguing that one needs to be wary of the powerful practices of academia, but that New Testament disciplines are available to wean us from dependence on worldly sorts of power. In fact, I suggested that academia can learn from the peaceful practices of communal correction found in the Radical Reformation heritage.

In this chapter, I shall further my investigation of the relations between knowledge and power by considering a particularly relevant body of knowledge, the social sciences. These disciplines are doubly interesting, in light of an analysis of the Principalities and Powers, because they are *about* the Powers that govern society: economic, political, social, legal. At the same time, the social sciences are themselves powerful practices—claiming scientific neutrality while subtly or not so subtly shaping public opinion and policy. As Walter Wink has noted, the methodological atheism of the social sciences makes them inevitably function as a defense for a "counter-evangel"—an apologetic for the message that society creates God.[2]

I shall consider two issues. First, how do the social sciences relate to the natural sciences? Can social behavior be explained in terms of individual dynamics, and ultimately in terms of genetics, as sociobiologists propose, or in terms of neuroscience, as has been argued more recently? Wink's analysis of the language of Power in the New Testament allows for an illuminating *redescription* and analysis of this debate.

Second, is social-scientific "truth" inevitably distorted? I shall argue that the divorce of the social sciences from the Christian tradition results in an inevitable distortion, insofar as *fallen* social realities are described as "normal" and thus legitimated. The co-opting of social scientists by the economic and political powers they study opens the door to further distortion.

Thus, I make a radical claim regarding the possibility of accurate knowledge of the social world we inhabit: Such knowledge would require not only that practitioners of social-scientific research follow the power-renouncing ways of Jesus' disciples, but also that they do their work from the epistemic standpoint of the gospel. As Wink says, true knowledge of good and evil requires a new mind, a new epistemic standpoint that cannot simply be added to the old.[3]

## THE HIERARCHY OF THE SCIENCES

Throughout the modern era, it has been common to think of reality in terms of a hierarchy of levels of organization or complexity, and to think of the sciences as capable of being organized hierarchically to reflect this "layered" feature of reality. The earliest (and most idiosyncratic) version was Thomas Hobbes's (1588–1679) hierarchy, with the "science" of geometry at the bottom and civil philosophy at the top. In the twentieth century, it has been widely agreed that the hierarchy of sciences begins with physics at the bottom and then adds chemistry and biology. Physics is at the bottom because it studies the most basic constituents of reality; chemistry studies these "atoms" as they relate in complex structures (molecules);[4] biology studies a number of levels of structure, from the biochemical through the levels of organelles, cells, tissues, organs and organisms to colonies of organisms in their environments.

There has been continuing debate in modern Western intellectual history over two issues: whether psychology and the social sciences can be added to the hierarchy above biology, and whether all of the sciences are ultimately reducible to physics—that is, whether the laws of physics ultimately determine everything that happens. The question of reductionism is complex and highly contentious. My goal here is not by any means to settle this debate, but rather to put this set of issues into a dialogue with Wink's writings on the Powers.

There are three analogous or parallel sets of arguments in philosophy and science, pertaining to the levels of biology, consciousness, and social structures. Early in the twentieth century, there was a heated three-way debate in the philosophy of biology among the mechanists, the vitalists, and the organicists. The vitalists maintained that life was a distinctive entity or substance, a nonmaterial agency that had to be added to inorganic matter to produce an organism. For example, Hans Driesch interpreted his experiments in embryology as evidence for a purposeful "entelechy" directing events in anticipation of future goals.[5] In sharp contrast, mechanists, throughout the modern era, have argued that living beings are merely complex machines, assemblies of moving particles that obey the same laws within the organism as they do outside it. That is, biological laws are reducible to the laws of chemistry and ultimately to physics.

Organicism has something in common with each of these contrasting theses yet in important ways opposes both. Organicists agree with mechanists in rejecting all nonmaterial vital agents. Instead, life arises as a result of complex organization and consists in special sorts of complex functioning. Thus, there is no impassable gulf between the living and the nonliving; rather, there is a continuity of levels. Organicists diverge from mechanists, though, in insisting that biology needs distinctive *biological* concepts, which cannot be defined in physicochemical terms. The term "organicism" comes from the insistence that biological terms refer to aspects of the whole, integrally functioning organism. A major theme of organicism is that the parts are influenced by the whole, as well as the reverse. And here is the contentious issue of reductionism—that of explaining how it can be the case that the behavior of the whole is *not* simply a product of the behavior of its parts. There is no widely accepted answer to this question, but a number of helpful analyses of so-called top-down or whole-part causation have been offered.[6]

Despite lack of agreement regarding downward causation, and despite a few outspoken reductionists, the mainstream philosophy of biology follows more in the footsteps of the organicists than the mechanists, and vitalism has been left behind entirely.

There is an analogous debate in full swing in neuroscience and philosophy of mind. Note that we are proceeding up the hierarchy of sciences and the corresponding hierarchy of complex systems. If it has been decided that no nonmaterial entity needs to be added to reach the organic level from the inorganic, then this next debate concerns the question of whether a nonmaterial entity (a mind or soul) needs to be added to living things to reach the level of sentience or consciousness. Here, again, there are three options.

According to informal surveys I do whenever I lecture on this topic, a large proportion of the general population holds either a dualist or trichotomist view of the human person: body and mind; or body, soul, and spirit. Parallel to the arguments of the vitalists, these views assume that something nonmaterial needs to be added to the physical organism to account for its special conscious abilities. The opposite view is reductive materialism. Here all mental functioning is attributed to the nervous system, and it is assumed, as well, that eventually neuroscience can explain all conscious processes and thus all of human behavior. The most extreme of the reductionist views is eliminative materialism, according to which all talk of consciousness, beliefs, and so forth is "folk psychology," which is destined to be replaced by the language of neuroscience.

Nonreductive physicalism is the third position, and it agrees with the materialists, against the dualists, that there is no *entity*, the mind or soul, in addition to the brain. But against the materialists, nonreductive physicists argue that mental processes—reasoning, decision making, aesthetic appreciation—are not reducible to the laws of neurobiology. Here, again, is the focus of the arguments: How can it *not* be the case that mental events are simply determined by the laws of neurobiology if mental events are all realized by physical events in the brain?[7]

## Wink's Contribution to the Debate

Now, if we move up the hierarchy of complexity from the individual level to the social level, we can relate these three-way arguments to Wink's account of the Principalities and Powers and to brief remarks he has made about the social sciences.

It is clear that Wink does not take a position analogous to that of the mechanists in biology or the reductive materialists in philosophy of mind. This is seen in his citing with approval antireductionist authors such as neuropsychologist Roger Sperry.[8] Although I believe Wink underestimates the difficulties involved in defeating reductionist arguments, the interesting feature of his contribution is his situating of the discussion of reductionism within his analysis of the biblical term *stoicheia* (elements). Included among the elements are both the basic building blocks of reality and the first principles by which things are ordered. We might now speak of basic particles and the laws of physics.

Reductionism, Wink says, is not only the tendency to explain phenomena at higher levels as if they were nothing more than the sum of their most fundamental parts.[9] It is, in addition, a form of idolatry. It takes the lowest elements in the chain of being to be the ultimate source of all else. Wink quotes Clement of Alexandria: "The great original, the maker of all things, and creator of the 'first principles' themselves, God without beginning, they [that is, the reductionists] know not, but offer adoration to these 'weak and beggarly elements'!"[10]

One of the values of Wink's association of reductionist ideologies with idolatry is the vantage point it gives us from which to unmask the social agendas of many reductionists. Logical positivism had as one of its goals the delegitimizing of religion. Current reductionist arguments, such as the sociobiologists' attempts to reduce morality to genetic programming, are often covert arguments for a moral vision of their own, counter to the more stringent demands of Christian morality.[11]

Now, one of my puzzlements in reading Wink's trilogy can be expressed by asking whether his account of the Powers places him with the vitalists and dualists or with the organicists and nonreductive physicalists. Many interpreters of the New Testament recognize that, for its writers, social structures are among the Powers, but the Powers also include nonphysical realities; the intertestamental world was populated with a variety of kinds of beings neither divine nor flesh and blood.

The gain for contemporary readers from recent studies of the Powers (Wink's included) is that we now have referents for many of these terms that we can make sense of in this deanimated worldview of ours, namely, social structures.

Wink's unique contribution is to distinguish a spiritual from a material element, which he calls the "interiority" or the "within" of the Powers. This move is based on analogy with human consciousness. The application of this concept to social structures is valuable for two reasons. First, it is an effective strategy, in our individualist culture, for calling attention to aspects of social entities that transcend the individuals involved in them. It does make sense to speak of the *personality*, or *moral character*, of an institution. Second, it helps us to see that these structures cannot simply be reduced to the individuals who make them up.

So far, all of this is compatible with, and in fact an extension of, a nonreductive physicalist account of the individual: no spiritual *entity* is postulated that might exist independently of the "team spirit" of the social organization. However, at other points Wink seems to be endorsing (not just reporting) a view of the spiritual aspect of Powers that is a closer analogy to dualism or vitalism. In a move comparable to those of Pierre Teilhard de Chardin and process philosophers, Wink argues that "interiority" is present in attenuated form in lower-level entities as well. For example, he speaks of "angels of nature," and his account here sounds surprisingly like a more intelligent version of a vital force or entelechy. Quoting Dorothy MacLean, he says that an angel can be the "species pattern of all wild violets and at the same time speak as the interiority or 'within' of a particular plant. The species-angel maintains the current form . . . and the plant's archetypal possibilities or vocation."[12] If "interiority" or "within" were said to be merely information internal to the individual plants, it could be taken as an odd way to refer to DNA and would then be consistent with an organicist view of biology. But to go on to quote a message from the St. John's Wort Angel and "take the rumors of these angels so seriously"[13] does indeed call for a new worldview, as Wink admits. But the legitimation of such a worldview would require much more argument than we find either in Wink's brief treatment (four pages) or in his sources—process theorists Charles Birch and John Cobb.

## THE DISTORTION OF SOCIAL-SCIENTIFIC "TRUTH"

George Ellis and I have argued in our coauthored book, *On the Moral Nature of the Universe*, that, contrary to claims of value neutrality, the social sciences inevitably incorporate ethical assumptions.[14] The so-called pure social sciences regularly employ ethically loaded conceptions of human nature, such as assumptions about the intrinsic egoism of individuals, the necessity of violence or the threat of violence in all social relations, concepts of human dignity, and, more broadly, conceptions of human good or flourishing. In our book, we argued that such moral assumptions needed to be recognized and evaluated from a point of view outside of the social sciences themselves. However, in light of Wink's analysis of social powers as *fallen*, I am inclined to make a stronger and somewhat paradoxical claim: To the extent that social sciences maintain a neutral stance toward the social powers they describe, they inevitably *mislead* us about the true nature of social reality and are likely to foster anti-Christian moral sensibilities. That is, insofar as fallen social structures are described as normal, we are deceived about the true nature of human sociality, and social practices that reflect rebellion against God are legitimated and promoted.

In our book, Ellis and I showed how combining the apparently innocuous and morally neutral assumptions of rational choice theory and game theory results in a powerful argument for the necessity of acting egoistically: (1) To be rational is to maximize my utility. (2) Economic exchange can be modeled by competitive games. (3) I must choose my moves on the basis of expectations of how my opponent will play. (4) I expect all (other) rational agents to act to maximize their own utility. (5) Therefore, I must always adopt the most egoistic strategy rather than the cooperative strategy. Thus, insofar as economists propose egoism as a theory about human motivation, it easily becomes part of a *justification* for egoism when combined with other assumptions of game theory and rational choice theory.

For another example of social-scientific legitimizing of counter-Christian morality, consider modern positions on the necessity of violent coercion in society. This assumption can be traced to Thomas Hobbes's social contract theory. Here is how organizational theorist James O'Toole describes Hobbes's view of the "state of nature" and the formation of the "social contract":

> In nature, man "finds no stop in doing what he has the will, desire or inclination to do." To Hobbes the "Natural Right" of every individual in this Edenic state is "the liberty each man has to use his own power for the preservation of his own nature, that is to say his own life . . . and consequently of doing anything which in his own judgment and reason he shall conceive to be the aptest means thereunto." Here, particularly in the concluding phrase, we see a statement of a modern notion of liberty. But in the next breath Hobbes gives it all away! Unhappily, he says, in this free and natural state the condition of life is "solitary, poor, nasty, brutish and short" because there is a perpetual "war . . . of every man against every man." Hence, to procure security, and the progress of civilization, humans reluctantly surrender the liberty of nature, entering into a "social contact to live under the rule of law."[15]

It is revealing that O'Toole uses the phrase "Edenic state" to describe the state of nature, for what we have in social contract theory is a new myth of origins at variance with the account in Genesis. In fact, Hobbes's myth is the antithesis of the biblical story. At least as we receive it through Augustine's interpretation, life for the original inhabitants in the biblical Eden is cooperative, not a state of war; bountiful, not poor; idyllic, not nasty; angelic, not brutish; and everlasting. It represents an aberration, a Fall, when the earth-creatures assert their will (against God, not one another) to take that for which they have a desire and inclination. These two myths of origin reveal antithetical theories of the nature of the person, two antithetical theologies.

A variety of social theorists since Hobbes have followed him in claiming that coercion is necessary to maintain society and that violence is merely the ultimate form of coercion. And so we have one of the most noted Christian ethicists of the twentieth century, Reinhold Niebuhr, arguing that the needs of an institution for its very survival require the people involved in them to do things they would not do (and would not be morally justified in doing) as individuals.[16] And this thesis has been given the congratulatory title of "Christian realism."

## SOCIOLOGY AS COUNTER-EVANGEL

I was intrigued by Wink's observation that, insofar as sociology "explains" religion as a product of human contrivance, it provides an apologetic for a counter-evangel—a message diametrically opposed to the good news that we are creatures of a loving God. A powerful voice furthering Wink's critique of sociology can be found in John Milbank's *Theology and Social Theory*. Addressing both theologians and social theorists, Milbank sets out to unmask the "counterbiblical" theology of the whole of modern social science:

> To social theorists I shall attempt to disclose the possibility of a skeptical demo-
> lition of modern, secular social theory from a perspective with which it is at
> variance: in this case, that of Christianity. I will try to demonstrate that all the
> most important governing assumptions of such theory are bound up with the
> modification or the rejection of orthodox Christian positions. These funda-
> mental intellectual shifts are, I shall argue, no more rationally "justifiable"
> than the Christian positions themselves. . . . "Scientific" social theories are
> themselves theologies or anti-theologies in disguise.[17]

I shall only be able to examine a small fraction of Milbank's argument here and thus will concentrate on one step in the argument that reinforces themes in Wink's *Engaging the Powers*.[18] In this step, Milbank sets out to show that scientific politics and political economy are "complicit with an 'ontology of violence,' a reading of the world which assumes the priority of force and tells how this force is best managed and confined by counter-force."[19] Orthodox Christianity, in contrast, recognizes no original violence. It construes the infinite not as chaos but as harmonic peace. Compare this to Wink's claim that the Domination System is not the original form of human sociality and has its origin in the "counterbiblical" creation myths of the Babylonians.[20]

Milbank's method is genealogical—that is, he calls secular social theory into question by uncovering the intellectual turns that shaped it and then showing that these were *unreasoned* changes. In brief, his argument is the following: Whereas the typical assumption of the social sciences is that the secular is the natural and religion is an intrusion or usurpation, it is more accurate to say that the secular realm had to be invented; it was created first by inventing the category of the natural over against the theological or religious.[21] Thus, Grotius, Hobbes, and Spinoza created a degree of autonomy for political theory over against theology. For moderns, the natural becomes a sealed-off totality, operating on the basis of invariable rules. Furthermore, these are rules precisely of power and passion.

A second step in the creation of the secular was to associate culture with human creation. This "sphere of the artificial," marked out by modern thinkers as the space of secularity, forms the "dominium" granted to Adam in the Garden.[22] "Both insofar as it was deemed natural and insofar as it was deemed artificial, the new autonomous object of political science was not, therefore, simply 'uncovered.' The space of the secular had to be invented as the space of 'pure power.' However, this invention was itself a . . . theological achievement."[23]

Milbank traces the development of a politics of pure power from ancient Greece, where *dominium* most commonly meant dominion over oneself, and it was in virtue of this self-possession that one could manage others and property. For Aquinas, dominion was subjected to the good of society in general. It is only in the modern period that we find a concept of pure power to do as one likes with one's person and one's property. This concept recognizes no providential purpose in the hands of God and, with its individualistic account of the will, has difficulty understanding any genuinely social process. "To keep notions of the state free from any suggestion of a collective essence or generally recognized *telos*, it must be constructed on the individualist model of *dominium*" (13).

These concepts of unrestricted dominion over private property, and of individual will restrainable only by means of absolute sovereignty (Hobbes), were given legitimacy by means of *theological* arguments. Human *dominium* as pure power could come to be seen as the essence of the human only because it was promoted as a reflection of the divine essence—an outworking of medieval voluntarist conceptions of God. "The later middle ages retrieved in a new and more drastic guise the antique connection between monotheism and monarchic unity which was affirmed in Christian tradition by the semi-Arian Eusebius and then became part of both imperial and papal ideology" (14). This is in contrast to concepts of the Trinity that emphasize relationship over will.

Milbank hopes that by showing the extent to which these and other secular social-scientific presuppositions are based on (unwarranted) theological positions, he will be able to call them into question, making room for the restoration of theology to its rightful position as metadiscourse for Western culture. He aims in this volume to pick up hints of a "counter-modern" position that is theologically realistic and orthodox. In such a position social knowledge will be

> the continuation of ecclesial practice, the imagination in action of a peaceful, reconciled social order. . . . It is this lived narrative which itself both projects and "represents" the triune God, who is transcendental peace through

differential relation. And the same narrative is also a continuous reading and positioning of other social realities. If truth is social, it can only be through a claim to offer the ultimate "social science" that theology can establish itself and give any content to the notion of "God." And in practice, providing such a content means making a historical difference in the world. (6)

This is no place to attempt an evaluation of Milbank's obscure tome. Suffice it to say that, insofar as his arguments are sound, his work provides striking evidence for the claim that there is no such thing as truly secular social science—that all so-called secular social theory is in fact imbued with theological positions. To bring his analysis together with Wink's: Social systems such as capitalism and the military-industrial complex have "interiorities" that are in rebellion against God (thus Wink). So social-scientific analyses of these spiritual powers cannot constitute theologically neutral descriptions; they are necessarily countertheologies (thus Milbank).

## ETHICS AND THEOLOGY IN THE HIERARCHY OF THE SCIENCES

A central thesis of *On the Moral Nature of the Universe* is that the hierarchy of the sciences is incomplete without ethics and theology. On the basis of the foregoing critique of social science, I can explain very briefly why Ellis and I have argued that this is the case. I have given examples of the ethical presuppositions built into modern social-scientific theories—for example, the normativity of egoism and the view that humankind's highest good can consist only in a social structure rooted in violence. These presuppositions need to be brought to light and examined. But even more so do alternative views of human nature and human possibilities need to be given credibility. Thus, Ellis and I argued for a scientific approach to ethics. Ethics provides visions of possibilities for the good life for humans, and these visions can be tested against empirical evidence. In our book, we marshaled some empirical evidence showing the possibilities for alternative forms of economic behavior, community governance, and justice systems. In particular we surveyed evidence for the effectiveness of nonviolence in both individual and social settings.

Thus, we argue that ethics belongs in the hierarchy of the sciences, directly above the social sciences. And this brings us back to the issue of reductionism with which I began. The rejection of reductionism means that each level of analysis draws profitably both from the levels below and from the levels above. For example, psychology profits from biological explanations of human behavior, such as the insight that chemical imbalances cause depression. But psychology is also essentially dependent on top-down explanations of a social-psychological nature, such as family-systems accounts of individual behavior. In an analogous way, the social sciences raise questions that they alone are not competent to answer—questions relating to the good for human life—and these questions are appropriately answered by (the science of) ethics.

Yet ethics itself raises questions that cannot be answered apart from an understanding of ultimate reality. That is, as Alasdair MacIntyre points out, to know what is the good for humankind requires an answer to the question of the purpose of human life.[24] Is it pleasure, as the utilitarians presume, or is there no purpose at all, as some scientific naturalists proclaim? The source of an answer to this question may be theological—for example: God made us to know, love, and serve him in this life and to be happy with him in the next (Baltimore Catechism). If no such theological account is provided, some other account, explicit or assumed, will take its place. Such an account, in Milbank's terms, is counter-theological, or in Wink's terms, a counter-evangel.

So, like it or not, social scientists and ethicists are always already involved in the doing of theology. Milbank is right—it is time they admitted it.

# Chapter 3

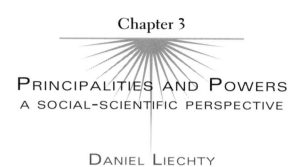

# PRINCIPALITIES AND POWERS
## A SOCIAL-SCIENTIFIC PERSPECTIVE

### DANIEL LIECHTY

In the religious environment in which I was raised, the Principalities and Powers were conceived in terms of a premodern worldview as personal, demonic forces, with both agency and volition, under the overall command of the archfoe Satan. This is still the view held by many Christians today, at least if what I see on the Christian Television Network is any indication. I first recall specifically encountering an interpretation of the Principalities and Powers as impersonal forces of the socioeconomic system in John Howard Yoder's book *The Politics of Jesus*.[1] That was my first year of college. By then I had already read other of Yoder's books, material by Art Gish, *Post-American/Sojourners* magazine, and other sources associated with radical Christian discipleship and ethics. It is likely, therefore, that I had been introduced to the concept of Principalities and Powers as impersonal, systemic socioeconomic forces even before.

This interpretation struck me as quite important, and I immediately started reading Yoder's sources, especially Hendrikus Berkhof's book *Christ and the Powers*.[2] I was attracted to exploring this view further, particularly because it gave direction to my struggle to be both Anabaptist Christian and actively involved in radical politics and also because I saw intuitively how this interpretation could free Christian faith, theology, and ethics from a worldview in which the universe was inhabited by all sorts of angels and demons and heavenly and underworld hosts and spirits. This mythological worldview had for me already become intellectually untenable. Yet it was so closely associated in my mind with what Christians believe that I hardly knew how to hold on to the one while letting go of the other. The Yoder/Berkhof treatment of the Principalities and Powers was a window into a much more intellectually rigorous Christianity than I had known before.

## PRINCIPALITIES AND POWERS AS
## SYSTEMIC SOCIOECONOMIC FORCES

According to the Yoder/Berkhof interpretation, Principalities and Powers are understood as social forces, encompassing "an inclusive vision of religious structure (especially the religious undergirdings of stable ancient and primitive societies), intellectual structures ('ologies and 'isms), moral structures (codes and customs), political structures (the tyrant, the market, the school, the courts, race, and nation)."[3] Walter Wink's voluminous work self-consciously builds on and extends this line of interpretation.[4] Wink's approach emphasizes the following points, which will also become our final points of comparison for a social-scientific view.

*The Powers are good.* Wink suggests that the Powers were created by God for the ordering of human community. The Powers, as part of the original creation of God, were created good, like all of God's original creation. If the Powers functioned according to God's original intention, they would be our ally in ensuring that people are fed and goods are distributed to those in need and, in general, that communal laws govern our life together for the common good.

*The Powers are fallen.* But these Powers are in rebellion against God's original intentions. As such, these Powers act in accordance with the "system of domination," creating vast inequalities and injustices in the economic order. They make themselves the hand servants of the worst of human emotions and motivations—greed, envy, revenge, and violence. They facilitate actions leading to ecological destruction and inequality and injustice, making such actions appear "logical" and "inevitable," and cause good people to act accordingly, even as they may personally regret the results.

*The Powers must be redeemed.* Christ has brought redemption from the Powers. They have been broken and shown in the cross to be a mockery of God's justice and goodness. The decisive battle against the Powers has been won in the cross of Christ. The task now is to bring the Powers to this recognition and to allow them again to function for the common good according to God's original intention.

The eschatological Christian community is God's tool to bring this redemption of the Powers into historical reality. Problems arise when Christians themselves fail to recognize this corporate and transpersonal element in God's salvation and retreat into satisfaction with personal salvation, the world be damned. When we do this, we ourselves become easy prey for the fallen Powers to seduce us into acting corporately and politically, according to their fallen dictates. Then we ourselves begin to value "patriotic duty" as equal to or above Christian commitments and lean toward the "expediency" of violent solutions to political problems. We begin to close our eyes to the systemic inequalities and injustices of our economic and political systems, however much we may regret the suffering that results. And worst of all, we begin to play power politics within our own communities on the model of the fallen Powers, rather than according to Christ's suffering love, thus diluting and negating the very high calling that God has entrusted to us.[5]

## A BASIS FOR DIALOGUE WITH THE SOCIAL SCIENCES

There would be near-consensus among social scientists that much or most of what occurs in human society is motivated by unseen forces and factors—forces and factors of which we are only vaguely aware and over which human beings have almost no control. This consensus diminishes as the discussion continues into areas of clarifying and explicating just what the nature and causes of these forces and factors are, which affairs are influenced by which forces and how much so, and how much these factors and forces could be brought, at least theoretically, under human control. This is the stuff over which schools of thought are formed within the social sciences, and some of these schools are very far from each other indeed. Nevertheless, one could do much worse than to define the cacophony of social science itself as the stumbling attempt of human beings to study, learn about, test, and seek increasingly refined understandings of exactly those unseen forces and factors of which we are only vaguely aware and over which human beings have almost no control—but which animate and motivate human social behavior. The category of Principality and Powers, therefore, is a particularly good focus for a dialogue and concept translation between an intellectually rigorous biblical and theological view and a view from the social sciences.

I cannot pretend to offer the one valid and definitive social-scientific understanding of the Principalities and Powers. What I can do is talk about how this concept looks to me, as a person with a foot in both the social-scientific and the biblical/theological camps. In order to do that, I now need to lay out briefly the basic social-scientific theory from which I work.

Perhaps because of my background in religious studies, I am most interested in social-scientific theory that takes in as much of life as possible without reductionism. There are those of a different temperament who studiously avoid exactly such broad theories because, being so broad, they feel mushy and soft. Such people much prefer the narrowly focused study that, in my opinion, doesn't say much about anything, but what it does say is rigorously tested by experimental and statistical methods. Again, these are the things around which social science divides itself. I have come to be satisfied with something between mushy but meaningful speculation and the narrowly focused, rigorously experimental study whose conclusions are not very meaningful. One theorist who explored this middle ground, and who paid the price of scorn from both ends of the continuum for doing so, was Ernest Becker.[6] Becker drew on Kierkegaard and Otto Rank to develop *a generative theory of death anxiety*, and it is to Becker's theory that I turn to cast a social-scientific eye on the biblical and theological concept of Principalities and Powers.

## DEATH ANXIETY AND THE REPRESSED UNCONSCIOUS

The theory of generative death anxiety is not difficult to understand. It is rooted in recognition of the biological, evolutionary aspect of our human heritage, but just as clearly it incorporates the social and cultural aspects of human heritage in what I see as an almost seamlessly integrated approach. The theory, in a nutshell, starts with the assumption that all species are driven by an overriding will to survive. If we want a fancy term for this drive, we can call it primary narcissism. If we prefer a colloquial term, we might simply refer to it as the survival instinct. Each species is endowed through the process of natural selection with specialized survival mechanisms for continued flourishing within the environment in which it exists.[7] For simple organic life, the survival mechanism is usually massive reproduction, so that, although extremely high percentages of the individual organisms of the species are consumed by more complex organisms in the food chain, enough survive to propagate a new generation. As we move toward more complexity, the survival mechanisms become such things as thick skin, teeth, speed, acute senses, and so on.

The human species is very limited in terms of these physical survival mechanisms. What the human species has is a very well-developed cerebral cortex that allows it to think abstractly, not simply reacting to the environment but actually creating new environments hospitable to survival. For example, that a cave provides shelter and fire provides warmth is something other higher primates may know by experience. But only humans can take those two facts and from them abstract something new, something that does not exist in the natural environment—a cave with a fire in it—and then create that in the natural environment.

As this ability to think abstractly developed among the species, however, it led directly to a major problem, even as it allowed the species to survive and flourish in a wide variety of climates and locations. The increasing consciousness of self (the ability to think of oneself in the third person—as that one sitting around that imaginary fire, for example) eventually led to a confrontation with the problem of death and mortality. In short, we are a species whose very specialized survival mechanism places it in direct and energetic confrontation with that overriding survival instinct shared by all species. Our minds are driven by the will to survive, while at the same time we are saddled with the knowledge that death is our inevitable end. The anxiety created by this contradiction in our very being is overwhelming. Were we unable to repress this anxiety, we would be constantly cowering in fear, psychotically stunned and unable to act at all.

According to the theory of generative death anxiety, it is this ability to repress from consciousness the fact of our own endangeredness, extreme vulnerability, and mortal nature that is the very foundation of human psychological existence. This theory suggests quite plausibly that the energy cooking away in the unconscious is not primarily sexual or aggressive urges, nor accumulative or mimetic urges, nor even the will to power. These are each, rather, culturally specific manifestations of a deeper energy, the energy of repressed mortality anxiety.[8]

We employ the entire array of psychological defenses to keep this mortality anxiety from bubbling up into consciousness, for, as noted, a person unable to repress his or her death awareness would be stunned and unable to act. Although there are mental problems resulting strictly from brain dysfunction, many of the neuroses and even many psychoses, as well as "normal" mental health, can be understood and interpreted as relative successes and failures at keeping this repressed death anxiety at bay—as psychological and behavioral habits constructed as trade-offs between anxiety and functionality in particular environments that are relatively problematic or unproblematic in the person's current environment.[9]

It is not individual psychology that interests us in relation to the biblical/theological category of Principalities and Powers, however, but the collective or social-psychological implications of this theory of generative death anxiety. In normal times, human culture acts as a massive buffer to raw mortality anxiety, allowing each person a sense of heroic place within a transcendently instituted project—that is, a sense of being a person of worth within a worthwhile scheme of living. The institutions of culture (religion, politics, art, economics, and so on) promise individual or species immortality by direct or vicarious participation in a divine plan. This is basically what the psychological literature refers to as *self-esteem*. Self-esteem is maintained so long as people believe the cultural stories, which tell us who we are, where we came from, where we are going, and why the way of life we are living is pleasing to the transcendent forces of the universe. Becker referred to such cultural narratives as *immortality ideologies*.[10]

When people have a firm sense of the plausibility of their cultural narratives and mythologies, the problem of death anxiety is more easily kept at bay and death can even be met as heroic sacrifice in support of the immortality ideology of the culture. This has sufficed for most people during most of human history. Obviously, even when the stories are told correctly and the rituals and ethics are followed meticulously, continued drought, plague, earthquakes, tidal waves, and other natural disasters, as well as historical events such as decisive military defeats or simply having the white man show up on your shore with vastly superior weapons, can cause widespread doubt about the cultural immortality ideology. But these moments of widespread doubt have been the exceptions rather than the rule for most human societies.

Probably the most important element in maintaining the intactness and plausibility of any particular cultural immortality ideology is the fact that everyone around you also believes in it.[11] In modern times, the deafening cacophony of competing and contradictory cultural immortality ideologies creates inevitable suspicion and doubt about the transcendent veracity of any one of them. Hence, we begin to see, coming to the surface in modern societies, a cultural malaise or anomie on one hand, and the frantic, meaning-grabbing compulsiveness on the other hand, as the cultural immortality ideologies no longer function to keep mortality anxiety at bay. People then desperately try to attach themselves to ersatz immortality ideologies (fundamentalisms of all sorts, nostalgia politics, technologism, Pyrrhic tragedies such as "heroic" school shootings, or, following the cultural narrative to its (il)logical conclusion, heretofore insane levels of capitalist accumulation and material display).

Becker himself was more or less indifferent to experimental testing of his theory. He was not trained, in the first place, in the experimental tradition, although he was firmly grounded in empiricism in the Jamesian sense. But secondly, he felt that the urge to reduce everything to small, testable pieces was one large reason why the social sciences had lost sight of the holistic understanding of human behavior and needs. There has been, however, a group of social psychologists who for the last twenty years have been putting an array of hypotheses spun from the collective psychological aspects of Becker's theory to a wide range of empirical investigation, amassing a considerable literature of both correlative and experimental data, and have been finding it to be a very robust theory, much more plausible (that is, more able to predict test-subject actions and reactions) than any of the leading theoretical behavioral alternatives.[12]

## Generative Death Anxiety and Representations of Immortality

What the theory of generative death anxiety strongly suggests is that there is a worm at the core of human existence of which we are mostly blissfully unaware. In effect, the evolutionary process seems to have played a cruel joke, having created a being with a transcending mind and imagination and then saddled that being with a very mortal and weak physical body that hungers, thirsts, defecates, ages, and finally dies, taking the transcending mind and imagination with it into the abyss of death. No wonder that a sensitive soul experiences panic and anxiety attacks! This theory suggests that we spend most of our psychic energy in the creation of symbols of immortality, symbols that allow us, at least momentarily, to suppress from consciousness the fact of who we really are. Our strivings are toward, as Ernest Becker put it, the denial of death.

As far as we know, we are the only species that knows and understands the reality of death years before it happens. Some animals never seem to understand death, even as the predator pounces or the butcher's blade is poised for the kill. Other of our animal siblings do seem to experience a kind of terror just prior to the mortal blow—and that look of terror on an animal face has haunted each and every one of us. But we are a species who must live with that furious terror within us, now simmering, now boiling, from early childhood until the day the death angel calls. Repressing this terror is quite literally *the central* human task, for without some success in taming this terror—in suppressing it from immediate consciousness—a person would be psychotically stunned and unable to maintain forward movement.

We are born into cultures that provide us with immortality narratives and symbols, and we tame the terror of mortality consciousness by vicarious identification with these narratives and symbols of transcendence. According to this basic theory of human nature, we all want to endure and prosper and in some sense gain or ensure our continued significance and immortality. Yet we are only mortal, plainly and undeniably. It is in this contradiction between who we are and what we want to be, a contradiction that rages within us at our deepest psychological and spiritual level of being, that we begin to see forming a social-scientific understanding of the biblical/theological category of Principalities and Powers.

> The thing that makes [humans] the most devastating animal that ever stuck his neck up into the sky is that he wants a stature and a destiny that is impossible for an animal; he wants an earth that is not an earth but a heaven, and the price for this kind of fanatic ambition is to make the earth an even more eager graveyard than it naturally is.[13]

We create cultural symbols representing immortality, which are "good" and assist us in maintaining self-esteem, keeping from consciousness the immediate awareness of death. But to keep ourselves from noticing that these transcending symbols themselves are human artifacts, we begin to treat the artifact as if it really had the power to bestow immortality upon us. It is the only way to keep from doubting its ability to do so.

Let us look, for example, at the immortality symbol of wealth accumulation, since that is so centrally a focus of the American immortality narrative. Wealth, in the form of accumulated goods and services, is a natural symbol of "more life," of immortality, as that which stands opposed to deprivation and starvation. This probably has deep roots in our collective psyche, given that deprivation and starvation were always very real short-term possibilities for human beings during most of their history (and continue to be so for much of the world even today). Money provides the power to command goods and services, and the symbol of wealth accumulation in our cultural immortality ideology has merged with the urge for money accumulation. However, the accumulation of money almost inexorably takes on a power of its own, a psychological investment that is all but disconnected from the accumulation of goods and services. It is pursued for its own sake, in a manner we can call a fetish. In this sense, a fetish is a "narrowing down" in our symbol picture that has become irrational. The accumulation of wealth in the form of goods and services, because it aids in survival, can be seen as rational, although it would surely also have a rational satiation point. But the pursuit of money for its own sake has no rational satiation point. More zeroes can always be added. In my own lifetime, I have watched the cultural immortality narrative as it concerns wealth—that is, whose money demonstrates who is really the winner, who is really on top, who is really more than mere human—move from millionaire to billionaire. And now that also seems to have been surpassed. "Sure he's a billionaire, but does he have only a few billions or lots of billions?"

It is important for our concerns here to notice that there is a clearly sacrificial element involved in this kind of fetishism. For as with ancient and pagan idolatry, that which we mortal humans have constructed becomes the consuming focus for life, a narrow constriction that comes to take precedence over all else.

It should be noted that some degree of narrowing down, of constricting, is necessary to human life, for there is simply too much to take in. Sitting alone in one closed room, it would be impossible to take in all that is truly there to experience. We focus attention on that which is important to the task of living, and only these things become conscious to us. Given the totality of possible experience in each moment, a mind unable to narrow down to this degree would be stunned by the multiplicity of everyday life.

But how narrowly must we narrow down? A life too narrow is crippling. To see a landscape only in terms of a prospective development site is crippling. To see a fellow human only as client, consumer, or possessor of desired sexual organs is crippling. It is to miss even that fullness of life that we, with our limited capacities, are able to experience.

## REPRESENTATIONS OF EVIL

We now draw a step closer to a social-scientific understanding of the Principalities and Powers by reflecting on the symbolic meaning of evil in human society.[14] Decay, feces, corpses, animality, stench—our symbolizations of evil in every society demonstrate clearly that what is just under the surface of consciousness is a direct association of evil with death and mortality. Evil comes to have a clear moral sense about it as well, for Satan is the archfoe of the Good, of God. God's will, the Good, is identified with that which is supportive of the community, society, and civilization. Evil becomes opposition to God's will, as acting contrary to "God's law," contrary to the good of society. Evil is wickedness, disorder, and chaos.

We are naturally predisposed to oppose evil, and rightly so. We oppose evil just as we oppose death! But here we come to the problem of evil from the other side. For even while we oppose evil as we oppose death, it is objectively demonstrable that nearly every stitch of human-caused evil in the world has been and is caused as a side effect of our attempts to maintain the "Good," in the form of maintaining the continued plausibility of one or another immortality ideology.

Now we are right on the edge of a social-scientific view of the Principalities and Powers. Let us recap. We rightly oppose evil. Few among us consciously embrace evil, and those who do we consider to be clinically pathological. The liberal humanist tradition is to that extent correct when it posits the innate goodness of human nature. Normal people choose the good and oppose evil.[15] Reality, however, is too much for us to bite off whole—we must narrow it down in order to get any grasp on it at all, but we remain consciously unaware of this narrowing habit of mind. Likewise, we unconsciously narrow down our compulsive struggle against mortality into a struggle against evil. Mortality we cannot oppose—but lawbreakers, yes! There is nothing we can do finally to halt death. But *this* enemy we can annihilate!

A social-scientific understanding of the Principalities and Powers, of the unseen forces that often transform even our best and most humanistic intentions into the service of violence and the system of domination in the world, comes down to this. In our opposition to evil, we must of necessity narrow down and focus on specific evils, which in turn come to represent mortality. Our motives in this are good, and it is certainly better that specific evils be opposed than that no evils are opposed, even if ultimately we cannot solve the enigma of death. However, our tendencies are to narrow too much in our focus, leading us to think that the specific evil we oppose is the ultimate evil and that all will be well (we will achieve salvation, heaven, utopia) if we can simply defeat and wipe out this one specific evil before us.

This tendency is coupled to another fetishistic urge to which we are prone in our manufacture of symbols, the creation of scapegoats. Scapegoating in this sense occurs once we have identified a specific, narrowly focused evil with absolute evil and then have identified that evil with a particular persona, group, race, or ideology. In seeking to fight against evil, human beings bring ever more evil into the world, because all but inevitably the evil we fight against has been too narrowly defined and too narrowly focused on other human beings and ideologies. The stage is then set for religiously and culturally sanctioned massacre.[16] Here is Becker's cogent summary of the situation:

> But if we add together the logic of the heroic struggle against evil with the necessary fetishization of evil, we get a formula that is no longer pathetic but terrifying. It explains almost by itself why humans, of all animals, have caused the most devastation on earth—the most real evil. The human alone struggles extra hard to be immune to death because he alone is conscious of it; but by being able to identify and isolate evil arbitrarily, he is capable of lashing out in all directions against imagined dangers of this world. . . . The human being is an animal who must fetishize in order to survive and have "normal mental health." But this shrinkage of vision that permits him to survive also at the same time prevents him from having the overall understanding he needs to plan for and control the effects of his shrinkage of experience.[17]

And here is the frightening power of the Principalities and Powers, the world systems of violence and domination. *Human beings commit their worst evil acts out of heroic intentions, the very desire to eradicate evil.* It is no wonder, then, that good people on both sides of any conflict see themselves as working toward the good, as fighting "evil," and as able to repeat with fullest conviction, "Gott mit uns!" "With God on our side!" Human beings will identify as "enemy" that which potentially threatens personal expansion or that of the group. When we recognize that our images of evil are culturally transmitted—that our immediate orientation toward good and evil is mediated to us by our environment rather than by rationally examined choices—we have essentially arrived at a social-scientific understanding of the biblical/theological category of the Principalities and Powers. For then we truly see that "it is not against flesh and blood that we wrestle." We wrestle, rather, against the power of culture to transmit to us for our consumption fetishized images of evil and a narrowly construed identification of our enemies that would lead us into becoming witting or unwitting perpetrators of ever-more-real human evil.

Though speaking from a biblical/theological position rather than from a position in the social sciences, Walter Wink definitely designates as Principalities and Powers the same unseen forces toward which a social scientist would point. Many paragraphs Wink has written on what he calls the World Domination System could have flowed from the pen of a phenomenological sociologist without any significant alterations.[18] Certainly these unseen forces include unjust economic arrangements, arrangements that lead some to feel they have a transcending (God-given) right to plenty, while masses of fellow human beings languish in poverty. Militarism is certainly included here, especially in our own cultural immortality ideology, where the end of the Cold War has only spurred an enthusiasm for higher military spending—more SDI and research and development for an entirely new array of weapons systems to "meet the unknown challenges of the post–Cold War period."[19] Racism, sexism, and homophobia also carry the power to have us falsely define evil in this world and therefore falsely align ourselves against each other.

The mass media is neither a positive nor a neutral force in our culture. The media more than anything else determines and transmits our cultural images of good and evil. In the grips of the profit-making system (itself an obvious fetish), the media, hiding behind a chimera of objectivity, spew into our environment a constant and daily dose of glamorized violence and killing, aimed not at adults, but rather, what is surely criminal, at our children and teenagers.

I find a particularly instructive example of social-scientific understanding of the Principalities and Powers in Lt. Col. Dave Grossman's book, *On Killing*.[20] Grossman worked for years as a military psychologist. It was his job to increase "fire ratio" among the foot soldiers—that is, to break down the natural inhibitions humans have in regard to killing other humans. Military psychologists like

Grossman developed established mechanisms for this assignment, including methods of classical conditioning, operant conditioning, desensitization, and role modeling. Then Grossman was startled to realize that, in the American media system of "violence as entertainment," in movies, television, and video games in particular, the culture is exposing and subjecting its children, from early age upward, to essentially the same kinds of conditioning techniques being used in the military to break down new recruits' inhibitions to point a gun at another human being and pull the trigger. Combine that fact with the availability of weapons, and we have a clear recipe for disaster among our teens and young people.

What Grossman's book makes even more startlingly clear, and what is directly related to the subject at hand, is the fact that it is impossible to point to any one person or group of people who made conscious decisions about creating violent chaos in the country. Each piece of the complex puzzle is created and set in place by good and respectable citizens, each simply trying to earn an honest and legal living by selling a legal product within the rules of the social system and protecting and defending the civil rights of people to enjoy those products. Yet the collective result of each of these pieces is a society in which children are being brought up with significantly decreased resistance to killing each other and significantly increased access to high-powered weapons for doing so. This is a lucid example of the force of Principalities and Powers at work.

Consumerism, the urge for "bigger and better," is one of those forces in our culture that disposes people to act against their enlightened best intentions. Spurred by advertising, the lifeblood of the mass media, people are subtly and not so subtly encouraged to feel restless and dissatisfied with the abundance they already have. Already the richest nation in the world by any measure other than social-quality-of-life indicators, we find it all but impossible to curb our desire for more stuff. Like a person on an alcoholic binge, we seem determined to fill our spiritual void by more and more "shopping," even as destruction of the environment devastates the land in which we live. The happiness promised by consumerism turns out not to be fulfillment at all, but a treadmill pursuit of an ever-receding aspiration point.

## THE WISDOM OF THE PACIFIST POSITION

If we return in conclusion to the major theses of Walter Wink's work on the Powers, it is easily seen by now how much common ground we have found between the biblical/theological category of Principalities and Powers and a social-scientific view of the phenomena.

***The Powers are good.*** As human self-consciousness developed, the concurrent awareness of death brought with it a crippling psychological burden of anxiety. The species would not have survived had it not developed psychological mechanisms to defend against this intolerable burden. These internal, psychological mechanisms were reinforced by evolving social and cultural forms that allowed each person to feel he or she was a significant actor on a transcendent, cosmic stage.

*The Powers are fallen.* As these social and cultural forms evolved, varying degrees of power and prestige accrued to those who could manipulate the structures most adeptly. Generation upon generation of this process created systems of domination; "pyramids of sacrifice" was sociologist Peter Berger's apt term for them.[21] These pyramids of sacrifice became embedded in the cultures themselves and came to mediate simple reality to the people born into them. The fundamentally unjust skewing of social wealth and benefits toward some and away from others is hidden behind a chimera of "common sense."[22] It comes to represent "order" as opposed to chaos and disorder.

Even more important than the skewing of prestige, privilege, and social wealth is the fact that, ultimately, the worm gnawing at the core of human beings is not the lack of material things or even social power and prestige. It is fundamentally a lack of being, an urgent mortality anxiety that informs even those at the top of the pyramid that there is something fundamentally "wrong" and evil with them.[23] There is a spiritual hunger at the core of each one of us that can be masked by the things of this world but cannot finally be sated.[24] Because of this, people are especially susceptible to immortality ideologies that identify the source of this gnawing sense of evil with a tangible enemy, present a program for moving against that enemy, and promise "salvation" once that enemy is conquered. Once the pyramidal structures of sacrifice are aligned in mutual support of any such immortality ideology, it becomes all but impossible to set limits on the levels of violence populations will be willing to employ against this enemy in pursuit of its eradication. Furthermore, the best and most carefully laid plans to foster peace, justice, and tolerance among people seem always to be dangerously fragile, easily destroyed in short order by any two-bit demagogue who comes down the pike.

In short, the strategic combination of Principalities (the structural pyramids of sacrifice) and Powers (the spiritual gnawing and sense of lack) is about as close to a social-scientific definition of demonic evil as we get. This is how an educated population in the heart of Christian Europe could tolerate extermination camps as an acceptable (though perhaps regrettable) price to be paid for salvation. This is how a Calvinistic, thrifty, enterprising, and God-fearing Christian nation could countenance the creation of the atomic weapon to fight that enemy, only to employ it mercilessly against another when it proved unnecessary against the enemy for which it was created. This is how an American military strategist during the Vietnam War, educated in the best humanistic tradition, can state with no redeeming sense of irony, "We had to destroy this village in order to save it."

*The Powers must be redeemed.* Here is where the biblical/theological conception begins to diverge most clearly from anything that can be said from the perspective of social science. The preacher is able to inspire his or her listeners with language honed over the centuries for just this purpose. The social scientist, qua social scientist, can only hear the preacher as expounding yet another salvation ideology among all the others that have made our world a massive fertilizer pit. Certainly the social scientist will agree with Wink that, most of the time, most people are rushing off to serve "false gods," to feed their sense of gnawing lack. There may be common ground enough in the project of identifying and exposing idols, even if agreement cannot be reached as to what is or is not the true God.

The dilemma is that if we as a species are ever to become more than each other's executioners, we will have to be mobilized in large numbers for the task. Religion has the vocabulary to inspire and mobilize large numbers in a way social science does not. Yet no matter what the intentions of the movement leaders, large, mobilized masses of people have a clear tendency to start listening to the demagogues. If even Jesus Christ was not able to speak a message of peace, love, and understanding clearly enough to prevent it from becoming very quickly perverted, even within his own lifetime, by his followers into yet one more immortality ideology, which would eventually give its ritual blessings to twenty centuries of killing fields, what chance do we have of success in that message now?

Speaking personally now, wearing neither Christian nor social scientist hat, I have come to shudder at talk of redemption and salvation. I place my hope now in simple human survival. Given who we are, that will be work enough for all of us. My hope is that as we come to understand the social and psychological mechanisms by which we are so easily manipulated by the demonic forces of this world, we will be able to take at least some conscious control over the strings being pulled to make us dance—that we might be better able to tolerate the gnawing lack if we understand more clearly whence it comes, and not be so prone to project the source onto others and then move against them with righteous zeal. If we were more able to sit with our gnawing sense of lack and befriend it, rather than moving immediately for salvation and redemption from it, then our mortality, since we know our time is limited, may itself become a source of depth and meaning in our lives, rather than the unconscious enemy. This is faint stuff when compared to ideologies of salvation and redemption, I know.

Finally, this has brought me back to the profound wisdom of the religiously nonviolent and pacifist tradition in which I was raised. I think it is significant—and perhaps indicative that the reservations I expressed in the above paragraphs concerning the language of salvation and redemption are more semantic than substantive—that Professor Wink arrives by his route at the same place of committed nonviolence and pacifism.[25]

Knowing we have this tendency to define too narrowly the focus of evil, leading us ever to see the "demonic" in the face of our enemies and making us therefore unable to place enduring limits on the degree of violence we are willing to employ to fight against that enemy, we begin to see the profound wisdom of moral traditions that set the parameters of these limits on an a priori basis. Such moral traditions then are seen not as strategies of withdrawal, retreat, cowardliness, or an intentional but ineffective righteousness, but rather as wise and judicious applications of political pragmatism. They may be placed on the same moral plane as the Hippocratic Oath in medicine—"Above all, do no harm!"

Given what we do know now about the unseen Powers that manipulate our perceptions, we can never be sure in any absolute sense that what we have identified as evil is in fact evil and not simply another partial and fetishized projection of our cultural salvation ideology. No matter how sure we seem to be in any given instance, we must humble ourselves before the evidence of history and admit that we are probably wrong and that a violent move against the evil we think we see will most likely only create more evil. Yet we also cannot stand by and do nothing when we see evil.

Here is where the wisdom of pacifist, nonviolent, moral tradition comes into focus. We employ the methods of nonviolent intervention to fight against the evil, injustice, and oppression we see. But we remain committed, a priori, to the strategy of nonviolence so that, if at any point in our political and personal struggles against these evils we begin to feel that we would be justified to kill, maim, or slay another human being, signal flags ought to appear on our mental horizons, warning us that we are constricting our view of evil too narrowly and scapegoating the cause of evil.

In the escalation of power tactics, in other words, the Principalities and Powers are getting ahold of our puppet strings. It is here then that self-examination and cultural criticism, an embracing of our mortal limitedness, and a rigorous wrestling once again with the Principalities and Powers, are called for. Only then are we spiritually and morally prepared to resume the struggle against evil. Failure to pay attention to the signal flags at that point will lead one into becoming yet another perpetrator of the atrocities of human history. To employ nonviolent direct action in the struggle against evil, guided by firmly committed principles, may not always succeed in short-term goals but at least makes it much less likely that one will do great harm.

# Chapter 4

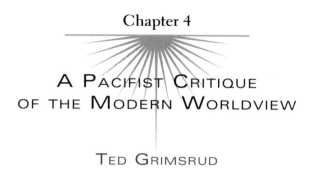

# A PACIFIST CRITIQUE
# OF THE MODERN WORLDVIEW

## TED GRIMSRUD

I have been learning from Walter Wink for years, going back half my lifetime to when I read his little book *The Bible in Human Transformation*,[1] which came at a crucial time for me as I was emerging from the literalistic fundamentalism I had been taught as a young Christian. In the early 1980s, I eagerly awaited his books on the Powers—I had been fascinated by John Howard Yoder's work on the Powers in *The Politics of Jesus*[2] and was delighted when I learned that Wink would be developing the analysis further. I was not disappointed. *Naming the Powers*[3] took the exegetical work done by Yoder and others to new depths, and *Unmasking the Powers*[4] provided new and exciting applications to social and psychological issues. However, impressed as I was by these books, I still could never have imagined the kind of book with which Wink would conclude his Powers trilogy.

That book, *Engaging the Powers*,[5] has energized me ever since I first read it in 1992 and more than any other book I can think of has directed my own thinking and research in the last number of years. Wink's analysis provides two especially crucial insights. The first is that one of the main effects that the fallen Powers have in the modern world is *concealment*—that is, they distort and hide from us the true nature of reality, the true nature of what binds us, and the true sources for our liberation. And the second is that the best criterion for discerning what is truth and what is deception in the swirl of ideas and values and theories and biases in which we are immersed in our world is *nonviolence*.

In this chapter I will reflect on the way we *look* at the world around us (our modern worldview) as a major expression of "concealment" in our culture today. Using the criterion of nonviolence (or, my preferred term, "pacifism"), I want to suggest that our culture's very worldview itself serves to alienate us from truth and life. Perhaps we fragile human beings feel the power of the fallen Powers most profoundly in the concealed assumptions of our worldview that lead to violence—violence against human beings, for sure, but even more fundamentally, violence against creation itself.

I conclude from this analysis that one of the major tasks of pacifists is simply to bring that which is concealed to awareness. That is, we are challenged to foster *dis-illusionment* with the modern worldview. We are challenged to discern how this worldview distorts and disguises and conceals and to expose such distortions for all people of goodwill to see. Such work plays a crucial role in human transformation and the healing of creation.

## A METAPHOR FOR THE MODERN WORLDVIEW

Yale University political scientist James C. Scott, a writer of deep humanity and unique insight, gives us a metaphor for illuminating the modern worldview. This story comes from his book *Seeing Like a State: How Certain Schemes to Improve the Human Condition Have Failed.*

By the late eighteenth century, the scientific revolution was in full sway in western Europe. The change in consciousness that we call modernity found expression in the human relationship with the natural world, one example being how people related to the forests of western Europe. Diderot's encyclopedia, produced in mid-eighteenth-century France, was a monument to modernity, and in its entry on "forests" the encyclopedia reflected the new thinking of the time. This entry focused almost entirely on the economic value of forests—the commercial products that could be extracted from the forests, possible tax revenues, ways forests could be exploited to yield profits. "Forests" were no longer thought of as places where a whole variety of life-forms live in ages-old harmony and balance.[6] The changes in the perception of the natural world in general (which also apply specifically to forests) can be seen simply in shifts in vocabulary. "Nature" becomes "natural resources," with the emphasis on the usefulness of nature for human usage. Trees that are understood to have economic value become known as "timber," and those without such value are labeled "trash trees" or "underbrush."[7]

"Scientific forestry" emerged at this time and exerted a profound influence on the landscape of western Europe, with major repercussions still being felt today. Scientific forestry began, not surprisingly, in Germany. In the late 1700s, foresters began to remake Germany's forests. They hoped to bring into being a more easily quantified forest through careful cultivation. They cleared the underbrush, reduced the numbers of species (often to monoculture), and did planting simultaneously and in straight rows on large tracts. Eventually the old-growth forests were transformed into truly "scientific forest," that is, neat and tidy monocultural, even-aged forests.[8]

The initial results of remaking Germany's forests were spectacular. Certainly, on an aesthetic level, the regularity and neatness of the appearance of the new forests resonated deeply with the values of modern Europe. At first, the new forests provided rich economic rewards as well. The Norway spruce became the tree of choice, because of its hardiness, rapid growth, and valuable wood. But because trees are long-term crops, it took some time for the full effects of this approach to forestry to become apparent. Only after the planting of the second rotation of the spruce did it become clear that something was wrong. The first generation had grown excellently because it could reap the benefits of the rich soil left behind by the old-growth forest in all its diversity. However, after that deposit of nutrients had been exhausted, the output of the forest shrank dramatically. A new German term was coined—*Waldsterben* (forest death)—to describe the effects.

It became clear that several of the practices of "scientific forestry" directly led to the problems. By clearing the underbrush, "trash trees," deadfalls, and snags, in the interest of neatness, foresters greatly reduced the diversity of insect, mammal, and bird populations so crucial for soil-building. By transforming old-growth biodiversity into a monoculture of same-age species, foresters made the forests much more vulnerable to massive storm damage and infestation of "pests" specialized to Norway spruce.[9]

Scott uses this story of the transformation of Germany's forests as a metaphor for the havoc wreaked by modern attempts to dismember "exceptionally complex and poorly understood set[s] of relations and processes in order to isolate a single element of instrumental value."[10]

In a similar way, this story may serve as a more general metaphor for symbolizing the modern worldview as a whole, and particularly, for the purposes of this chapter, for symbolizing the impulses toward coercion and even violence characteristic of this worldview. I will begin with some provisional definitions, then illustrate further my critique of the modern worldview by considering several aspects of that worldview, and conclude with a brief outline of an alternative way of looking at the world, what I call a pacifist way of knowing.

## A PACIFIST BASIS FOR CRITIQUE

For all my appreciation for his profound insights, I do have one clear disagreement with Walter Wink. This disagreement arises over the use of the term "pacifism." I do not have space here to discuss this difference beyond acknowledging it. I do suspect Wink would not necessarily be happy to be associated with "a *pacifist* way of knowing," as he rejects this term as a characterization of his position.[11]

All I can do here is to briefly justify my usage. The root of the word "pacifism" is the Latin *pacis*: "peace" (not "passivity"). I understand "pacifism" to mean the love of peace, making peace the highest value. To me, the "-ism" connotes *ultimacy*—"peace" is an ultimate value. Now, placing ultimate weight on "peace" could surely be problematic, depending on what we mean by it. If "peace" means avoidance of conflict, for example, then Wink surely correctly rejects "pacifism" as a useful term (the avoidance of conflict as the ultimate value may accurately describe some so-called pacifists but is actually a quite unhealthy and ultimately violence-*fostering* approach to life).

As a Christian, I argue for a *different*, biblically oriented understanding of "peace"—"shalom." I see peace as a holistic concept best understood in relation to a constellation of concepts such as the well-being, wholeness, and health of the entire community on all levels. We may think of respect and harmony in relationships among human beings and between human beings and the rest of creation. Pacifism, then, is a *positive* concept, reflecting a vision for how life can and should be. For pacifism, nothing is as important as love, kindness, restorative justice, and healthy relationships with all of creation. A pacifist approach to life privileges holistic peace above any other value or goal—be it economic wealth, the nation-state, moral purity, or the survival of any particular human institution. Consequently, for pacifists, violence of any kind is never acceptable since there are no values that take precedence over holistic peace. So *nonviolence* is certainly part of the pacifist commitment. However, to me, the term "nonviolence" is less all-encompassing and positive than the term "pacifism." The vision of life I am trying to comprehend and articulate centers not primarily on the absence of violence but on the positive reality of holistic peace.

In our work of seeking to critique and overcome the ways our modern worldview serves the Powers' efforts at concealment and delusion, pacifism becomes a central criterion of discernment. We evaluate values and practices in terms of how they do or do not foster peace. The presence of violence serves as a warning, tipping us off that something is wrong with the system—similar to the way the death of the songbirds tipped people off to the devastating effects of DDT on the ecosystem. The presence of violence indicates for the pacifist that penultimate values are being given too high a priority. And we assume that when this happens, many other problems undermining the well-being of life will arise.

## THE "MODERN WORLDVIEW"

Numerous historians argue that the "modern worldview" can best be seen as emerging in its fullness in the early seventeenth century. They pinpoint the transition from the Middle Ages to the modern era in the West as the period from the late fifteenth to the early seventeenth century. Columbus, Copernicus, and Luther were the providers of the final blows that ended the medieval period, with their discoveries of the New World, the solar system, and a new doctrinal system freed from church control, respectively.[12]

Less than a generation later, the modern era began, with the laying of a theoretical foundation for a new worldview. Francis Bacon was a key initiator of this new worldview; he was followed by René Descartes and John Locke. All three thinkers pled for a new order and derived much energy from their indictment of medieval disorder, the duress of daily life, the deadwood of tradition, and the oppression of hierarchy and community. They urged a new fundamental agreement, one that razed the tottering and constricting medieval structures and began anew on a solid fundament.[13]

Richard Tarnas, in *The Passion of the Western Mind: Understanding the Ideas That Have Shaped Our World View*, provides a helpful synopsis of the modern worldview. The modern view contrasts with the medieval in seeing the cosmos as "an impersonal phenomenon, governed by regular natural laws, and understandable in exclusively physical and mathematical terms." In the medieval view, a personal and all-powerful God ruled the cosmos. The modern cosmos has more autonomy.[14]

Science came to be the central intellectual authority, dethroning religion as the "definer, judge, and guardian of the culture world view." In the scientific approach to truth, reason and observation take the place of revelation and theological doctrine. Religion evolves to be more a matter of personal and subjective sensibilities, leaving public knowledge to scientifically verifiable understandings. Faith and reason are sharply divided.[15]

With the modern view, the cosmos is comprehended by human rationality alone. Other aspects of human nature—emotional, aesthetic, relational, imaginative—are no longer seen as relevant for genuine understanding of the world. The universe is known through sober impersonal scientific investigation. Such knowledge results "not so much in an experience of spiritual liberation but in intellectual mastery and material improvement." The domination of nature becomes the goal of intellectual activity.[16]

The final aspect of the modern worldview emerged with the integration of the theory of evolution and its many consequences in other fields. Now, human origins and the processes of nature's changes were seen as exclusively attributable to natural causes and empirically observable processes. With this step, the drift toward seeing the earth no longer as the center of creation but simply as another planet was followed by the drift toward seeing the human being also no longer as the center of creation but simply as another animal.[17]

## CRITIQUE OF THREE ASPECTS OF THE MODERN WORLDVIEW

To illustrate problematic aspects of the modern worldview, I will briefly discuss three interrelated elements in that worldview—the view of the universe as impersonal, the quest to dominate nature, and the impact of rationalism on how we approach life.

I want to be clear that I do not mean this critique to be a wholesale rejection of modernity, nor of our Western way of life. At this point, I am simply seeking to gain some orientation. I am deeply troubled by the pervasiveness of violence and alienation in our society and believe that a big part of our problem stems from how we view the world. This concern pushes me to ask questions and to try to make connections between my pacifist convictions and the violence toward human beings and nature that so permeates the air we breathe in our world.

Even if we might wish we could, I know that we cannot (and probably, when it came down to it, would not want to) join the premodern world or the nonmodern world of the small, marginalized aboriginal cultures that exist today. However, I do think we might learn much from pre- and nonmodern cultures. By drawing on their wisdom, we may find help as we seek to make some adjustments in the culture of which we are all inextricably a part. There is no long-term future for the dominating, totalitarian, inherently violent modern worldview as it has found expression in the West over the past four centuries. Either it will be transformed into a more sustainable, holistically peaceable worldview, or it will lead to the destruction of human life as we know it.

Perhaps a starting point in challenging the concealment of this worldview is to deny the assumption that the rapid pace with which Western society has depleted the national order is simply an inevitable product of human evolution. In fact, human beings lived for tens of thousands of years in an essentially steady-state harmony with the rest of creation.[18] Only with modernity did human culture declare widespread war on the natural order. That is, what changed were human consciousness and the worldview of a large enough group of people to have a major impact. I happen to believe that this consciousness can change again. We are not trapped in a suicidal worldview. But while the first step in breaking free from this suicidal spiral of violence may be simple, it is anything but easy. This first step, I think (following Wink), is simply *seeing* what is going on.

**An impersonal universe.** David Abram, in his provocative book *The Spell of the Sensuous*,[19] argues persuasively that the key issue for human well-being in the world is finding the way somehow to restore our mutuality with what he calls the "more-than-human world." The objectification of the world outside of ourselves, he believes, was a move with profoundly destructive ramifications. For Abram, one of the key aspects of this separation between human beings and the rest of the world—and with that separation the attributing of consciousness only to human beings—came with the emergence of an abstract written alphabet. As cultures shift to printed letters, "the stones fall silent." As our senses focus their enlivening perceptions on the written word, "the trees become mute, the other animals dumb."[20]

This shift began with the ancient Greeks and gained impetus when Christianity (with its Greek-language scriptures) spread throughout the Western world. Only with the advent of the printing press, however, did this process come to dominate an entire civilization. The printing press brought in the Enlightenment and, with it, a deeply detached view of the more-than-human world—the view that came to characterize the modern period.[21] A particularly influential tenet of the Enlightenment along these lines found expression in Descartes' explicit separation of the thinking mind, or subject, from the nonhuman material world, which Descartes understood to be the world of "things" or "objects."[22]

Such a separation turned the world into an impersonal entity, understood primarily in objective, impersonal, physical, and mathematical terms. No longer were the inner mind and the outer world understood as inextricably related, wherein understanding in one realm heightened understanding in the other. They were separated, seen to be operating on different principles.[23] This separation between human consciousness and the other-than-human world and the consequent redefinition of nature opened the gates to massive disregard for other forms of life in the world. The collapse of complex ecosystems, the poisoning of waters, the extinction of species—these all stem from our forgetting our human inherence in a more-than-human world.[24] Abram points out that for at least ten thousand years prior to 1492, human cultures had continuously inhabited North America. These peoples "gathered, hunted, fished, and settled these lands without severely degrading the continent's wild integrity." The relatively brief time since Columbus set foot has seen the destruction of much of the natural wealth of this continent.[25]

The destructive impact of Western settlement transformed the Australian continent much more quickly even than North America, as European cultures came to dominate Australia about three hundred years after the settling of North America. We find an illustration of the costly consequences of this settling—and of the way the notion of the universe as impersonal and human beings as separate that is characteristic of the modern worldview filtered down to common people— in Robert Hughes's book *The Fatal Shore*, an account of western European settlement of Australia.

Hughes tells of the unimaginable abundance of aquatic life in the southern ocean, the previously undisturbed sanctuary for the black whale, the sperm whale, and the fur seals. Focusing on the fate of these sea mammals, he tells how every season millions traveled north from Antarctica to mate and calve along the coasts of New Zealand and Australia. These animals had no natural enemies and knew nothing of human beings. They had economic value, and they were defenseless. Tens of millions of them were wiped out in less than thirty years.

The new European settlers exploited these sea mammals without mercy, killing them year-round, clubbing their prey to death. The sealers never stopped, observing no off-season for mating and pupping time. Pregnant seals were killed by the thousands, and the pups were left milkless on the rocks to starve. "Disturbed in their ancestral rookeries, which soon became bogs of putrefaction—for the sealers took only the skins and left hills of flayed carcasses behind—the seals stopped breeding and abandoned their haunts."[26] In time, several of these species ceased to exist. They had simply been a resource to extract from the earth. The Western worldview understood nature as having no intrinsic value or spiritual connection with human beings but as simply part of the impersonal, clockwork universe.

*The domination of nature.* Once human beings depersonalize and objectify nature, they easily think of their relationship with nature as one of domination. At the very beginning of the modern era, Francis Bacon, one of the founders of the modern worldview, gave voice to this dynamic. In his influential book *The New Atlantis,* Bacon speaks of torturing, extorting, and subjugating nature for human benefit. In doing so, he sets the tone for the modern approach to reality, to daily life, and to the physical world.

Albert Borgmann, in his book *Crossing the Postmodern Divide,*[27] argues that the modern and largely successful quest to dominate nature began with the voyages of discovery at the beginning of the modern period. The Baconian philosophy found expression in the Herculean efforts of Western culture to advance in the face of nature's resistance. Borgmann cites several examples—the voyages of discovery beginning at the end of the fifteenth century, the extensive harnessing of wind and water power, the establishment of manufacturing supporting mass consumption, and the development of bookkeeping methods and financial instruments. "In each case, expansion faced major barriers—which were overcome by force."[28] Dynamite, massive construction equipment, pesticides, herbicides, the mobilizing of financial and physical resources—all are examples of the use of brute force to subdue, control, and dominate nature.

Borgmann uses the building of the railroad across the northern United States as a metaphor for the modern quest to dominate and subdue nature. One barrier railroad builders faced was gaining right-of-way for the tracks, and at least in parts of Montana this land was simply taken from Native American reservations with the threat of military force. Another barrier was geographical. Getting through the mountains in western Montana into Idaho required massive and brutal force. This force came from both heavy use of dynamite and use of human laborers. The chief engineer had nearly two thousand workers, most of whom were Chinese, fresh "from the steerage of immigrant ships," who "were used for construction and discarded when no longer needed."[29]

The massive amounts of earth that had to be moved were unprecedented. The development and application of explosives for such work were prerequisites for the transcontinental railroad. Human beings no longer had to be deterred by geographical barriers. The domination of nature required that distance and terrain, weather and season, be subdued. An extraordinarily aggressive attitude toward reality propelled this conquest. And this attitude has rarely been questioned in the face of assumptions about the necessity of safe, cheap, and dependable transportation to fuel our nation's economic development.[30]

Ironically, one hundred years later, the work of the railroads is pretty much over. Borgmann mentions the Milwaukee Road that used to span the continent. It is now bankrupt and has had its line dismantled. The Northern Pacific merged with the Great Northern and the Burlington. Eventually the line through Missoula, Montana, was sold to a local businessman.

The major legacy that the Northern Pacific left to Missoula is a threat to its water supply. Since the 1950s, when locomotives were switched from steam to diesel, tens of thousands of gallons of fuel were spilled in the train yard. They soaked into the soil and now float on the water table. Pesticides, paint, and solvents are working their way down to the community's source of drinking water.[31]

Following the building of the railroad, in the late 1950s, the U.S. government embarked on another exercise in taming the continent, building the interstate highway system that in many places in western mountain ranges parallels the railroad. "A four-lane, controlled-access highway is a much broader and more massive structure than a railroad. Hence highway construction was even more aggressively intrusive on the land than its railroad predecessors."[32]

**Rationalism.** Ultimately, the modern worldview is probably best characterized in terms of its understanding of rationality. At the beginning of the modern era, scientists in the seventeenth century established that "rationality" would be understood in a fairly narrow manner, limited, in Stephen Toulmin's words, "to theoretical arguments that achieved a quasi-geometrical certainty or necessity."[33] This rationalistic form of knowledge and control requires a narrowing of vision. Such tunnel vision brings into sharp focus certain limited aspects of an otherwise far more complex and unwieldy reality. This focus makes the phenomenon at the center of the field of vision legible and hence more easily and carefully quantified, analyzed, and controlled. This "rational" method seeks to "purify" the work of reason by separating this work from particular historical and cultural situations.[34]

James Scott labels the practical implementation of rationalism "high modernism." Characteristics of high modernism include commitment to consistent movement forward (progress), absolute truths, and rational planning of ideal social orders under standardized conditions of knowledge and production.[35] High modernism's problematic elements follow, first of all, from its claim that it is backed by the authority of scientific knowledge in its quest to "improve" the human condition. Secondly, high modernism uses this authoritative claim to silence competing sources of judgment.[36]

However, the use high modernism makes of science is narrow and totalitarian. "*Nothing* is known until and unless it is proven in a tightly controlled experiment." Knowledge gained through other means is not taken seriously. "Traditional practices, codified as they are in practice and in folk sayings," simply do not matter. They exist under the radar of modernity.[37]

Scott provides an example of one of many cases in which this rationalistic imperviousness to context has exacted a terrible toll in recent years. In the fifteen years following World War II, people reflecting the mind-set of the high modernists sprayed enormous quantities of DDT with the intent of killing mosquito populations and controlling mosquito-borne diseases. In preparation for these actions, scientific experiments focused only on determining the dosage concentrations and application conditions required for eradicating mosquito populations. Within that framework, DDT worked quite well. It did kill mosquitoes and significantly reduce disease. But the experimental framework left out important considerations—with tragic consequences. It gradually became apparent that DDT had a devastating ecological impact. Residues were absorbed by organisms all along the food chain, with deadly poisonous effects.

One aspect of the problem was the way side effects multiplied. "A first-order effect—say, the decline or disappearance of a local insect population—led to changes in flowering plants, which changed the habitat for other plants and for rodents, and so on." Secondly, scientists had examined the effects of DDT on other species only under experimental, not field, conditions—even though its application occurred in the latter context. Scientists "had no idea what the interactive effects of pesticides were when they were mixed with water and soil and acted upon by sunlight."[38] The problem with DDT shows how the narrowness of rationalistic vision does lead directly to violence against the world. We could cite innumerable other examples, including many practices in modern warfare, such as chemical defoliation and the use of land mines.

One of the very early critics of rationalism, Blaise Pascal, raised a concern that remains apropos today. The great failure of rationalism, Pascal said, is "not its recognition of technical knowledge, but its failure to recognize any other."[39] These three elements of the modern worldview, seeing the universe as impersonal, dominating nature, and privileging rationalistic science as determinative of acceptable knowledge, combine to foster a tremendous amount of violence. Yet, they are simply part of the air that educated people in the West breathe. What is required is some major *dis-illusionment*.

## A PACIFIST WAY OF KNOWING

As an alternative to uncritical living within the modern worldview, I want to propose a pacifist way of knowing. Let me repeat what I mean by pacifism: a holistic concept best understood in relation to a constellation of concepts such as the well-being, wholeness, and health of the entire community on all levels. We can think of respect and harmony in relationships among human beings and between human beings and the rest of creation. Pacifism is a *positive* concept, reflecting a vision for how life is meant to be. Nothing is as important as love, kindness, restorative justice, and healthy relationships with all of creation. A pacifist approach to life privileges holistic peace above any other value or goal. In concluding my chapter, I want to mention briefly two elements of a pacifist way of knowing that specifically relate to what I have been saying about the inherent violence of the modern worldview.

*The web of life.* The first recognizes the *interconnectedness* of all of life. Native American philosopher Gabriel Horn writes of the contrast between two ways of knowing. The first coheres with what Horn calls "our Original Intention." "Take only what you need, live in harmony and balance with your environment, love the Earth. Such a thought process does not allow artificial extensions, like the tools we create or even the weapons we make, to become actual extensions of the self." People whose thought processes follow this path do not believe they are superior to other life-forms. All things are necessary parts of wholeness.[40] The other way of knowing "travels on an asphalt road." For this path, people's artificial extensions, on which they increasingly depend, are linked with their very identity. This leads to an ever-widening separation not only from non-Western peoples but also from other life-forms. The wheel is seen no longer as something sacred but simply as an instrument for moving faster.[41]

Wendell Berry argues that we must resist the modernist urge to reduce everything to abstract classifications. "Without some use of abstractions, thought is incoherent or unintelligible, perhaps unthinkable. But abstraction alone is merely dead."[42] Instead, we must understand ourselves as intimately connected with the other-than-human world. "If we are to protect the world's multitude of places and creatures, then we must know them . . . with affection, 'by heart,' so that in seeing or remembering them the heart may be said to 'sing,' to make a music peculiar to its recognition of each particular place or creature that it knows well."[43]

*Eloquent reality.* The second aspect of a pacifist way of knowing is openness to the richness of life, what Albert Borgmann calls "eloquent reality."[44] Many people have characterized the twentieth century as a century of deep alienation and brokenness. Such alienation seems to follow from a worldview that has abstracted from the nonhuman world all conscious intelligence and purpose and meaning and then projected onto the world a soulless machine. Richard Tarnas writes, "This is the ultimate anthropomorphic projection: a [human]-made machine, something not in fact ever found in nature. From this perspective, it is the modern world's own impersonal soullessness that has been projected from within onto the world."[45]

A pacifist way of knowing argues that this modern interpretation of the universe is only one particular *perspective*. Other perspectives are possible. "Eloquent reality" consists of those things, in this life, this world, that are genuinely beautiful, healing, soulful, invigorating. Reality understood thus is not totally orderly, objective, controllable, or quantifiable.

Martin Buber articulated an understanding of the world focused on relationships as the core of what is most real—in contrast to the world of use, control, and exploitation (the "It-world"). Buber argued that the world we live in is where we will encounter our peaceable God:

I know nothing of a "world" and of "worldly life" that separate us from God. What is designated that way is life with an alienated It-world, the life of experience and use. Whatever goes out in truth to the world, goes forth to God. Only he that believes in the world achieves contact with it; and if he commits himself he cannot remain godless. Let us love that actual world that never wishes to be annulled; . . . in all its terror, [daring] to embrace it with our spirit's arms—and our hands encounter the hands that hold it.[46]

Gordon Kaufman is another who profoundly and painstakingly articulates a pacifist way of knowing in relation to the big issues of God and the world. Seeking peace on earth—what Kaufman calls a "humane order," characterized by love, justice, creativity, and mutual respect—goes *with the grain* of the universe. Reality is not soulless, arbitrary, meaningless. "Our deepest human aspirations are not alien to this ecological-historical order into which we have been born: the world in which we live is a humane-seeking order. We can give ourselves wholeheartedly to responsible life and work within it."[47]

A pacifist way of knowing, then, makes two strongly countermodern assertions. First, all of life is interconnected. We are called to respect that interconnectedness and to seek harmony with all of creation. Second, life *in* this world is where we encounter the divine. Let us love this actual world, and in that way we will be loving the God who made it and enlivens it.

# Part Two

# Understanding the Powers

# Chapter 5

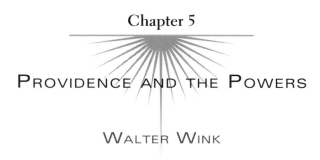

# PROVIDENCE AND THE POWERS

## WALTER WINK

Nicolai Berdyaev was right: the world is not in such a state as to justify an optimistic view of divine providence.[1] For every story of divine intervention, there are dozens of counterstories of divine absence. Why else would "miracles" seem so marvelous and unusual? Prayers are answered, yes, but they also go unanswered. The guardian angels of middle-class children seem to be more efficient than the ones guarding children in the ghetto. There is an issue of class and race here. In a world of causally ordered events, each with its own antecedent, there appears to be no room for God to "step in" and "interfere" with the consequences.

Even more devastating to the idea of God's beneficent care is the Holocaust. How can we speak of God's answers to prayer when millions of God's people died—among them a third of world Jewry—many with prayers on their lips, while the ovens roared remorselessly on? And what of the gays, the retarded, the communists, and the Jehovah's Witnesses who also were killed? God did not clog up the ovens at Belsen or cause the trains carrying victims to Auschwitz to break down (or, if they did, they were soon repaired). The bullet aimed at the heart of Martin Luther King Jr. sped unswervingly to its target, but the antitank shell aimed at the Chilean dictator Augusto Pinochet failed to detonate. Many who survived the bombing of the World Trade Center testify to how they stopped for coffee, which they normally did not do, or called in sick, or had a glitch in child care, and their lives were spared. But then what about the other three thousand who died?

When a tornado struck the Goshen United Methodist Church in Alabama, killing twenty and injuring scores, the whole first row of the soprano section was lifted up and set down in safety. But Diane Molock died protecting two little boys by covering them with her body. The pastor's two-year-old daughter was killed when a wall fell in instead of out. Individual cases of survival remain unintelligible in the face of those killed. The press repeatedly attempted to get the clergy to ascribe, not only the survivals, but the deaths, to God. But the clergy insisted that it was chance, no matter how many were able to find tiny zones of safety in the face of such raw tragedy.[2]

If that were the whole story, we could simply write off the idea of divine providence as bad theology. But people all over the world have had incontestable experiences of providence that require explanation. Not all of these experiences pass muster as believable, but enough do so that we are obliged to take them seriously. My interest in this chapter is to juxtapose the notion of providence with that of the Principalities and Powers. For when we treat providence in isolation from the Powers, we turn providence into privileged treatment granted by God to the righteous, the chosen, and the few.

Curiously, the idea of divine providence was far more central to Greek and Roman paganism than to Judaism or early Christianity.[3] Providence was a god in Rome, one of the Virtues (Latin: "Powers") who, along with Victory, Peace, Fortune, and so on, composed an impersonal rank of gods known only by the specific benefit they conferred. Victory was a god because it produced victory.[4] "Providentia" provided political legitimation for the ascent of an emperor to power and was constantly invoked as the superhuman agency by which the ruler cared for and provided for his subjects.[5] The emperor's Providence was skillfully stressed in order to ingratiate the masses. It followed from this that any conspiracy against Caesar became a conspiracy against the heavenly beneficence that he dispensed and a threat to the eternity of the state.[6] Though, of course, if an emperor was overthrown, the god Providence had clearly changed sides and blessed the usurper.

"Providence" in Roman usage was merely an optimistic view of Fate, held by the winners. Whoever won in battle, whoever ascended to the principate, whoever overthrew the emperor, had manifestly been blessed by the spiritual Powers That Be.[7] Belief in the Virtues is just a variant on the myth of redemptive violence. These gods rode on the victors, and whoever won could, without fear of contradiction, be named the gods' chosen, simply because he had won.[8]

We find this same attitude toward providence continuing right up to modern times. In economics, Adam Smith made providence the central principle of the capitalist system, an "invisible hand" that bestows beneficence on all through the greed of each. In biology, we meet the same idea in the principle of "survival of the fittest": a species is fit because it survived, and it survived because it was fit. This is the same tautology found in the Roman worship of the Virtues: one was beloved of the gods because one was blessed, and one was blessed because one was beloved of the gods. Benefits conferred provided the clearest proof of the existence of the gods; one's knowledge of divine power could be drawn from no better source than the certain evidence of benefits received from the gods. Behind all this lies an unmistakable worship of power and the benefits it confers.[9] In each case, the fundamental notion is that whatever is, is right, and has succeeded through might, so that might makes right.

Superpatriot fundamentalists in the United States appeal to providence to maintain the status quo. Bill Bright asks, for example, "Do you thank God when you are discriminated against . . . racially?" You should, Bright says, because God is using racial prejudice to develop Christlike patience in you. Changing racist structures would deprive God of this great tool for character development! Or Merlin Carothers can announce cheerfully that "God didn't just *allow* the Chaldeans to conquer, He *raised* them up. What about Napoleon? Hitler? . . . Are we willing to thank God for raising them up? Can we accept His word that He is doing it for our good?"[10]

In the same vein, the theosophist Rudolf Steiner could write, "The American Indians died out, not because of European persecutions, but because they were destined to succumb to those forces which hastened their extinction."[11] And few modern capitalists have been so frank in their dependence on God as George Gilder: "Faith in man, faith in the future, faith in the rising returns of giving, faith in the mutual benefits of trade, faith in the providence of God are all essential to successful capitalism."[12] In short, whether it be businessmen thumping for the profit motive or a televangelist declaring God's preferential option for the wealthy, the American worship of success is nothing less than a throwback to the Roman worship of the Powers.

One generally finds among these devotees of providence a common presumption: the good of the whole system is a higher value than the good of any individuals in it. If they must be sacrificed for the preservation of the system (which is, incidentally, usually highly advantageous to the persons making these statements), then they must stoically or joyously offer themselves up. Thus is society preserved in peace and good order for the powerful, and all is right with the world.

## THE PROVIDENCE OF GOD

All notions of providence as a kind of divine favor, or karma, or special preference, are incompatible with the New Testament understanding of God's providence. Jesus' God plays no favorites but causes the sun to rise on the evil and on the good and sends rain on the just and unjust alike (Matt 5:45//Luke 6:35). Jesus spoke of trusting the created order like the lilies of the fields and the birds of the air (Luke 12:22-31//Matt 6:25-34), but this was not a way to hoard wealth. It was the assertion, against the demonic structures that let many starve while the few overeat, that even in the midst of the Domination System it is still possible to live in harmony with nature and by sharing with each other: "Set your mind on God's kingdom and God's justice before everything else, and all the rest will come to you as well" (Matt 6:33 REB alt.).

In an otherwise dark saying, Jesus stated categorically that the accidental death of people killed by a falling tower and Pilate's murder of Galileans in the temple were not God's will or doing (Luke 13:1-5). Nor is it God's will that even a sparrow fall dead to the ground. The RSV created a false impression when it translated Matt 10:29 as "Not one of them [the sparrows] will fall to the ground without your Father's *will*." The Greek reads simply "without your Father" (also KJV; NRSV reads "apart from your Father"). Other translations supply what they feel to be the word implied after "Father's": JB, "knowing"; Phillips, "knowledge"; NEB, "leave"; TEV, "consent." Jesus' meaning is clear from Luke's parallel in the RSV: "And not one of them is *forgotten before God*" (Luke 12:6). God is with even the smallest sufferer.

The early churches could confirm from their own experiences that those who leave behind "house or brothers or sisters or mother or father or children or lands, for my sake and for the gospel, [will] receive a hundredfold now in this time, houses and brothers and sisters and mothers and children and lands, *with persecutions*, and in the age to come eternal life" (Mark 10:29-30 RSV). This was not an early recipe for attaining wealth by striking a deal with God. It simply reflected the church's experience that those who abandoned everything for the sake of proclaiming the gospel were supported and enfolded by the body of Christ wherever their journeys took them. The ironic aside, "with persecutions," emphasizes the infinite gulf between the New Testament understanding of providence and the naïve view of those who accept the world as it is. The early Christians *expected* to be assaulted by the Powers That Be. They scarcely seemed puzzled by this fact. It would have been unthinkable for them to ask, "Why do bad things happen to good people?" The Powers that crucified Jesus had a stake in crushing this new movement, and anyone who joined it knew full well that they might be persecuted.

I have long been struck by the absence of a thoroughgoing attempt to explain evil ("theodicy") in the New Testament. Nowhere, not in a single sentence, do suffering or persecuted Christians raise the question so incessantly asked of pastors in hospitals and at funerals, "How could God have let this happen?" The question was not voiced even under the impact of what the church regarded as the most incomprehensible evil of all: the crucifixion of Jesus. They did not ask *why*—about that they seemed clear from the outset, prior even to theological reflection. It was obvious: he was crucified by the Powers because what he said and did threatened their power. The burning question for them was not *why* but *how*: How has God used this evil for good? How has God turned sin into salvation? How has God unmasked the Powers through the cross?

Likewise, persecution did not evoke surprised reactions of "Why me?" Because the early Christians *expected* to be persecuted (Matt 5:10-12//Luke 6:22-23; Matt 23:34-36//Luke 11:49-51; Rom 8:18; 2 Cor 1:5-7; Phil 3:10; Col 1:24; 1 Tim 1:12; 1 Pet 5:10; etc.), they were surprised when they were not! For them the question was not *why* but *how long*: "How long will it be before you judge and avenge our blood on the inhabitants of the earth?" (Rev 6:10).

Paul does not rejoice that God's providence delivers us *from* affliction; clearly it did not deliver him (2 Cor 11:23-33)! Rather he celebrates God's comforting us *in* our afflictions (2 Cor 1:3-7). When he was almost killed in Asia, he did not rail at God for mistreating him, since he knew that it was the Powers, not God, that wanted him destroyed. He even found a lesson in the ordeal. It was "so that we would rely not on ourselves but on God who raises the dead" (2 Cor 1:9). So free was he from the fear of the Powers and their final sanction, death, that he could avow: "If we live, we live to the Lord, and if we die, we die to the Lord; so then, whether we live or whether we die, we are the Lord's" (Rom 14:8).

So we can assert this: *Whenever Christian theology ignores the Powers, the notion of divine providence reverts to paganism.* Providence then becomes victory, prosperity, success, special treatment. At the cross, the chief priests and scribes behaved as if they had a clearer understanding of how providence is supposed to work than Jesus: "He saved others; he cannot save himself. Let the Messiah, the King of Israel, come down from the cross now, so that we may see and believe" (Mark 15:31-32). Matthew makes their taunt still more piercing: "He trusts in God; let God deliver him now, if he wants to" (Matt 27:43).

Here is how Acts depicts Paul responding to providence: The Holy Spirit does not say, "Paul, go to Macedonia." Instead, it seems to him to prevent his going to Asia (Acts 16:6). Then, when he turns toward Bithynia, it does not allow him entry there either (16:7). Only when he has bounced from one closed door to another and has arrived at Troas does a vision come from across the waters: "Come over to Macedonia and help us" (16:8-10). Even to the person of faith, the world does not cease to be a place where God's providence unfolds only in stages and indirectly.

Paul is not for all that a passive instrument in the hand of God. He himself is free to choose, sometimes against the option God offers. On one occasion, according to Acts, Paul writes, "When I came to Troas to proclaim the good news of Christ, a door was opened for me in the Lord"—he uses the divine passive, meaning that *God* had opened a door for the gospel— "but my mind could not rest because I did not find my brother Titus there. So I said farewell to them and went on to Macedonia" (2 Cor 2:12-13). Paul walks away from the door God has opened! He is a cocreator in the gospel with God and knows God can perfectly well open other doors elsewhere. He even regards the hour of his death as his to choose, as other great spiritual masters have done: "Yet which I shall choose [life or death] I cannot tell. I am hard pressed between the two" (Phil 1:22-23 RSV).

When Paul departs from Achaia to take the collection to Jerusalem (Rom 15:22-29), "bound in the Spirit" to go, he reports that the Holy Spirit "testifies to me in every city that imprisonment and persecutions are waiting for me" (Acts 20:22-23). In Tyre, where he and his party stayed seven days, "through the Spirit they told Paul not to go on to Jerusalem," a message apparently echoed by the four prophetesses in Caesarea (21:4, 9). Agabus even comes down from Jerusalem and warns him in the Holy Spirit of certain arrest if he persists in going to Jerusalem (Acts 21:9-11). But Paul is portrayed as convinced that he himself must present the collection as a gesture of solidarity and reconciliation within the church and cries out against these well-meaning prophets and their warnings, "What are you doing, weeping and breaking my heart? For I am ready not only to be bound but even to die at Jerusalem" (21:13).[13] His friends assume that the warnings of the Holy Spirit imply that he must choose safety and make his escape, whereas Paul is depicted as interpreting these warnings merely as occasions to test his resolve and reconfirm his choice, for which he is prepared to die. So far is he from confusing providence with personal protection!

In short, for the early church, the problem of justifying the existence of evil in a world under the sway of the Powers can scarcely be said to have existed. The cross had placed evil in a wholly new light. The crucifixion had become for them, as it were, a hologram of the universe, as if the meaning of every given segment could be discerned in the violent opposition of the rebellious Powers to God's purposes and God's exposure of their evil through the cross.

So James could write, "Count it all joy when you meet various trials" (1:2 RSV). Luke echoes the same refrain: "Blessed are you when people hate you, and when they exclude you, revile you, and defame you on account of the Son of Man. Rejoice in that day and leap for joy, for surely your reward is great in heaven" (Luke 6:22-23). Of course the Powers will oppose you; of course you will be brought before the rulers and authorities (literally, "principalities and powers," *tas archas kai tas exousias*, Luke 12:11); of course they will hunt you down like animals, deliver you to torturers, and even kill you for threatening the spirituality of an alienating world. Not one writer of the New Testament shows the slightest surprise over this. In a world under the practical daily dominion of the Powers, nothing else is to be expected—unless, of course, one has sold out to the Powers.

To restate my thesis more precisely, then: *Whenever discussion of divine providence takes place without reference to the Powers, it simply serves to legitimate the Domination System.*

## THE PROVIDENCE OF THE POWERS

Given the massiveness and ubiquity of the Powers, the wonder is not that there is so much evil in the world, but that good should ever prevail at all! With so much might at their disposal, the Powers are able to create a providence all their own. This is an issue theologians would rather not touch. It seems to imply a dualism in which Satan, or evil, or the dark side, operates with impunity. The objection to this "negative providence" stems at least in part from pagan ideas of providence. Like pagans, we react to illness, persecution, blacklisting, or death as if we had a right to be exempted from such things.

The New Testament certainly understands this negative providence. For example, when Judas decided to betray Jesus, he went to the chief priests, who offered him a fee. From that moment "he began to look for an opportunity to betray him" (Mark 14:11). What do these simple words suggest about the providential character of the universe? "Opportunity" in Greek is *eukairos*, literally a good (*eu*) time (*kairos*), a suitable, convenient, favorable time. Judas was seeking the *right time*. So the world is constituted such that a good *kairos* comes to the enemy of God as well as to God's friends. The fullness of time waits not only for the son of the man but for the son of the man's betrayer (Mark 14:21).

There is a providence of the Powers as well as a providence of God. No doubt there is in the universe a gradual process of selection that judges species by their adaptability to the requirements of life. But within that vast and encompassing constraint, individuals appear to be free to use the good *kairoi* that are provided—to do evil! And God does not prevent them. The world is so far from being ordered providentially for the good that the betrayer of Jesus is "blessed" in his search for the "right" time. His fidelity in betrayal is rewarded. Time opens to him a moment rich in opportunity: midnight. "This is your hour, and the power of darkness!" Jesus says to Judas and the arresting party, and passes into night (Luke 22:53).

From that point on in the story, every opening that might have procured Jesus' release slams shut. Pilate, who could have released him, will not. The crowd, which might have clamored for his freedom, howls for death. Judas might have changed his mind before the arrest instead of after it. He might have been unable to find Jesus among the throngs camped on the Mount of Olives. The Sanhedrin might have exonerated him. In short, the *eukairos* so spectacularly favorable to Judas is wholly unfavorable to Jesus. God is unable to provide escape for this beleaguered servant. The "right time" (*eukairos*) seems more often to favor the Powers, who have the means to exploit the moment, than the righteous, whoever they might be.

We must give the Powers their due. They are not only persistent and adamant, but they have a spiritual power all their own. It was one of the great errors of the Enlightenment to believe that the spiritual realm is wholly good. This fallacy led to the identification of spirit with reason. And since evil is irrational, reason was defenseless before the onslaught of evil. When people idolize a Power, treating it as ultimate, the very intensity of their focus is equivalent to prayer. They exude an energy that is available for evil ends. Sorcery, black magic, the occult, pogroms, inquisitions, witch hunts, Satanism—all these release forces in the psyche and society that quickly spin out of control and take on a momentum of their own. But these are a bit unusual. The more banal forms of idolatry are what provide the Powers stability and longevity: careerism, overweening ambition, status seeking, social climbing, jingoism, greed.

It is as if a Power that has turned aside from its heavenly vocation and devotes itself with utter abandon to its own demonic goals is assisted by a kind of malevolent providence. A nation, when it has focused its energies on evil, experiences an almost supernatural chain of interventions on its behalf. Satan assumes, as it were, the nation's angelic guardianship. A nation's priestly caste (identified in Rev 13:11-18 as the "Beast from the Earth") is able to "perform great signs, even making fire come down from heaven," and guarantee that its willing subjects prosper. Consider how the churches and synagogues of the United States have consistently fallen in line behind America's wars, providing the necessary legitimation by means of an uncritical application of the "just war" theory.

All things seemed to work together for good for Hitler during his ascent. There were occasions when Hitler's intuition saved his life with a peremptory warning, much as Nero was saved from death plots by an idol that "spoke" to him.[14] Once, during World War I, when he was in the trenches, Hitler felt he had to move at once. "No sooner had he gone than a shell burst where he had been standing."[15] On another occasion, after he had taken power, the fused time bomb that was to have killed Hitler as he flew from Smolensk to East Prussia failed to ignite. The next week, on May 21, 1943, Major von Gersdorff was prepared with two bombs in his own coat pockets to sacrifice his life and kill Hitler while he was inspecting an arsenal. But he was unable to get into position before Hitler unexpectedly left.[16] Hitler survived a dozen abortive assassination attempts. He came to believe in the superiority of his inner voice: "I carry out the commands that Providence [!] has laid upon me." "Unless I have the incorruptible conviction—this is the solution—I do nothing. Not even if the whole Party tried to drive me to action. I will not act. I will wait, no matter what happens. But if the voice speaks, then I know the time has come to act."[17]

Another example is much closer to home for me, since it was one of the early school shootings that subsequently turned into something of an epidemic, and it took place on the campus where our Quaker meeting was held. In December 1992, Wayne Low, an eighteen-year-old student at Simons Rock College, killed a professor and a student and wounded several others. Had the semiautomatic weapon not jammed (providentially?), he later admitted, he would have shot many more. The story he later told came down to this: He received a divine message to go to the gun store, order the ammunition with his mother's credit card, then lie and deceive and kill. He was so convinced that he was justified in his acts that he raged at his lawyers during his trial because they insisted on asserting that he was insane. Instead, he argued, his lawyers should have investigated his victims to uncover why a heavenly power had selected them to be shot. The ease with which he had bought the gun, ordered the ammunition, and fooled Simon's Rock officials had convinced him that his mission was guided by a divine force. "It all worked so seamlessly," he said. Apparently he was not insane; at least he has been able to feel remorse and to doubt the divine origin of his command to kill. Osama bin Laden unfortunately did not reach the same conclusion. For him, Allah was the architect of terrorism.

Here again, the perpetrators of terrible evils can cite divine providence as accounting for the ease and success that seems to flow, effortlessly, to them. Are they simply wrong, so that we need not invoke providence as an explanation? But that ignores the sense of being guided, of it all working "so seamlessly." There does seem to be an "evil providence" that mortals can evoke; but ultimately, God's providence prevails over the providence of the Powers, and, in Martin Luther King Jr.'s words, the universe does bend toward justice.

## GOD'S PROVIDENCE VERSUS THE PROVIDENCE OF THE POWERS

Providence, then, is not simply a gracious intervention or unexpected grace. It not only can aid the working out of God's will in the world but also can serve the malevolent goals of the Powers as well. It is simply one of the characteristics of reality and can be used by God on our behalf the same way God uses prayer, medicine, and surgery to heal us. It is merely one of the spiritual facts built by God into the creation, to be utilized in our freedom for the benefit of life or the victory of death, however we choose.

Carl Jung observed something akin to providence in his work with patients and dubbed it "synchronicity." According to Jung, synchronicity is "a concurrence or meaningful coincidence of events not causally connected with one another."[18] The characteristic feature of all such phenomena is *meaningful coincidence* between an inner image that has arisen from the unconscious and an outer event that coincides with this unconscious content. Causality is merely a statistical hypothesis of how events evolve one out of another, whereas synchronicity takes the coincidence of events in space and time as meaning something more than mere chance, namely, a peculiar interdependence of objective events among themselves as well as with the subjective (psychic) states of the observer or observers.[19] Synchronicity is thus a neutral element in the constitution of the universe, capable of being evoked for good or evil purposes.

For synchronous events to occur, Jung continues, there must be an intense focus and receptivity in the subject. Because synchronous events are acausal, it is impossible to predict in advance when the synchrony will occur. All we can say at this point is that they seem to occur more often at the beginning of an experiment; are heightened by excitement, faith, prayer, a personal stake, or other states of affectivity; and tend to occur at rates that exceed probability. They cannot be regarded as pure chance but possess a meaningful quality—and not only have no perceivable cause but cannot even be *thought* of as having a cause. Indeed, unbelievability is one of the characteristic features of synchronous events.[20]

The meaning of synchronous events is not one that we impose on the events, says Jung, but appears to inhere in the phenomena themselves. "Synchronicity postulates a meaning which is *a priori* in relation to human consciousness and apparently exists outside" of us.[21] It is this objective quality that imposes on us the conviction that the universe must have meaning. And meaning arises not from causality but from freedom, that is, from acausality. In short, synchronicity provides a space for providence in a highly determined world. If there were no causality, reality would dissolve into chaos. If causality were absolute rather than statistically probable, there would be no room for freedom. It may well be, Jung concludes, that the traditional belief in the efficacy of prayer is based on the experience of concomitant synchronistic phenomena.[22]

What scientists have called chance might sometimes be more precisely designated synchronicity. For example, if two helium atoms strike and, during the millionth of a second that they stay together, are hit by a third, a carbon atom is created—the building block of all life. All the carbon in the universe was formed by such highly improbable collisions. But the population is so large that they do happen. In that sense they are chance events; they are synchronous only from the perspective of the life that subsequently emerged from them. This suggests, against Jung's statement above, that synchronous events do not have their meaning objectively given, as if imposed by the situation, but that they are interpretations, and as such are open to a variety of interpretations.

So, one might say, God bombards us with potentially synchronous events, but our failure to be receptive means that we fail to bring our "third helium atom" to the mix, so to speak, and thus the creative event fails to materialize. But when it does, the transformation is so dramatic that we may feel God is surely in it, which is true—but no more than in the lost occasions. God does not intervene occasionally; God is the constant possibility of transformation in *every* occasion.[23]

## THE SIGNIFICANCE OF SYNCHRONICITY

Perhaps it will be helpful to document some actual cases of synchronous events and then to draw up a set of conclusions or thesis statements on the basis of the actual instances. I have drawn the first two accounts from my own experience, for no other reason than that I have firsthand knowledge of them and know they are true. Of course, my stories will not carry equal conviction for others. I have included the stories of several others as well, because they reveal how God's providence comes to our aid in our encounters with the Powers.

I will begin with the least significant episode, because it is a good illustration of pure synchronicity unencumbered by religious concerns. On December 2, 1978, I was jogging in Riverside Park in New York City. My mind lapsed into a reverie on synchronicity and on how important it had been in events earlier in my life. I recalled that great emphasis is placed on it by my mentoring group, the Guild for Psychological Studies, and I resolved to make it a matter of deliberate attention.

The next morning, I took a writing break at 11:30 a.m. and decided to make a picture as a way of opening myself to the kind of right-brain influences that might stir up synchronous events in my life. I started at the center of the page, working out with great energy, making what looked like a sun, red at the center and tapering off to yellow on the perimeter. At 12:30, I pulled a magazine out of a stack to read over lunch; it fell open to an article by Arthur Koestler on synchronicity! (I was unaware that he had written two books on the subject.)

At 4:30 p.m., my wife, June, came home, telling me she had bought an early Christmas present for me and couldn't resist giving it to me right then. Out of her bag she drew two potholders: they were roughly the same colors and size (eight inches in diameter) as my picture but arranged in concentric circles of red/yellow/red/yellow. She had bought them on her lunch break, at 12:30.[24]

Nothing much was riding on this. In the next account, however, more was at stake. Richard Deats, of the U.S. Fellowship of Reconciliation, and I had been invited to South Africa to do workshops on nonviolence, but the apartheid government blocked our attempt to get visas. To circumvent the visa problem, our workshop was planned for 1988 in Lesotho (a pseudoindependent state surrounded by South Africa, requiring no visas), and people from South Africa and other parts of southern Africa were invited to come there for the workshop.

After repeated interviews and phone calls, Richard (who had not been to South Africa before and thus was not so suspect) was granted a visa a week before we left. I appealed the refusal of my visa, but to no effect. Rob Robertson, a leading advocate of nonviolence in South Africa, proposed that I enter illegally, as a protest against a government policy that has periodically excluded peace activists from the country since 1967.

On the opening session of the Lesotho workshop, we sang the hymn, "Thine is the glory, risen, conquering Son! Endless is the victory thou o'er death hast won," set to a melody from Handel's *Judas Maccabaeus*. This then served as our theme song for the rest of the workshop.

The last day, Rob and I were to attempt to get across the border. People in our group and others in the States were praying that we would get in. As we came in sight of the border, we stopped and prayed that, as God had opened the prison doors and let Peter and Paul and Silas out, God would let us in! Then, in a pouring rain, we drove up to the border post, jumped out, and ran under the shelter of the porch, where the black Transkei soldier in charge was whistling the hymn "Thine is the glory, risen, conquering Son." At that moment I knew we would get in. The rain-darkened room was so dim that I had to read my passport to the other soldier; he never even looked for the nonexistent visa.[25]

Synchronicity, indeed—but it is rather awkward to give praise and thanksgiving to synchronicity. There is more here than the mechanics of impersonal systems. As Jean Shinoda Bolen wisely remarks, "Every time I have become aware of a synchronistic experience, I have had an accompanying feeling that some grace came along with it."[26] The sheer unexpectedness and the awestruck sense that something—no, *someone*—has done this, is virtually irresistible, and it can be a life-transforming experience. One can make too much of such things, to be sure; God does not always seem so able to bend the Powers to the divine design. (Am I right even to assume it was God's design?) Yet we heard other such stories, far weightier. Three of our Lesotho group—Emma Mashinini, McGlory Speckman, and Joe Seremane—told how, amazingly, each of their captors had suddenly stopped torturing them when they desperately cried out within themselves to God. (But what of all the others whose prayers were not answered? Once again, the arbitrariness and favoritism in the idea of providence is both repulsive and yet an undeniable fact of experience.)

Out of a number of other stories of positive providence or positive synchronicity, I have chosen a few that involve illegal entry into military bases or factories to protest weapons of mass destruction. It is here that the issue of providence runs up against the Powers That Be, and providence is rid of any selfish motivations. In classical Christian terms, here providence is subjected to the acid bath of suffering, and the miracle of divine intervention is placed under the sign of the cross.

On Holy Saturday, 1983, a group of friends cut the barbed-wire fence and entered the Strategic Air Command Center at Wurtsmith Air Force Base to protest the policy of nuclear deterrence. Pausing, they renewed their baptismal vow to "renounce Satan and all his works." Then they proceeded to the heart of the base. As they report it:

> Here an astonishing phenomenon occurred, one reportedly not uncommon in such undertakings: We passed unseen. On one side were the bunkers, encircled with barbed-wire, lit like perpetual noon-day, driven roundabout by a constant patrol of vehicles, and observed from above by watchtowers, beneath which we processed. On the other side, parked for maintenance or refueling, huge bombers stood in a line equally well-lit. It was as though the water had parted. We walked unhindered to the open entrance of the high security area where planes on alert stood ready to fly on command. . . . There, measured by a sudden flurry of activity within, we were finally noticed. Armored vehicles and pickup trucks rushed to surround us. We spread our altar cloth of intercessions on the runway. About it we scattered blood, brought in small bottles, to signify the blood of the innocents, the blood of the Lamb. Producing the elements of the eucharist, we completed the service at gunpoint.[27]

The second story took place in Tucson, Arizona, during the summer and fall of 1983. The site was the Davis-Monthan Air Force Base, the only military base in the world where people were trained to use the ground-launched cruise missile. After weeks of picketing outside the base,

> two souls, dressed in black, scared to death, but who had nevertheless talked it through beforehand, climbed over the 7-foot cyclone fence topped with

barbed wire in the wee hours of the morning. One carried a live Christmas tree, three presents, and a nativity scene. The other carried a bag of household goods—an apron, children's toys, a large ham bone, curtains, all drenched in kerosene. There was a fire extinguisher, and a large chain and padlock. . . . They came to the open area a few hundred feet in plain sight of the guardhouse. The length of a football field needed to be traversed in full lighting. To run was to risk being shot. To walk was perhaps never to reach the parking lot. They ran, for better or for worse, set up the tree, presents, nativity scene, and a message to Herod pleading with him not to incinerate the innocents. The other lit her bag in the middle of an empty concrete parking lot and left the fire extinguisher nearby. Also, and in hindsight, thank God, they were invisible. [Again, invisibility!] No one saw the two shepherds of new tidings. No one saw the 3-foot flames rise in the darkness. So they went and chained themselves to the cruise missile building doors, while a group gathered outside the gate singing songs into the early morning hours. . . . Supporters on the outside grew anxious, and suggested that the press call the base and find out what had happened. The base denied any trespassing, but sent security out anyway. Security had the trespassers full in his headlights, and they raised their hands, but he drove on by . . . invisible. The second patrol also failed. Security finally found and arrested them.[28]

When Louis Vitale and ten others clandestinely entered the Los Alamos nuclear research laboratories, they headed straight for the front doors, though they were normally chained shut during non-working hours. Curiously, they were unchained; they later learned that the Los Alamos office had chosen that morning to have the carpets cleaned, and the cleaners had neglected to lock the doors behind them.

Since they, too, had passed unseen into the facility, they called their supporters, who phoned the local media. Security at the site learned of the presence of the "intruders" while listening to a live radio interview with them. "People started coming up the walk with automatic weapons," says Vitale. "We decided to pray until they arrested us. They didn't want to arrest us until we were through praying." Vitale and friends spent three days in the Beatty jail, where he celebrated Mass using the toast from breakfast and small packets of grape jelly for "wine."[29]

## CHARACTERISTICS OF SYNCHRONOUS ACTIONS

There are many more such stories, and someone should be gathering them. Themes common to them all include the intensity of prayer before and during the actions; the invisibility of the protestors; the way locked doors opened; and their not knowing where the target was located and being "led" to it. These are all conditions or characteristics of synchronous actions. Invisibility is especially interesting to me. In Acts 12, Peter is in jail expecting to be executed the following day. The story seems to be embellished with fanciful details (he is sleeping between two guards, while others guarded the door to the prison; the prison door opened of its own accord). But the common element in these details is the invisibility of the protestors.

Such stories prove nothing, explain nothing. But they are immeasurably powerful confirmations, to those to whom they happen, that God is still sovereign over the Powers. They are like stars shining in the darkness, and the darkness cannot put out their light.

What conclusions can we draw from these examples and our general discussion? It appears to me that we can make the following assertions:

1. Events are providential in and of themselves, but they are ineffectual if they are not recognized as such.
2. Synchronicities cannot be caused, since they are acausal, but prayer and focused action, or action focused by prayer, tends to evoke synchronicities.
3. In those moments when we are attuned to the will of God and free from major resistance or ambivalence, there does seem to be a "flowing with God" that is almost effortless (for example, our entering South Africa). But it is also characteristic of negative providence (Wayne Low).
4. The difference between negative and positive providence is the difference between a providence conceived of as for the privileged (Gilder) and a providence serving a higher good (demonstrators at military bases).
5. Positive providence is possible even under the worst conditions, but only within terrible constraints (Viktor Frankl in the Nazi death camps, described below).
6. God's ability to intervene in a situation is limited by choices of other self-determining agents.
7. When a system becomes virulently demonic, God can intervene in small ways but may be unable to preempt the system itself (Nazi Germany).
8. To change a system, large numbers of those most immediately affected by that system must normally be involved.
9. We must be prepared to find God's providence in what we may ourselves initially regard as evil.
10. God can bring good out of evil, but God does not cause evil.

Even in the midst of the Holocaust there were numerous little providences that sustained people in the heart of that darkness. Viktor Frankl tells of one such moment in a Nazi death camp when a light was lit in a nearby farmhouse. At that very moment, in answer to his question whether there existed an ultimate purpose, a voice within him said a victorious "Yes!" And with the lighting of the candle, the phrase came: *"Et lux in tenebris lucet"* ("And the light shines in the darkness"). At that moment a bird flew down, perched on the soil he had been digging from the ditch, and looked steadily at him.[30] It was enough. And it was next to nothing.

The astronomer Nikolai Aleksandrovich Kozyrev prayed in a Russian prison for help, and an astronomy book came into his hands! But God was unable to open the gates of the Gulag prison system itself.[31] Mihajlo Mihajlov, writing about people who underwent mystical experiences in Hitler's labor camps, notes that "arrest, prison, and camp—simply to say, the loss of freedom—have formed the most profound and significant experience in their lives. The paradox is complicated by the fact that, although they underwent the most extreme spiritual and physical suffering during their imprisonment, they also experienced a fulfilling happiness, undreamed of by people outside the prison walls."[32]

In workshops we sometimes have participants do a time-line drawing on which they depict all the key events of their lives. Then we ask them to go back over their picture and identify the times when they felt closest to God. The results are striking: the dark areas, signifying divorces, diseases, death, and other crises, were almost always the times when God's presence was most pronounced.

But nothing can ameliorate the horror of the Holocaust or the Soviet Gulag. An aspect of the suffering of God is the constraints placed on God's ability to intervene effectively when evil has, as it were, gained a monopoly on power and those who should be in the vanguard of spiritual opposition have fallen silent or been muzzled. As we saw earlier, the very concentratedness of those whose minds are set on evil seems to conjure up an "evil providence," surrounding and protecting them from well-intended attempts to remove them from power. God is no more able to vanquish evil in such a time than the body is able to reject cancer cells when the immune system is suppressed. "O Jerusalem, Jerusalem, killing the prophets and stoning those who are sent to you! How often would I have gathered your children together as a hen gathers her brood under her wings, and you would not!" (Luke 13:34 RSV).[33] God, who longs for Jerusalem's well-being, is unable to save it because the city itself, as the center of the corrupt temple system, is not open to God's justice and peace.

And yet the very premise on which nonviolent direct action is based is that the oppressor *always* has a monopoly on power. From the Israelites' exodus from Egypt to the civil rights movement in the American South, from the struggle for nationhood led by Gandhi to the effort to gain economic democracy led by Cesar Chavez, small numbers of people (in fact, usually one to six) have succeeded in slowly gathering a critical mass of people, usually less than 5 percent of the population, who are capable of bringing about desired change.[34]

## SYNCHRONICITY, PROVIDENCE, AND PRAYER

Rather than living within empirical reality, where experience confirms that God's capacity to intervene is highly restricted by our own choices and those of the Powers, people imagine that God has all the power there is, and therefore blame God for the social evils they themselves refuse to correct. In its most perverted form, this belief turns into a justification of these very evils as willed by God, since, according to this view, all that is can exist at all only because God wills or permits it. The very idea of an omnipotent God is deeply contaminated by dreams of domination: an ultimate and irresistible power able to impose our view of what is "right" on the entire universe.

The belief that God's providence means that God will set everything right, here and now, is a form of religious infantilism. God cannot fix everything, because the people and the Powers that unfixed them in the first place have a stake in keeping them unfixed to their advantage. It is not just that God *will not* intervene more often (as in the proposition that if God healed every sick person, we never would have developed medical science). The point is that God *cannot* heal every sick person. Since we do not know when healing is possible, we simply pray for healing and leave the rest to God. As one of my teachers, John Bennett, put it, God does not will everything, but God wills something *in* everything.

---

I find myself pinioned between two widely attested experiences. On the one hand, it is undeniable that there is divine providence in the world. This fact, or rather, experience, is almost universally attested. On the other hand, it is undeniable that providence is indefensible. It is arbitrary, erratic, capricious, unpredictable, inconsistent, and unreliable. Nevertheless, synchronous events do happen, and when they do they are often among the most significant events that can take place in a person's entire lifetime.

The longer I struggle with the issue of providence, the more it strikes me as insoluble. We seem to have here a genuine antinomy, which is to say, a contradiction between two apparently equally valid principles. And an antinomy cannot be resolved by means of logic. People experience what feels like a gracious intervention that quite literally saves their lives, while others die in the same place at the same time (the Alabama tornado). All we can do is make a kind of existential sense out of this bewildering problem. For providence is not only acausal but irrational. As Jung noted earlier, synchronous events are by definition unbelievable. We simply have to accept the fact that synchronicities happen, even though we cannot explain them.

Perhaps some of the more troublesome aspects of providence can be ameliorated if we treat it as a subcategory of prayer. Like synchronicity, prayer is acausal. We cannot cause acausal events. We can never say, "Prayer did this." But prayer seems to make a difference, perhaps in part by sharpening the inner eye to *perceive* meaningful coincidences that we might otherwise let pass unnoticed, perhaps in part by alerting us to ways that may actually help precipitate such events.[35] Coincidences seem to come to the prepared mind, and reality seems to be so constituted that we are able to draw what we need to us—the way books I know nothing about have a way of "finding" me when I am concentrating on a problem. As Goethe put it, "The moment one definitely commits oneself, then Providence moves too. All sorts of things occur to help one that never otherwise would have occurred."[36] This statement is as true of negative providence, however, as of positive.

In prayer we wrestle with God and the Powers with resolute determination. With synchronicity, however, a convergence of outer event and inner meaning is so surprising and unexpectedly gracious that we can only describe it as divine intervention. Prayer is proactive, a thing we do. Divine providence is pure gift. Yet synchronous events tend to occur to those whose whole being is focused, laserlike, on a desired outcome. The fact that a Hitler could avail himself of negative providence the same way a Mother Theresa could does not, then, negate the idea of providence. But it does limit what God can do in a situation. Recognizing that limit is the beginning of wisdom.

Since God is sometimes able to work so unforeseeably to bring transformation out of distress, it only makes sense to pray for miracles: to refuse to submit to the world's limited grasp of possibilities, to call forth the divine presence in the darkest regions of evil, and to cry to God with a world-defying ring that shatters the iron mountain of unbelief and grants an opening to God.

## Chapter 6

# TRADITIONS, PRACTICES, AND THE POWERS

## NANCEY MURPHY

Not often in academia does one encounter an idea that changes one's view of the world. One such idea, for me, was the biblical concept of the Principalities and Powers, as understood by John Howard Yoder and James Wm. McClendon Jr. and most recently and fully elaborated by Walter Wink. The individualism of our culture makes it difficult for us to come to terms with social structures—that is, to see them as anything over and above the individuals who participate in them. Paul Feyerabend, my mentor at the University of California, Berkeley, often pointed out that facts are not just there to be found. It is often only in light of some new theory that the relevant facts appear. And so for me, the New Testament theory of the Principalities and Powers has served to bring facts to my attention that I otherwise would have overlooked—facts about the moral character of social realities.

Awareness of the existence and character of the Powers has important implications for church life, for ethics, for social action. Other chapters here address some of these. My attention will focus on the area I know best: epistemology, or theory of knowledge. One of the defining features of modern epistemology has been its individualism. It is striking to read the writings of René Descartes, "father" of modern philosophy, and see the extent to which he has emphasized the *solitude* of his epistemological inquiries. In *Meditations on First Philosophy* he wrote: "Today I have expressly rid my mind of all worries and arranged for myself a clear stretch of free time. I am here quite alone, and at last I will devote myself sincerely and without reservation to the general demolition of my opinions."[1] Descartes wrote that his *Discourse on Method* was conceived while he "stayed all day shut up alone in a stove-heated room, where [he] was completely free to converse with [him]self about [his] own thoughts."[2]

On the far side of modernity we have been helped to see the oddity of the solitary knower by critics of Descartes, from Ludwig Wittgenstein to Stephen Toulmin and Alasdair MacIntyre. So "postmodern" thinkers in the Anglo-American tradition are well aware of the essentially *social* character of our epistemic practices. What is yet lacking, I shall argue in this chapter, is a just measure of the moral status of the social entities involved in knowledge acquisition. And it is here that I shall be helped by Wink's analysis of the Powers.

What I shall do is, first, present a thumbnail sketch of what I judge to be the most sophisticated account, to date, of human reason—that of Alasdair MacIntyre. I will then criticize his overly optimistic account of social practices in light of Wink's theory of the Powers. Along the way, I shall argue that the sort of critique I bring to bear on MacIntyre's position points to an understanding of human reason consistent with the Radical Reformation tradition.

## ALASDAIR MACINTYRE ON
## TRADITION-CONSTITUTED RATIONALITY

No philosopher provides better resources for thinking about rationality and knowledge, at the end of the modern era, than Alasdair MacIntyre. MacIntyre has worked in a number of areas in philosophy but is currently best known for his work in philosophical ethics. In *After Virtue*, he concluded that it is not possible to justify ethical claims apart from some *tradition* of moral reasoning.[3] It was then necessary, to avoid moral relativism, to address the question of how moral traditions, such as the Aristotelian or Enlightenment tradition, were to be evaluated. One feature of these traditions is that they incorporate their own standards of rationality. Thus, he was faced with a problem similar to the one raised in philosophy of science by Thomas Kuhn. Kuhn's question was how one can evaluate scientific paradigms when the *standards* of good science are themselves *paradigm-dependent.*[4]

I shall describe MacIntyre's contributions to epistemology by tracing the development of his thought through several works. In an early article, titled "Epistemological Crises, Dramatic Narrative, and the Philosophy of Science," he argued that justification of theories in science depends on our being able to construct a historical narrative that makes the transition from the old theory to the new theory intelligible: "What the scientific genius, such as Galileo, achieves in his transition, then, is not only a new way of understanding nature, but also and inseparably a new way of understanding the old science's way of understanding nature." It is only from the standpoint of the new science that the inadequacy of the old science can be characterized. This points to an asymmetry between the old and the new and provides grounds for recognizing the new science to be more adequate than the old. "It is from the standpoint of the new science that the continuities of narrative history are re-established."[5]

Thus, he claims, scientific reason turns out to be subordinate to, and intelligible only in terms of, historical reason. That is, our ability to judge which scientific theory is better turns on our ability to judge which narrative account of the history of science does it more justice. Let us call this aspect of justification the diachronic dimension. Here MacIntyre is answering the question of how one justifies a modification within a given tradition.

However, a second question is how one justifies the tradition as a whole over against its rivals. And here he has moved into the sphere of practical reasoning. Recall what I said earlier: In *After Virtue*, he recognized that settling moral disputes requires, ultimately, a way to judge competing *traditions*. He takes up this issue in *Whose Justice? Which Rationality?*[6] Traditions, he says, generally originate with an authority of some sort, usually a text or set of texts. The tradition develops in successive attempts to interpret and apply the texts in new contexts. Application is essential: traditions are *socially embodied* in the life stories of the individuals and communities who share them, in institutions and social practices. So traditions go through phases. First, the authority is unquestioned. Then a crisis comes along (such as incoherence or a new experience that cannot be explained) and the authority has to be either rejected or reinterpreted.

One aspect of the adjudication between competing traditions, then, is to construct a narrative account of each—of the crises it has encountered and how it has or has not overcome them. Has it been possible to reformulate the tradition in such a way as to overcome its crises without losing its identity? Comparison of these narratives may show that one tradition is clearly superior to another: that is, it may turn out that one is making progress while its rival has become sterile, has failed *on its own terms*.

In addition, if there are participants within the traditions with enough empathy and imagination to understand the rival point of view in its own terms, then

> protagonists of each tradition, having considered in what ways their own tradition has by its own standards of achievement . . . found it difficult to develop its enquiries beyond a certain point, or has produced in some area insoluble antinomies, ask whether the alternative and rival tradition may not be able to provide resources to characterize and to explain the failings and defects of their own tradition more adequately than they, using the resources of that tradition, have been able to do.[7]

Let us refer to this aspect as synchronic justification. Notice that it involves diachronic evaluation of each tradition as an intrinsic element, but a crucial ingredient is the claim that it is sometimes easier to diagnose the rival's failures from the point of view of one's own tradition than from the point of view of the rival itself. Returning to Galileo: MacIntyre's point here is that once you have the heliocentric theory, you can explain both the successes and the failures of the geocentric model. You can see *why* it would work for the limited purposes it did.

MacIntyre's favorite historical example of this ability to see things from the point of view of two traditions is Thomas Aquinas, with his appreciation for both the Augustinian and Aristotelian traditions. For a contemporary illustration of MacIntyre's account of tradition-constituted rationality, consider the justification he provides for his own position in ethics. In *After Virtue*, he argued that his own reformulation of virtue theory is justified because it solves the problems neither Aristotle's nor Thomas's version could solve. This is the diachronic aspect. But this very approach to the justification of an ethical position is an instance of a broader theory of rationality, according to which a tradition is vindicated by the fact that it has managed to come through its epistemological crises while its competitors have failed to do so.

This epistemological theory itself needs to be justified by showing that it is part of a large-scale tradition and that this large-scale tradition is justified. This MacIntyre does by means of a historical narrative in which he recounts the crises faced by the Aristotelian-Thomist tradition and how (with MacIntyre's help, of course) it has overcome them.

A second narrative concerns the Thomist tradition's main contemporary competitor, modern Enlightenment reason, and the crises into which it has fallen. And here is the crucial point: From the perspective of *his* account of tradition-constituted rationality, MacIntyre is able to argue not only that the Enlightenment tradition has failed but that it was bound to fail, *and fail on its own terms*. In short, being "the tradition of traditionless reason," it was bound to misperceive its own capacities and limitations.

MacIntyre's views have important consequences for contemporary discussions of knowledge. In contrast to the prevalent relativism of our day, he maintains that it is at least sometimes possible to provide a rational justification for accepting one tradition and rejecting its rivals. This allows him to make truth claims regarding his own tradition, but it does not, of course, place him back in the Enlightenment camp, because he recognizes the historical conditioning of all knowledge. All that this sort of justification allows one to claim is that this tradition's point of view is the best so far. So he offers a genuine alternative to both relativism and the absolutist position of the Enlightenment. The critically important (and perhaps unique) feature of his work is his ability to show that the fact of our necessarily speaking from the point of view of some particular tradition does not mean that we cannot make compelling and rationally justified truth claims in the public domain—even though we recognize that standards for rational justification are themselves tradition-laden.

## IS THEOLOGY PRIOR TO EPISTEMOLOGY?

An intriguing consequence of MacIntyre's historico-philosophical research is the hint that epistemological positions, such as theories of truth, are, in fact, dependent on *theological* accounts of reality. This is the lead I intend to pursue in the remainder of this chapter.

In his book *Three Rival Versions of Moral Enquiry*, MacIntyre distinguishes three major traditions in contemporary Western thought, which he labels Encyclopaedia, Genealogy, and Tradition.[8] The first is named for what he designates as its classic text, *The Encyclopaedia Britannica* (ninth edition). This text enshrined the Enlightenment view of objective standards of rationality and universal morals. This Encyclopaedist tradition, he claims, has been effectively criticized by the Genealogists—that is, by Friedrich Nietzsche and his followers.[9] As a current competitor to the Nietzschean view that all moralities need to be unmasked to reveal the interests behind them, MacIntyre offers his renewed version of the Aristotelian-Thomist tradition. Thus, he sees two live options for the future of academia: Thomas or Nietzsche.

I, however, see three. I suggest that MacIntyre's account is, in a certain respect, typically Catholic, while the Genealogical tradition is *in the line of descent* from Augustine to the mainline Reformers. The fact that these two options can be associated with major theological positions suggests that we might find other possibilities by considering a different *theology*.

In general, Catholic theologians have been more optimistic than Protestants regarding human capacities for knowledge. This optimism can be traced in part to the fact that Thomas developed an account of the capacities of the soul that was different from the account Protestants inherited from Augustine. For both Augustine and Thomas, the soul was conceived as hierarchically ordered, and the proper "chain of command" was from higher faculties to lower. For Augustine, the will was the highest faculty of the soul, above the intellect. Thus, when the will falls, it corrupts all lower faculties, including the intellect; in Calvin's terms, the fall entails total depravity. For Thomas, in contrast, the corruption of the will does not affect the intellect directly. Humans can still fall into error, such as when the will leads them to form judgments prematurely, but the capacities for knowledge are not intrinsically darkened or depraved.

MacIntyre's version of Thomist epistemology accepts Thomas's account of truth as adequacy of the mind to reality, and emphasizes the social character of the pursuit of knowledge. Following Aristotle, he understands philosophy as a craft. Participation in a craft requires apprenticeship to a teacher, shared standards of achievement, and the acquisition of virtues necessary for successful participation in the craft. Thus, MacIntyre promotes a concept of the intellect as embodied in *social practices*.

The concept of a social practice is an important one for MacIntyre for a variety of reasons. He defines it as follows:

> By a "practice" I am going to mean any coherent and complex form of socially established cooperative human activity through which goods internal to that form of activity are realized in the course of trying to achieve those standards of excellence which are appropriate to, and partially definitive of, that form of

activity, with the result that human powers to achieve excellence, and human conceptions of the ends and goods involved, are systematically extended.[10]

What is important for our purposes is the specification that social practices aim inherently at the realization of *goods* internal to those practices. Thus, MacIntyre's account of the socially embodied intellect is one in which the intellect itself aims intrinsically at a variety of goods—including truth. This is not to say that social practices, including those relating to the acquisition of knowledge, cannot be deformed or distorted (for example, by corrupt institutions or by the lack of appropriate virtues on the part of participants), but it is a more optimistic view of the nature of social practices than we find in the Genealogical tradition.

Nietzsche set out to show that the will to power conceals itself under the guise of the will to truth. If we redescribe Nietzsche's will to power in theological terms as wanting to be like God (cf. Gen 3:5), his account is strikingly like what an Augustinian Christian would expect—apart from any concepts of grace, regeneration, or revelation.

Michel Foucault, an important interpreter of Nietzsche, has developed a view of knowledge parallel to MacIntyre's in many respects, and these very similarities make the difference at one point all the more striking. Both are thoroughly historicist in their understandings of epistemology; both employ a genealogical method; both regard knowledge as originating from social practices. But whereas MacIntyre takes such practices to aim intrinsically at truth, Foucault concentrates on practices of social control and aims to show how they distort human knowledge. For Foucault, there is an essential connection between knowledge and power, and it inevitably deludes us.

## AN ALTERNATIVE: POWER, THE POWERS, AND PEACEFUL PRACTICES

I now sketch some outlines of an alternative to both Thomas and Nietzsche with roots in the Radical Reformation. MacIntyre's epistemological proposal has at least two major weaknesses. First is the overly optimistic evaluation of social practices and thus of the capacities of the (socially embodied) intellect. A second is that he has not been able (in his own estimation) to provide conclusive reasons to reject the Genealogical tradition.[11] I claim that his epistemological account can be repaired by two moves. The first is to *acknowledge* a measure of truth in the Genealogists' account, namely, the epistemic distortions caused by the will to power. The second is to provide a more nuanced account of social practices.

For a better account of social practices, I turn to the writings of theologians James Wm. McClendon Jr. and Walter Wink. McClendon, in the first volume of his three-volume systematic theology, *Ethics*, makes use of MacIntyre's account of a social practice but calls into question "the generally optimistic and progressive ring of MacIntyre's overall account of practices."[12] By invoking the biblical concept of Principalities and Powers, McClendon forges a concept of *powerful practices* that has neither the essential optimism of MacIntyre's nor the essential pessimism of Foucault's account of the relations between power and knowledge.

McClendon's account of the Principalities and Powers (first published in 1986) is indebted to both John Howard Yoder's *The Politics of Jesus*[13] and to the first volume of Wink's trilogy, *Naming the Powers*.[14] The following summary of McClendon's account will show it to be in close agreement with Wink's as regards the nature and influence of social structures.

McClendon, along with numerous predecessors, traces the biblical concept of the Powers to the alien gods of Old Testament understanding. In the Near East, power was inevitably associated with gods, and gods were linked with politics and society. "In the New Testament" he says, "the powers retain their status subordinate to God, and also their political role: they are God's creatures (Col 1:15-17), fallen and rebellious (Eph 2:1ff; Gal 4:1-11), and may be identical with empire and its lords (Rom 13:1-4)" (174). The mission of Jesus is understood as conflict with and conquest of these Powers. In the epistles, this conflict is typically represented in summary form, as in Col 2:15 (REB): "There he disarmed the cosmic powers and authorities and made a public spectacle of them, leading them as captives in his triumphal procession." In the Gospels, this conflict is portrayed in narrative form, and the opponents are no longer called the "Principalities and Powers" but are human overlords of state and temple, or demonic forces that sponsor illness and madness. McClendon says, "Note further that the contra-power that Jesus . . . mounts against these is nothing less than the whole course of his obedient life, with its successive moments of proclamation, healing, instruction, the gathering of a redemptive community, and costly submission to the way of the cross and its death and resurrection."[15]

Wherever Christ's victory is proclaimed, the corrupted reign of the Powers is challenged, and yet they remain in being—in the time between the resurrection and the final coming of Christ, they remain in an ambiguous state. They delimit and define the social morality of Jesus' followers; to them the disciple must witness concerning the reversal of power achieved in Christ's resurrection. There is a hint in the New Testament that the final destiny of all these Powers—civil, military, economic, traditional, cultural, social, *and religious*—will be not their abolition but their full restoration (Eph 1:10; 3:10). "So the task of Christians confronting a world of *powerful practices* . . . requires almost infinite adjustments, distinction, and gradations."[16]

So, as far as it goes, McClendon's account of the Powers agrees essentially with Wink's, both in its interpretation of the biblical data and in conclusions drawn for Christian ethics.[17] The distinctive feature of Wink's work, though, is his focus on the spiritual aspect of the Powers—the "within" as opposed to the empirical-material manifestations.[18]

Wink's emphasis on the "within" of organizations provides an understanding, in light of the concept of the Powers, of the social practices involved in the acquisition of knowledge. My proposal is that we begin with MacIntyre's account of tradition-based rationality, including his (and Foucault's) recognition of the role of social practices in the acquisition of knowledge. However, we need to use McClendon's account of powerful practices, illuminated by Wink's proposals concerning nonviolent direct action, to correct both MacIntyre and Foucault. That is, although the social practices of research and education not only *can* be corrupted but (pace MacIntyre) are *likely* to be corrupted, they *need not be* (pace Foucault) if only the will to power can be tamed.

## INSIGHTS FROM THE RADICAL REFORMATION HERITAGE

I further suggest that a set of social practices characteristic of the Radical Reformation heritage provides just exactly the remedy needed to curb and redirect the will to power. I will mention four practices that together constitute distinctive characteristics of Radical Reformation churches: pacifism, revolutionary subordination, free-church polity, and simple lifestyle. Pacifism is the refusal to go to war, but also the refusal to use physical force in any case against another. What John Howard Yoder describes as "revolutionary subordination" is a strategy for righting injustices without the use of any power other than that of the imagination. It is valuable to emphasize that while "pacifism" and "revolutionary subordination" can both refer to isolated individual actions (or refusals to act), these are better understood communally. With the development of strategies for nonviolent resistance and nonviolent action, these activities meet the criteria for a social practice in MacIntyre's technical sense. Wink provides engaging and convincing arguments tracing these strategies directly to the teachings of Jesus.[19]

Free church polity, that is, the separation of church and state, is the rejection of institutional longing for alliance with the power of the state. Finally, learning to live simply reduces the need for power to defend one's economic privileges. So all of these elements go together to help form a community that does not need to rely on the usual sorts of worldly power to survive and flourish.

In addition, Radical Reformation churches have contributed to the development of what might be called a "Christian epistemic practice"—a communal practice aimed at the pursuit of truth. This practice involves procedures and criteria for judging teaching, prophecy, and decisions as being or not being of the spirit of Christ.[20] A comparable practice is known in the Catholic tradition as discernment of spirits, and the American theologian of the Great Awakening, Jonathan Edwards, wrote similarly on "the distinguishing marks of a work of the Spirit of God."

Consistency with Scripture has served as the primary *criterion* for decision making among Radical Reformation Christians. However, the *practical test* of consistency is the agreement of the entire community—whether the issue be the conduct of an individual in the local community, the distinctive characteristics of the Radical movement as a whole, or a theological debate with outsiders. The *means* of reaching agreement is open discussion in the context of prayer. Note that this discernment process, too, is an instance of a social practice as defined by MacIntyre. Wink's treatment of the importance of intercessory prayer[21] and Yoder's discussion of "the rule of Paul" (or the "sacrament" of open conversation)[22] expand on this point.

There is an important connection between discernment, as the Radicals understood it, and the power-limiting practices described above. Anabaptist leader Pilgram Marpeck (1495?–1556) was committed to the *sola Scriptura* principle, but without the aid of the Holy Spirit, he maintained, the Scriptures could not be interpreted or explained. The subtlest temptation besetting the Christian, he says, is to ascribe to the Holy Spirit what is actually one's own human opinion. "Ah, my brethren," he warns, "how diligently and carefully we have to take heed that we do not consider our own impulses the impulse of the Holy Spirit, our own course the course and walk of Christ."[23] We might say, how easy it is to be self-deceived about self-serving teachings, and how tempting it is to invoke the authority of the Holy Spirit to augment one's own power. Consequently, Marpeck offered four signs by which to judge the impulses behind one's own or a fellow Christian's teaching:

> First is love for God and to grant to my neighbor that which God has granted and given me for His praise and the salvation of my soul. Second is a devaluation and giving up of life unto death to suffer for the sake of Christ and the Gospel and all patience. Third, to realize when God unlocks or opens a door that one may enter the same with the teaching of the Gospel. No one shall open a door which God has not opened, in order that the office of the Holy Spirit remain His own and free. . . . Fourth, that one be free and sound in teaching and judgments and in truth, in order that none speak unless Christ work through his Holy Spirit. . . . These four parts are the true proof that the compulsion is of the Holy Spirit; also that it brings forth fruit at each season.[24]

The criterion of willingness to suffer and even to die is particularly interesting, for our purposes, in that it is a clear acknowledgment of the potential connection between theological teaching and self-interest. Consequently, teaching that is clearly in *disregard* of one's own survival has greater warrant to be accepted as authentic. The fourth criterion, the freedom of the teacher, arose from Marpeck's reaction to teaching distorted by the attempt to maintain church-state unity.

I suggest that what we see here is a social practice aimed at discerning truth that adequately takes account of the distorting influences of the will to power and, in the happy case, counteracts it in a variety of ways: by listening to the least of the brethren (and sisters), by requiring unity, by deliberately favoring teaching that flies in the face of the will to survive. And all of this is taken to be a means of allowing the Holy Spirit (rather than self-interested individuals) to have the last word. In Wink's terms, it is a means of allowing the Holy Spirit to function as the interiority of the gathered community, the body of Christ.

Although the practice of discernment was developed for practical decisions within the church, it is not irrelevant to scholarly inquiry, as its adaptation to the theological disputation demonstrates. What epistemological consequences follow from the Radical Reformation tradition's attitude toward the Powers, especially the Powers of academia? Most important, there is no a priori reason (as in the Augustinian tradition) to attribute sin to those who believe differently. Nonetheless, beliefs that (from the Radical Christian's standpoint) diverge from the truth *may* be a result of failure to exercise proper communal judgment and hence failure to be obedient to the Spirit. In current terms, a hermeneutic of suspicion is in order. Yet that same suspicion must always be directed toward the Radicals' own beliefs, since they, too, may be the product of self-interest (see the quotation from Marpeck above).

It follows from these convictions that the communal discussion, which for the Radicals normally included all members of the church, must be broadened to include the voices of outsiders, those participating in rival traditions, as well. This is, in fact, what was seen in the public disputations, as practiced by Balthasar Hubmaier and others. In our own day, a dialogue with a broader range of rival traditions is called for, and here problems of incommensurability—that is, of different standards of rationality and discrepant conceptual schemes—are likely to be a factor. Thus, the procedures MacIntyre recommends for dialogue between rival traditions, including learning of the language of the other as an insider, will be a necessary prerequisite.

The next step recommended by MacIntyre is to become familiar with any intellectual crises recognized by the participants in the rival tradition and to attempt to account for them on the basis of resources within one's own tradition. One important resource that the Radical tradition brings to bear here is to ask whether the crisis is a result of attachment to particular points of view that have been incorporated into the rival largely because they served the interests of power. In fact, Radical Reformation approaches to the history of doctrine regularly attend to sociopolitical factors: who stood to gain from one outcome or the other in the resolution of doctrinal controversies?

## CONCLUSION

MacIntyre's recommendation for the dialectical questioning of one's own tradition by subjecting it to critique from the point of view of rival traditions follows naturally from the Radicals' recognition that they themselves might be deluded by self-interest, despite communal practices designed to minimize this danger. The attempt to diagnose errors within rival traditions and especially to expose them as the fruits of the will to power follows, as well, from Radical teaching on the need for communal discernment and renunciation of worldly power.

Thus, MacIntyre's criteria can be employed with irenic rather than "agonistic" intent.[25] The "defeat" of rival traditions might better be thought of in terms of *conversion* of their adherents to a point of view that they themselves, as a result of dialogue and critique, have come to appreciate as a more inclusive and illuminating perspective. The differences, in the end, come down to different accounts of the training in moral virtue required for the intellectual life. For MacIntyre, the virtue most needed is humility. For the Radicals, humility is important, but more important is learning to curb the will to power by participating in the practices of peacemaking, revolutionary subordination, and simple living and by distancing oneself from reliance on worldly power structures.

Notice that while MacIntyre advocates a social or communal view of scholarship (belief-justifying *social* practices), his writings by themselves do little to overturn the individualistic and competitive modes of scholarship to which academia has become accustomed. The Radical tradition, with its emphasis on the judgment of the community in scholarly disputation, may provide insights for current scholarly practices that would be more social and less competitive.[26]

---

Alasdair MacIntyre recognizes two ways ahead for those of us who see the limitations of Enlightenment absolutism—his own renewed version of Thomist epistemology or the postmodernity that takes its cues from Nietzsche. Although MacIntyre argues in an ingenious way for his own position, he readily admits that he has not defeated his Nietzschean competitors.

Using resources provided by Wink and others, I have provided a theological interpretation of the impasse. Christians in the Reformed tradition would rightly criticize MacIntyre's essential optimism regarding the intellect, inherited from Aristotle and Thomas Aquinas. Christians in the Radical tradition, in general, would agree, but on somewhat different grounds. For the Radicals, the effects of the fall are found not in any innate perversion of the intellect but in willfully chosen acts of disobedience. The remedy for sin (beyond Christ's universal atonement) is found in practical matters of community discipline—in the practices based on Matthew 18 and 1 Corinthians mentioned above. More significant, then, than the fallen state of the individual is the fact that the church itself—designed by God to provide direction and support—is fallen; specifically fallen into collusion with the Powers most famously at the time of Constantine. Rejecting this tie to earthly power structures, rejecting violence as a means to one's ends, and learning to live without grasping for possessions are all essential ingredients of a lifestyle in which the will to power is diverted into Christlike channels.

The academic world, along with the rest of the social order, is a congeries of powerful social practices. When academic practices seek their own internal goods, they promote the kingdom of God. But they are easily corrupted by the interests of the powerful (as the Genealogists rightly remind us). I have argued that a recovery of New Testament forms of social life, as highlighted in some of the Anabaptist communities, provides hope for the restoration of fallen powers, including those involved in the pursuit of knowledge.[27]

## Chapter 7

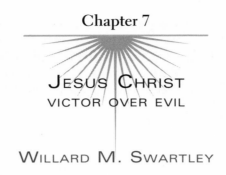

# JESUS CHRIST
## VICTOR OVER EVIL

# WILLARD M. SWARTLEY

The context for my contribution to this topic arises from three areas of experience. First, for over twenty-five years I have taught a course on war and peace in the Bible (often with an Old Testament colleague). From this I have come to see the Bible's peace teaching within the larger context of God's combat against the forces of evil. Millard Lind's book *Yahweh Is a Warrior* has influenced me significantly.

Second, for five years I served as a theological consultant on an Indiana-Michigan Mennonite Conference–appointed committee for Dean Hochstetler, who has engaged in exorcism ministry for over thirty years. By attending sessions, praying, and participating, I have come to see the reality of the spirit world and to recognize that deliverance ministry is an important component of the Christian life.

Third, I have been interested in the writings and thought of René Girard and Walter Wink. These writers urge us to think about the depth and nature of evil. Girard has unmasked the hidden mechanisms of human behavior that lead to violence, which in turn is regarded, through human blindness toward the innocent victim, as a sacrificial ritual producing peace for a time in the rivalrous community. Wink has done extensive analysis of the New Testament's depiction of the Powers. In the third volume of his trilogy, he has helped us see how pervasive evil is in the systemic, structural dimensions of our modern culture.

My contribution to this topic thus combines biblical theology on war and peace with practical contemporary deliverance ministry, as well as an appropriation of Christ's victory into the structural, psychic, and spiritual dimensions—personal, social, and collective.[1]

My presentation traverses three of the typologies on Christian approaches to the Powers, as developed by Thomas McAlpine.[2] McAlpine identifies four main approaches: Reformed, which is transformational in objective; Anabaptist, which emphasizes the importance of the church as a contrast community to the Powers; and the Third Wave approach (Peter Wagner), which employs as its chief means in missionary strategy the binding of evil powers possessing territorial control.[3] McAlpine's fourth approach is sociological-anthropological, which is for the most part comparatively descriptive of evil as understood and dealt with in various societies in relation to differing worldviews.

First, I summarize my basic biblical theological convictions that inform this chapter's focus on Jesus Christ as victor over evil. Second, I focus on New Testament teachings and understandings to assist us in understanding Jesus Christ's victory over the Powers. Third, I take up some analysis of the early church's interactions with the Powers, since their stance, I believe, integrates three of the approaches that McAlpine identifies: exorcistic, contrast communities, and transformatist approaches. Borrowing Wink's terminology, I suggest that the early church had an *integral* or holistic approach to the Powers, though their practices differed from Wink's emphases.

## BIBLICAL THEOLOGICAL CONVICTIONS AND BELIEFS

1. The overarching emphasis of Scripture presents God as both peacemaker and divine warrior who fights against evil to establish and maintain peace and justice. God's people are called to trust in God for divine victory and are not to take vengeance and judgment into their own hands. "Holy war" is motivated by divine judgment on idolatry and God's jealousy for Israel, that they not worship other gods or engage in pagan practices of sorcery (see Deut 18:9-14). Witness Israel's fight against idolatry, of which Ps 106:36-37 says, "They served their idols. . . . They sacrificed their sons and their daughters to the demons." God's expected role for Israel was to stand still, watch, and see God's victory. Victory is "not by your sword or by your bow" (Josh 24:12).

2. Jesus comes as divine warrior to overcome and defeat the powers of evil. Exorcisms and healings play a major role in Jesus' ministry; they announce the in-breaking of the kingdom-reign of God.

   Jesus' ministry in its entirety is an encounter against demonic power: demon possession of individual persons; temptations from Satan, even through his disciples; the hostility and blindness of religious leaders; and the political powers that crucified Jesus. Though the demonic sabotaged God's shalom upon earth,[4] Jesus confronted and depowered Satan's forces and work in this world. Walter Wink describes this dimension of Jesus' ministry:

   > Jesus' healings and exorcisms, which play such a major role in his ministry, are not simply patches on a body destined for death regardless; they are manifestations of God's reign now, an inbreaking of eternity into time, a revelation of God's merciful nature, a promise of the restitution of all things in the heart of the loving Author of the universe. . . . God's

nonviolent reign is the overcoming of demonic powers through nonviolent means.[5]

Kathleen M. Fischer and Urban C. von Walde note that, in the miracles
of Mark 4–5, including the exorcism of the Gadarene demonic, "Jesus is acting in ways similar to Yahweh in re-creating the harmony of the universe in
reclaiming it from Satan." They rightly contend:

> The miracles are not simply demonstrations of divine power but are exor-
> cisms, the means by which . . . God's sovereignty over Satan reasserts
> itself. And this sovereignty controls all areas of life. Thus Mark presents a
> Jesus who has power greater than any human malady, a power from God
> which exerts itself to right the order of creation by expelling and control-
> ling Satan's grip over man and the world.[6]

Jesus' liberation is indeed shown to be comprehensive and complete.

3. In Jesus' combat against and victory over evil, the disciples are called not to
   fear but to believe and have faith, echoing the Old Testament call to trust in
   God for victory and defense (see Ps 18:1-3). Here the New Testament Greek
   *pisteuo* matches the Old Testament Hebrew *batach*; both are a call to faith
   in God's power to demolish the strongholds of evil.

4. Jesus refuses to identify with the militaristic Jewish strands of messianic hope
   (Mark 8:29-33) because those hopes depended on violence against enemies
   for fulfillment. In Wink's terms, in *Engaging the Powers*, that view is the
   domination system fired by a redeemer myth that lives by violence. Instead,
   Jesus teaches the ethics of a contrast society, to be discussed later. Jesus' entry
   into Jerusalem on a donkey, in accord with Zech 9:9, shows Jesus as the nonviolent, humble King of peace, who trusts and manifests God's way.

5. Jesus includes "the enemy" into his circle of ministry—the marginal-
   ized Jews, the Samaritans, and the Gentiles. This incarnates his teaching:
   "Blessed are the peacemakers, for they shall be called the children of God."
   Love of the enemy and nonretaliation are cardinal teachings of the gospel.[7]
   So also is confrontation of and expulsion of demonic spirits—God's king-
   dom against Satan's kingdom.

6. Luke's gospel develops twin emphases in his travel narrative: onslaught
   against and victory over Satan and the demonic powers and the proffering of
   peace and justice as gifts of the gospel.[8] Further, each major new section of
   Acts shows confrontation with evil spirit-powers as the first stage of ministry
   in the evangelistic spread of the gospel: Acts 8 in Samaria, Acts 13 in Asia
   Minor, Acts 16 in Macedonia, and Acts 19 in the culmination of Paul's ministry in Ephesus.[9]

7. The Pauline teaching on the Powers is a gospel proclamation of the theological meaning of Jesus' ministry (see especially Col 2:12-15). Walter Wink is

correct that the method of Christ's defeat of the Powers is the nonviolence of the cross. But he is less correct when he views the Powers primarily in the spirit-personality manifestations of structures and institutions.

Herein lies some difference between my perceptions and Wink's emphases, specifically, in what all needs attention when discussing Jesus' victory over the Powers. Wink does speak about "outer personal possession" in *Unmasking the Powers* and gives seven helpful points about exorcism of demons from persons. Further, I know that Wink has witnessed such an exorcism of demons from a person, where Jesus' power liberated a person from demonic oppression.[10] Thus, both of us recognize manifold manifestations of the demonic, but our writings show different balances in emphasis.

*Hear, O People: Jesus is Lord and Victor.*

## FOCUS ON THE NEW TESTAMENT

Many aspects of New Testament teaching relate to this topic, but I focus specifically on selected teachings of Jesus in the Gospels, Pauline theological perspectives regarding evil, the "Principalities and Powers," and a brief statement about Revelation.

### 1. Jesus in the Gospels: forming communities of values contrasting with those of the empire.
The Beatitudes (Matt 5:3-11) mark out the fundamental nature of life in the kingdom of God:

> Blessed are the poor in spirit, for theirs is the kingdom of heaven.
> Blessed are those who mourn, for they will be comforted.
> Blessed are the meek, for they will inherit the earth.
> Blessed are those who hunger and thirst for righteousness, for they will be filled.
> Blessed are the merciful, for they will receive mercy.
> Blessed are the pure in heart, for they will see God.
> Blessed are the peacemakers, for they will be called children of God.
> Blessed are those who are persecuted for righteousness' sake, for theirs is the kingdom of heaven.
> Blessed are you when people revile you and persecute you and utter all kinds of evil against you falsely on my account. Rejoice and be glad, for your reward is great in heaven, for in the same way they persecuted the prophets who were before you. (Matthew 5:3-11)

These truly represent upside-down kingdom thinking and, like Mary's Magnificat, promise a reversal of suffering or deprivation, or at least a joy and blessedness in the midst of poverty, mourning, and the quest for peace and justice.

*Blessed are the peacemakers!* Here is the charter for our vocation, if we indeed reflect the nature of being God's children. Jesus called disciples who were to be trained in this radical new way of thinking about reality. The Gospel narratives are to a great extent Jesus' catechism for the disciples.

Second, Jesus taught his disciples to do the unthinkable: to love enemies. Wink cites a wonderful testimony from Sheila Cassidy in *When the Powers Fall*: "Hatred is a devil to be cast out, and we must pray for the power to forgive, for it is in forgiving our enemies that we are healed."[11] Of all the strategies that we may advocate for response to the Powers, this command to love our enemies must ever be kept in view, since it is so easy to absorb the very evil we seek to resist, as Wink points out.[12] The goal of all nonresistance or nonviolent resistance is to overcome evil with good, pervasive in New Testament *paraenesis*, and to transform hostile relationships into reconciliation, through truth telling and forgiveness.

Third, Jesus sought to convert his disciples from rivalry to renunciation of violence. When James and John vied for the top seats in Jesus' coming messianic kingdom, Jesus stopped short their rivalry by calling them to renounce the politics of the so-called great rulers: They *lord* it over others and *rule oppressively*. Instead, he told them, your *greatness* lies in your humble service to others. Model your lives, therefore, after the example of "the Son of Man [who] came not be served but to serve, and give his life a ransom for many" (Mark 10:45). Here James and John echoed the mimetic desire of Cain, the murderer of his brother. Rivalry, born from acquisitive mimetic desire, is the mother of violence (à la René Girard).[13]

From Mark 11 on, Jesus refuses all options to rule by violence, rather suffering death on the shameful cross. The cross is the power of God unto salvation. The shed blood of Jesus defeats the demons and releases humans from their grip because Jesus is now the once-and-for-all sacrifice for sin. When pointed to the cross, the demons flee, for they know that in the cross is their defeat. Demons thrive on rivalry, violence, and sacrifice of good people, but Jesus is the final, once-for-all sacrifice. Thus, the demons lose their powers. The cross breaks the spiral of violence. The "foolishness" of the cross is the wisdom of God; it opens the way to reconciliation and peace with enemies. Quoting Erick Dinkler: "Peace and reconciliation are tied to Jesus Christ in such a way that the cause for peace is anchored in the blood of Christ, in his crucifixion. Peace is constituted through the cross and at the same time the crucifixion with its offensive character as *skandalon* is interpreted as peace."[14]

Jesus and his disciples are indissolubly linked in this new creation of transformed desire. The overall context demands that we stress the binding relationship between the Redeemer and the redeemed. The redeemed, that is, the followers of Jesus, are linked to Jesus as the servant-head who leads the ransomed into lives of servant-living. Certainly this was one of Mark's primary aims in writing the gospel: to set forth Jesus' life, death, and resurrection as a call to and an empowerment for faithful discipleship,[15] consisting of transformed desires so that the natural human acquisitive desire is refused in the name and power of Jesus as the Servant of the Lord who leads us into the new creation.

James Williams puts it well: "I think Mark probably intends to say, in effect, 'The human condition is such that only the price of the Son of Man's suffering and death will have the effect of loosing the bonds of the sacred social structure [Wink's Domination System], enabling human beings to see what their predicament is and the kind of faith and action that will bring liberation.'"[16]

The inclusio images to Jesus' teaching in Mark 8:27–10:52 are *hodos-cross* (8:34) and *giving his life as a ransom* (10:45). Both point to suffering and death, and both point also toward gaining life and ransoming life. The way of the Messiah's—Son of humanity's—own victory and the way of victory for his followers are bound together by the cross and resurrection. The section as a whole shows that God's victory[17] comes in a most unsuspecting way: the way of self-denial, humble service, and the very giving of one's life for others.[18] This is the *way of Jesus*. Jesus' resurrection is a vital part of every passion prediction on the way. Jesus' road is not only a way to death, but also a way to God's victory (note "go before" [*proagein*] in 16:7). This victory is assured by Jesus' death as a "ransom for many." This is victory through nonviolence, as Girard puts it: "Jesus had to die because continuing to live would mean a compromise with violence. . . . Here we have the difference between the religions that remain subordinated to the powers and the act of destroying those powers through a form of transcendence that never acts by means of violence, is never responsible for any violence, and remains radically opposed to violence."[19] This refusal of violence, and victory over it, empowers Christians to resist the Powers, even when the Powers persecute Christians, as Acts demonstrates.[20]

*Hear, O People: Jesus is Lord and Victor.*

**2. Pauline theological perspectives regarding evil.** Paul's writings powerfully proclaim Christ's triumph over all the powers of evil. They celebrate and proclaim the gospel of Jesus Christ, "the power of God unto salvation" (Rom 1:16-17). God's salvation in Jesus is *the* power that delivers us from "the dominion [or authority—*exousia*] of darkness and transfers us [in]to the kingdom of his beloved Son, in whom we have redemption, the forgiveness of sins" (Col 1:13-14 RSV). By the power of this gospel alone, humans can be delivered from the bondages of sin, evil, devil, and demons—manifested in many forms, be it personal oppression or possession, or structural and systemic manifestations of the demonic powers.

Paul speaks of evil power in five ways.[21] The first of these is Satan or the devil. A most striking text occurs at the end of Romans where Paul calls believers to be wise about what is good and guileless about what is evil (*kerapous*, translated "simple" by the KJV): "Then the God of peace will soon crush Satan under your feet" (16:20 RSV). Notably, this pronouncement combines the unique New

Testament term "God of peace" with the crushing of Satan's power. In one short declaration, it unites two major trajectories in biblical theology: God as Warrior and God as Peacemaker. They meet in the life of the Christian and the believing community when the power of Satan is crushed by the power of God through Jesus Christ. In this way God triumphs over evil and establishes peace.[22]

Paul's letters speak of Satan or the devil numerous other times as well. The incestuous man is to be turned over to Satan "for the destruction of the flesh, so that his spirit may be saved in the day of the Lord" (1 Cor 5:5). Many texts speak of the believers' resistance against Satan (Eph 4:26-27; 1 Cor 7:5; 2 Cor 2:11; 11:14; 12:7; 1 Thess 2:18). The ways of Satan are deceitful; he masks himself as an "angel of light" (2 Cor 11:14) and with deceitful designs seeks to get an advantage over the believer (2 Cor 2:11). In 1 Thess 2:18, Paul says that Satan hindered the missionary team from visiting the Thessalonians (if this refers to persecution, it is thus an instance of Satan's working through political powers). Also, the believer is to give no place to the devil, thus not letting the sun go down on his or her anger (Eph 4:26-27).

Paul's second reference to evil powers is his repeated use of the word "demons." Paul uses the word on only one occasion (1 Cor 10:20-21, occurring four times). Echoing the Old Testament connection between idolatry and demon power, Paul draws a parallel between the Israelites' worship of idols (1 Cor 10:6-13) and the Corinthian believers' potential idolatry through participating in cultic meals, dedicated to pagan gods (1 Cor 10:14-22). Paul asserts, "You cannot partake of the table of the Lord and the table of demons" (1 Cor 10:21). Although in 8:5ff. Paul says that pagan gods actually have no real existence,[23] in chapter 10 he does not flirt with the power of demons. He recognizes their power and calls Christian believers away from their influence.

A third way in which Paul speaks of evil is in the categories of sin, flesh, and death. The evil impulse of "the flesh" (Rom 7:5-18) is in opposition to God's Spirit (Rom 8:3-9; Gal 5:16-18, 24; 6:8). Through the impulse of the flesh, the law itself becomes an occasion for humans to sin and come under the power of death (Rom 7:5-25). Indeed, Romans 7 reflects a deep psychological despair—fanned by a sin, flesh, law syndrome—which can be overcome only by deliverance through Jesus Christ. Paul frequently calls for a "putting off" of the old and a "putting on" of the new. That which is to be put off are the sins of the flesh; that which is to be put on is the fruit of the Spirit (Gal 5:16-23; Col 3:1-17; Eph 5:25-32). Paul nowhere calls any of these sins demons; yet his overall theology is such as to recognize that demonic power works through sin and preys upon human weakness.

A fourth face of evil appears in the forces that lie behind pagan religions and philosophies, as well as behind the law as means for self-justification. Paul speaks of being redeemed from under the law and being freed from "the elemental spirits [*stoicheia*] of the universe" (Gal 4:5, 8-9; see also Col 2:8, 18-23). These structures and rituals were powers that dominated life and thus destroyed free-dom. For the Jews, it was the law—not the law itself, but the works of the law as a means of salvation. For the Greeks, the *stoicheia* consisted of astrological fate and fortune, powers governing the cycles of nature, imparted secret knowledge, and certain beliefs about how the cosmos is held together.[24]

From these texts we gain a basic understanding of idolatry itself. Structures that are deemed good and that provide the basis for natural or social order that enables life (for the Jews, the law) are turned into ultimate values, ends in themselves, and thus are elevated to powers over one's life and then worshiped as gods.[25] Romans 1 shows the same pattern: Through sinful impulses, humans fail to see God's rev-elation in nature and therefore turn to idolatry, worship the creation and creature instead of the Creator. Hence, God gives them over—repeated three times (Rom 1:24, 26, 28)—to the course and consequences of their wickedness. Only the power of the liberating gospel can free humans from this chain of sin. Indeed, Jesus "gave himself for our sins to set us free from the present evil age" (Gal 1:4).

In the fifth way, related to the above, evil is identified through a variety of terms denoting types of *rulership*: principalities, powers, dominions, thrones, and so on. Although these Powers have a positive function within the world outside of Christ—restraining evil as agents of God's wrath (Rom 13:4, reflecting likely the Old Testament link between the wrath of God and the demonic; cf. 2 Sam 24:1 with 1 Chr 21:1)—they readily become instruments of the demonic. Indeed, these Powers crucified the Lord of Glory (1 Cor 2:6-9). Here we examine a series of texts that contain this power language and focus then on Colossians. They proclaim Jesus Christ's victory over the Powers.

*Hear, O People: Jesus is Lord and Victor!*

**3. Victory over the Principalities and Powers.** Three differing views of the Powers are present in the New Testament.[26] It is clear that political powers may be viewed both negatively and positively in their functions. But the third stream is most important, since it presents Jesus' victory over the Powers and guides the Christians' understanding of their position, authority, and witness in relation to the Powers. The key texts with their core claims include the following:

1 Cor 15:24-27. Every authority, rule, and power has been put in subjection to Christ; when Jesus hands over the kingdom to the Father, they will be stripped of all power.

Col 1:15-16, 20. The Powers, in all their variant expressions, owe their origin to God's creative work through Jesus Christ as agent of creation and are included in the ultimate reconciliation of all things in Christ.

Col 2:10, 15. Here Jesus is said to be head over the Powers (v. 10) and has also disarmed them, triumphing over them and making a public exposure of them (i.e., of how they operated in the cross).

Eph 1:19-23. The exalted Lord Jesus Christ is reigning far above all rule and authority. All such Powers are subject to Christ for the sake of the church, to enable it to fulfill the spread of knowledge of God and radiate his love to all (3:17-19).

Eph 3:9-10. The call of the church includes witness to the Powers of the manifold wisdom of God in uniting formerly hostile parties in Christ.

Eph 6:12-18. Believers must take a stand against the strategies of the Powers to trick, deceive, and defeat us. The armor of resistance is the same as God's in his long battle against evil.

Rom 8:35-39. Nothing in all God's creation, not even the Powers, can separate believers from the love of God that is in Christ Jesus our Lord.

1 Pet 3:22. All angels, authorities, and Powers are subject to Jesus Christ, who is in heaven, at the right hand of God.

Rev 18:2b, 10c. "Fallen, fallen is Babylon the great! . . . For in one hour your judgment has come."

Scholarly study of this stream of emphasis has turned up numerous interpretive issues, some of which I identify here.

1. Are the Powers benign (according to Carr) or adversarial (most writers) to God's purposes?
2. Are the powers to be demythologized and relegated to a primitive worldview (Bultmann), or are they to be viewed as spirit powers, superintelligent demons opposing God's purposes, often associated with idolatry (Arnold, O'Brien)?[27]
3. Are the demonic Powers in terms of and virtually identified with socio-economic-political structures (Berkhof, Yoder, Tambasco, Wink),[28] and/or should these structures, systems, and institutions be understood in both inner and outer dimensions, invisible and visible, to ascertain their spirit "personality" (Tambasco, Wink)?[29]

The Christus Victor view of the atonement emphasizes Jesus' binding and plundering of the demons' powers.[30] In Paul's writings, the death and resurrection of Jesus mean cosmic victory over evil spiritual powers.[31]

How should we understand the Powers today? In a sermon at Associated Mennonite Biblical Seminary, Metropolitan Paulos Mar Gregorios[32] of India spoke on Col 1:15-20 under the title, "The Comprehensiveness of Christ." The metropolitan put it well:

I think the people of Colossae did not live in our kind of secular world. They could understand many things which we cannot understand—like thrones, powers, principalities, authorities. These are lost to us, but for the Colossians these were important concepts because in the prevailing culture of that time. . . . the belief was that there were other beings besides ourselves in this cosmos—visible as well as invisible. We don't believe that. Our secular civilization tries to teach us that whatever is open to our senses is all that there is. . . . But that is not what the Colossian people believed. They believed in a whole hierarchy of beings surrounding the human community.

In a later dinner conversation on this subject, a pastoral counseling professor said, "Granted there are these various phenomena that we must consider." Gregorios incisively cut into the sentence, "Not phenomena, but *beings*." The incident exemplifies how steeped we are in our scientific worldview, and how prone we are to reduce all reality to the empirical. Even God-talk points only to function of belief, not to an actual being, whose reality determines the reality of the empirical, as traditional Christian faith holds.

The most explicit description of Christ's triumph over the Powers says he "disarmed the principalities and powers and made a public example of them" (Col 2:15 RSV). In his recent commentary on Colossians, Ernest Martin illumines the structure of this text, showing a parallel pattern for vv. 13-15.[33] Philip Bender holds that here Jesus stripped himself off from the Powers' power, the means to divine warfare and victory.[34]

In another important text (Eph 1:20-23), Christ is the head, the church is his body, and all the Powers are put under Christ's feet. The writer of Ephesians sees the new Christian community, composed of previously hostile parties, as God's witness to the Principalities and Powers, a demonstration of God's power over all other so-called Powers (Eph 3:9-10). The frequent use of Ps 110:1 throughout the New Testament, speaking of Christ's rule at God's right hand, further testifies to Christ's victory over the Powers.[35]

The consummation also has consequence for the Powers, but here emerge two emphases not easily harmonized. In some texts, the picture is that of "destroying" (or better, "rendering powerless") every rule and authority (1 Cor 15:24-28; cf. 2 Thess 2:3-11), but other texts speak of a reconciliation of the Powers to God's purpose (Col 1:19-20; Eph 1:9-10).

*Hear, O People: Jesus is Lord and Victor!*

**4. Revelation: the church amid demonic chaos.** Current scholarship disagrees about whether Christians were programmatically persecuted when Revelation was written, during the reign of Domitian. In my opinion, John's exile on Patmos, Antipas's martyrdom as a faithful witness (2:13), and expressions like those in 17:5-6 and 18:24 make it difficult to think that persecution was only sporadic: "'Babylon the great, mother of harlots and of earth's abominations.' And I saw the woman, drunk with the blood of the saints and the blood of the martyrs of Jesus" (17:5-6 RSV); further, in the fallen city, Babylon, "was found the blood of prophets and of saints" (18:24).

Whether feared as imminent or actually experienced, Revelation portrays the Powers in determined revolt against and opposition to God. The Powers at work through the emperor are demonic. The key issue of the book is, who is the true Lord of this world? The book forces a choice between loyalty to the rule of God and loyalty to the rule of Rome.[36]

Finally, Revelation presents us with a paradigm of proper response when the demonic appears in wild control: Worship God only. Endure faithfully amid persecution—even when all hell seems to have broken loose. Through faith and hope, envision God's victory; celebrate it now through song and prayer.

*Hear, O People: Jesus Christ is Lord and Victor. Praise the name of Jesus.*

## LEARNING FROM THE EARLY CHURCH

We look now to the beliefs and practices of the early church (from the second to the fourth century) to ascertain a fuller view of the Powers and how Christians claimed Christ's victory over them. Notice that I did not write "confront" the Powers. John Yoder wrote in his *Politics of Jesus*, following Hendrikus Berkhof, that we need not/should not confront the Powers because Jesus Christ has done that. We only bear witness to his victory over the Powers. We bear this witness most truly when we are truly the church, with Jesus as Lord, with freedom from the tyranny of the Powers.[37]

The portrait of early church life that I here develop bears out this point. The church of the first three centuries did not so much confront the Powers as manifest the reality of a contrast community. It witnessed to the power of Jesus' victory on the cross, God's resurrection of Jesus from the dead, and God's exaltation of Jesus to God's right hand, with all powers subject to him (1 Pet 3:22). In the name of this authority, the early church cast out demons, made exorcism a standard element in baptismal preparation, and claimed freedom from the Powers. The church was thus freed and empowered to proclaim this victory in all dimensions of its life. The early church confronted the oppression of the Powers in both political and personal spheres. We will discuss four ways that this happened.

*1. Exorcisms.* Everett Ferguson, a respected church historian, has shown in his thorough study, *Demonology of the Early Christian World*,[38] that exorcism of evil spirits from men and women, especially from those coming to Christian faith, was an essential feature of the attraction, power, and growth of early Christianity, even amid a political situation in which the political powers were oppressive of Christian life. Quoting Ferguson, "The most notable mark of the early church was its ability to deal with the spirit world in the Roman Empire. . . . I am persuaded that an important factor in the Christian church's success in the Roman world was the promise which it made of deliverance from demons."[39]

In his careful study of the means by which early Christianity grew and prepared members for baptism, Alan Kreider, concurring with Ramsay MacMullen, says that exorcism was the chief factor in conversion, attracting people from the pagan world to Christianity because of its power over evil spirits. Kreider cites numerous sources from the Fathers, including a report from Origen. He tells of a case in which someone attending Origen's instruction of catechumens suddenly cried out under the power of an impure spirit when Origen cited the words of Hannah: "My heart has exulted in the Lord." Origen continued to instruct from Hannah's hymn of praise, while others spoke to the woman, who, under the power of Origen's continued exposition of Hannah's hymn of praise to God, was eventually set free. Such episodes were not infrequent in early Christianity and became a key factor in the church's growth. Of this event, Origen says, "Things like this lead many people to be converted to God, many to reform themselves, many to come to the faith."[40]

Kreider describes the early church's practices in instructing catechumens preparing for baptism. In some parts of the church, especially the Eastern sector and prior to Constantine, the instruction would last for three to five years and regularly include exorcistic prayers for candidates. Not only was the final act of the bishop before baptism an exorcistic prayer, but the baptismal vow included a renunciation of Satan as well as confession of faith in God as Father, Son, and Holy Spirit. Upon ascending from baptism by immersion, after years of preparation in teaching and exorcism, the person entered the life of the church as a full member, eligible to partake of the Eucharist.[41] Wink, too, asserts that, for the early Christians, baptism was viewed as exorcism.[42] In *The Powers That Be*, Wink quotes Justin Martyr, saying that the "Son of God became man 'for the destruction of the devil.'"[43]

This thorough reorientation of life to prepare for baptism boggles our modern minds, since today baptism is often viewed as social acculturation only. To be sure, it was that in early Christianity, but this involved forsaking a pagan, idolatrous culture and learning a new culture shaped by the teachings of Jesus and his victorious power over evil. Truly was a person as Paul says, a totally new creation (2 Cor 5:17; Gal 6:15).

Indeed, the Roman world did not provide a Hotel Hilton or Hyatt Regency environment for early Christianity. In fact, often the early Christians experienced harassment, ostracism, and sometimes outright persecution from the empire. The gods of the Roman world and the God of the Christian community had little in common. One could not simultaneously serve the gods of the cultural environment and the God of the Lord Jesus Christ. The only means of changing allegiance and worship was through conversion, and that involved a retraining for and renewal of all of life, including the expelling of demons from the catechumens. In this drama of changing old self to new self, it became crystal clear that Jesus is the victor over sin and evil. Unhindered praise of God and the Lord Jesus became the sterling sign that one's life was set free from demonic powers and remade for the life of the Christian community. Conversion itself was a testimony to the Powers.

*Hear, O People: Jesus Christ is Lord and Victor. The name of Jesus be praised.*

*2. Early church ethics contrasted with empire ethics.* Living under the Powers of the Roman Empire, the early church came into sharp conflict with the Powers. Prior to C.E. 171, Christians consistently refused service in the military, and all church fathers taught against participation in the military up to the time of Constantine. Why was this? Here is where scholars debate one another. Representative voices are Cadoux and Hornus, who identify the chief reason as refusal to kill another human being in light of Jesus' teaching to love the enemy.[44] Helgeland, Daly, and Burns argue, conversely, that Christians refused to participate in the military because military life involved idolatry in that time and culture. But that gives no reason for Christians theologically and in principle to refuse the military.[45]

My response to this debate is yes! Why so? From study of numerous Old Testament passages, such as Isaiah 2:6ff. (following the great "swords to plowshares" passage), I conclude that amassing weapons of war and idolatry are bedfellows. The war arsenal means that humans no longer trust the Lord Yahweh. Other gods have nudged their way into their hearts. Thus, the early Christians' refusal to participate in war was precisely because it involved both idolatry *and* killing of the enemy, which Jesus forbade when he taught us to trust only in God and to love our enemies.

For a current variation on this discussion, Walter Wink and Richard Horsley face off in a debate over whether it is permissible for Christians to use violence to accomplish the goal of justice.[46] Though Horsley grew up as a Quaker pacifist, he argues for a yes response, especially for oppressed developing countries. Wink, who does not consider himself a pacifist, argues for a no response, since he now regards Jesus' teaching on nonviolence as nonnegotiable. For Wink, nonviolent resistance is the means to work for justice and truth-telling in this world of evil and violence.

Important to the early church's refusal of war is the case the church fathers made for their positive contribution to the empire. When pagan philosopher Celsus criticized Christians for not doing their duty for the empire but only reaping its benefits, they gave a threefold defense: (1) they are duty-bound to follow the "law of Christ," which consists of "beating swords into plowshares," refusing military warfare, and doing good to, even loving, the enemy;[47] (2) because the army required an oath to the emperor and sometimes emperor worship, they could not participate in war, since Jesus forbade all oaths and all Scripture forbids idolatry;[48] (3) their warfare was on a more significant level, namely, praying against the demons that incite fighting and war.[49]

The Christians thus argued that they were the true defenders of the peace of the empire because they prayed against the evil powers that incite war and violence. Moreover, they defended peace by worshiping the true God who gives earthly kings their power, and, further, they prayed that the armies would maintain the peace of the land in accord with God's sovereign purpose.[50] The story of Marcellus (who died in C.E. 298 and whose martyr bones lie in the Notre Dame

Basilica crypt in South Bend, Indiana) illustrates well the early Christian resistance to war. To the judge he declared: "I threw down [my arms]; for it was not seemly that a Christian man, who renders military service to the Lord Christ, should render it [also] by [inflicting] earthly injuries."[51]

The question I now raise is, was this confronting the Powers? In some respects, yes, but in a way different than we first think. I contend that the early Christians' response confounded the Powers because it witnessed to a unique strength and power among Christians, apart from the protection of the empire. In effect, the Christians said what Jesus taught them: We are the salt of the earth; we are the light of the world. *Our* existence is *essential*; the Powers are contingent. Our loyalty is to the sovereign Creator and Redeemer of the world. The true and abundant life is in our communities. We give allegiance to the Lord Jesus Christ, Victor over the Powers.

They did not make confrontation their goal, however. As Luise Schottroff points out, they promised submission and a degree of allegiance to the empire, but for the empire it was never enough.[52] Schottroff explains, "The root of the problem was their resistance against Satan and sin as the true rulers of this world, the resistance that had shaped Christian practice through and through."[53] Their unique blend of nonresistance and resistance to evil befuddled the Powers and gave Christians strength against evil. The peace of Jesus Christ was more powerful in confronting both human sin and the social structural evils of the time than was the Pax Romana.[54]

*Hear, O People: Jesus Christ is Lord and Victor. Praise be to the name of Jesus.*

### 3. Practice of charity and mutual aid: a contrast culture.

Early Christianity witnessed to Jesus' victory over the Powers by means of the church's incredible practice of charity and mutual aid. The Roman world treated human life with contempt in many instances, allowing especially female infants to die and their bodies to decay in open sewers running down the middle of the city streets.

Rodney Stark, from his sociological study of early Christianity, says, "We've unearthed sewers clogged with the bones of newborn girls." The early Christians "had to live with a trench running down the middle of the road, in which you could find dead bodies decomposing."[55] Christians did not put sewer systems in the cities, but they did speak out against infanticide; they cared for each other and for the weak in a society that otherwise blinded itself to human need. Though agnostic in his personal stance toward Christianity, Stark is convinced that the early Christians made a striking difference in their world, by standing for life over against death, by caring for each other, and by valuing women and children, granting them dignity and worth that manifested God's kingdom values amid an immoral, degenerate social order.[56]

In my own study, "Mutual Aid Based in Jesus and Early Christianity," I was amazed to learn the depth of conviction and practice among early Christians to care for each other. I cite one short paragraph from my article in *Building Communities of Compassion* to illustrate what this commitment demonstrated, a brilliant enactment of what Paul says, that through the church the manifold wisdom of God is to be made known to the Principalities and Powers (Eph 3:10): "In A.D. 251, the church in Rome had a massive program of care for the widows and the poor. The church, consisting of many house fellowships throughout the city, had 1,500 people on its roll for support. Bishop Cornelius was aided by six presbyters, seven deacons, seven more subdeacons, and ninety-four people in minor roles [aiding the ministry of care for the needy]."[57]

Caring for the poor and conferring human dignity upon women and children became a powerful testimony to Jesus that unmasked the illusions of the Powers. When Constantine became emperor under the banner of his Christian conversion—though he was baptized only at his death—he simply took over the Christian charity patterns already developed, trying to maintain them as a welfare system. Certainly the life of the Christian community that enacts the new creation of the gospel of Jesus will bear not only a nonviolent testimony to the Powers but also a positive demonstration of how Christian faith and life order society through love and honor of the dignity of each human being.

*Hear, O People: Jesus Christ is Lord and Victor. Praise be to the name of Jesus.*

**4. The nature of early Christian worship.** The fourth force that made Christianity an unrivaled power against the Powers of the empire was the nature of early Christian worship. This is a huge topic, and I can treat it only in broad strokes. As Robert Webber has shown, the worship of early Christianity celebrated Jesus' triumph over the powers of evil. Worship, especially celebrating the Eucharist, freed believers from the devil's power, enabling them to live free from the empire's means of ordering society. The sign of the cross was used to indicate the sealing of the catechumen to Jesus Christ, against all bondage to every spiritual power. Imposition of hands upon the candidate may have been itself an exorcistic act, the mediation of divine power against all other power. The priest/minister also gave salt to the candidate, a sign of hospitality welcoming the person into the covenant. Also used was a rite of breathing, in which the candidate blew out every evil spirit and inhaled the Holy Spirit.[58] Webber summarizes:

> The period of purification and enlightenment, of spiritual journey preceding baptism, emphasizes not instruction, but spiritual recollection and readiness. It brings before the converting person the essence of what it means to be converted to Christ and equips the new convert with the weapons of spiritual warfare. It calls the convert into an ultimate rejection of Satan and all works of evil. It bids the convert to receive the tradition of faith and prayer that has been handed down in the church from the beginnings of Christianity. Rejecting Satan and accepting the tradition is absolutely essential to conversion.

The period of purification and enlightenment with its exorcisms and presentations provides the converting person with one more opportunity to deepen his or her commitment to Jesus Christ as Lord and Savior.[59]

Similarly, Alan Kreider and Taylor Burton-Edwards, in studying early Christian liturgy, show how basic the celebration of Christ's peace was in the liturgies, including the Eucharist.[60]

*Hear, O People: Jesus Christ is Lord and Victor. Praise be to the name of Jesus.*

---

Through Jesus' comprehensive confrontation with the powers of evil, culminating in the cross and resurrection, God has paved the way to bestow shalom, a divine gift, upon earth. We are called into the same nonviolent warfare, depending upon the Word of God, in the name and authority of Jesus, to stand against the powers of evil and thus celebrate God's gift of shalom through Jesus.

Jesus, through his life, death, and resurrection, has been exalted to God's regal right hand, and all the powers and authorities have been subjugated under his feet.

This is the reason for Paul's shocking, perhaps offensive, new birth ethic. The reason believers are to be subject is because these authorities, even in their rebellion, have been subjected under Christ's rule. The realm of Christ's victory is universal; nothing escapes it. But the locus of the victory is with the believers. They know the victory and new order of life. Their new life is a demonstration that war is over, that the enmity of enemy relationships has been defeated. We do not attack or fight the Powers; God has done that in Christ. We proclaim the victory by the new way of love that overcomes evil with good. I conclude with two stories, illustrating Jesus' victory over the Powers in both the personal dimension of freedom from the demonic and the structural political triumph of good over evil.

First, one afternoon I received a call from a colleague in deliverance ministry asking me to immediately pray and bind the demon of murder in a certain man in the area who had just threatened to come to his church and murder the pastor. Both he and I, and the pastor, did accordingly. The man came into the church parking lot and started toward the church with a gun, then suddenly stopped, got back into his pickup, tore out of the church lot, went home, called the pastor on the phone, and said, "I need help. I am overcome with this evil energy to murder you." The pastor arranged a meeting for the same evening and invited several of us to come and assist.

During my twelve-mile drive to the church that evening, I struggled with how a nonresistant Mennonite would handle the violence likely to be manifested. I believe Jesus: "Love your enemies." How does this figure when one is confronted with violence? Not long into the session, I thought I was a goner. The man, much bigger than me, lunged toward me with his fist aimed at my head.

The words I thought about in the car burst out of my mouth, "Jesus said, 'Love your enemies.'" The man collapsed to the floor, his swinging arm gone limp.

Then we learned from the demon, when commanded to speak the truth, that someone had murdered this man's father when the man was twelve years old and that he had nurtured the desire to find and kill the man who had killed his father all these twenty-five-plus years. We told this to the man when he had come out from under the demonic spell, to check the truth, and he broke down and said, "How do you know this? I've told no one. It's true, and I am overcome by the spirit of murder." He then confessed his sin and asked God's forgiveness. From then on, we knew what we were dealing with, and expulsion of that demon from the man came quickly in the next round of command-confrontation. The spirit of murder cannot withstand being confronted with Jesus' command to love our enemies.

Second, one of the most moving stories of our time is what happened in East Germany in 1989. The church in East Germany became the place where people gathered for prayer, to cry out to God for help in changing the tyranny of their political system. Believers and unbelievers came together to pray and to search for God's help and way. As one East German–born Christian from Grand Rapids, Michigan, put it, with tears in her eyes, the people who had never come to church came and began to call upon God for help — in simple but powerful and earnest prayers. In the Nicholas Church (Nikolaikirche) in Leipzig, for example, many began to meet regularly on Monday nights.

Then the political situation became very tense, and the people began to think that the troops of the Communist Party would come and crush their hopes by force. But the church called on both the government and the people to refrain from violence. This petition not to resort to violence was read from every pulpit in the city and over the municipal public address system. The petition called all those who wanted to do something for their country to come that night to the church. Amazingly, seventy thousand people showed up. After the secret police felt the power of this faith movement, they left the mass of people. The people, weeping with joy, praised God for a new Red Sea miracle.[61]

This to me is a modern Scripture story. The church honored its Lord and trusted God for victory over the powers of evil. Now it is also true that in some cases, perhaps even similar to this one, evil continues to triumph for a while, and believers do get crushed and killed. This, too, is part of the Christian history. Even then the church exclaims in worship: "Worthy is the Lamb who was slain, to receive power and wealth  and wisdom and might and honor and glory and blessing!" (Rev 5:12 RSV). "The kingdom of the world has become the kingdom of our Lord and of his Christ, and he shall reign for ever and ever" (Rev 11:15 RSV).

*Hear, O People: Jesus Christ is Lord and Victor. Praise be to the name of Jesus.*

# Chapter 8

# THE ECONOMICS AND POLITICS OF VIOLENCE
## TOWARD A THEOLOGY FOR
## TRANSFORMING THE POWERS

## RAY GINGERICH

I intend here to broaden the categories of the Powers as developed by Walter Wink[1] and to make the concept of the Powers more readily available as a tool for doing ethics. Most of what is being done in ethics today is done as personal (individual) ethics. Even when social ethics are taken seriously, the structures are usually taken for granted. Largely neglected are corporate and cultural ethics that examine the structures determining the larger patterns of our lives. I argue that the subject of the Powers offers the most promising entrance for doing theological ethics at this largely subconscious level of corporate, structural ethics.

The practical, historical focus of this chapter, at the intersection of theology, ethics, and the political sciences, is on economic systems of covert violence and the politics of war—overt violence.[2] The interests in both economics and politics lie at a structural level, one that is largely subconscious to its participants, while creating an ethos that dominates us as a church, a society, and a nation. This interest in political, corporate-driven economics and politics dovetails with Wink's treatment of the Powers within the "Domination System."[3]

Economics was central in the political message of the eighth-century Hebrew prophets. Economic justice was a dominant thread woven into the fabric of Jesus' ministry.[4] The particular historic episode of this essay, however, begins with the early stages of capitalism and the breakup of feudalism—a system that shares the principle components of later capitalism but is less complex in form.

I begin with a historical sketch. The episode of the early sixteenth-century South German–Austrian Peasants' War stands as an example of the economics of oppression and the politics of violence. After developing a socially "thickened" understanding of the Powers using Clifford Geertz's thought alongside that of Wink, I show that both the economics of covert violence and the politics of overt violence belong to the fallen Powers—the Powers gone amok. Then, using Thomas Kuhn's theoretical framework of "paradigm shifts," I examine what happened in the aftermath of the Peasants' War. Many of those involved in the war also showed up as leaders in the nonviolent Anabaptist movement, while hundreds of others constituted the rank and file of that movement of economic sharing. If the first parts of this chapter are the warp of the fabric I am weaving, then the paradigm shift I suggest constitutes the woof.

At another level, this chapter may be seen as a conversation among Walter Wink (the Jungian theologian), Clifford Geertz (the functionalist[5] philosopher of social anthropology), and Thomas Kuhn (historian of science, contributing to the theory of a cosmology or worldview).[6]

## THE ECONOMICS OF COVERT VIOLENCE AND POLITICS OF OVERT VIOLENCE: A CASE STUDY

*The economics of covert violence: nascent capitalism.* In the spring of 1525, the peasants of Swabia (with the help of a learned sympathizer[7]) drew up the Twelve Articles, which they presented to the princes and nobility of the area in their opposition to an oppressive and covertly violent economic system. These articles reflected a wide range of hardships and abuses imposed on the peasants by the nobility. As Peter Blickle notes, they constituted "a list of grievances, a reform program, and a political manifesto all in one."[8] The peasants' concerns ranged from their being denied participation in the selection of the local parish pastor,[9] to equitable distribution of the income from the tithe, to their desire to ensure that the needs of the poor were met.[10] Other articles called for restored fishing and hunting rights for the poor[11] and for access to firewood cut from trees on public lands and a return of meadows to the "entire community—meadows that had been expropriated as private property by the princes and bishops."[12]

Still other articles related to unjust servitude and the suffering of indignities: "It has been the custom for men to hold us as their own property."[13] "We are grievously oppressed by the free labor which we are required to provide for our lords."[14] And for the peasant to be in possession of his holdings so that "the lord shall not . . . demand anything else from him without payment."[15]

Several additional observations about these articles are in order:

1. The entire document is in a *religious context* with Scripture references in the margins. Some of the articles end with a special appeal to the authority of Scripture, most notably the following: "We have no doubt that since they [the lords] are true and genuine Christians, they will gladly release us from serfdom, or show us in the gospel that we are serfs."[16] The final and culminating article underscores the peasants' willingness to have everything tested on the basis of Scripture.[17]

2. Nine of the articles are related to *economic justice*, dealing with various components that relate to the basic necessities of life. The two remaining articles concern leadership in the congregation (Article 1) and the legal

system, calling for justice in the courts in which differences are resolved (Article 9).

3. No dualistic ethic is reflected. Nowhere is the assumption made that there is one standard for the public arena and another for the private sphere, or one ethic for the church and another for the state. There is no separation of civic from churchly responsibilities, nor of the sacred from the secular, nor of the religious from the political.[18] Neither are arguments based on a dualistic ontology. They reflect a communally unified understanding of society, strongly bound by the cords of economics and ordered by the teachings of Jesus. This is in contrast not only to later seventeenth and eighteenth-century Enlightenment thought[19] but also to Luther's own two-kingdom theology in which he differentiates between the public and the private spheres of life, relegating the ethics of the Sermon on the Mount to be applicable only in the private sphere.[20]

By April 1525 the cities of Erfurt and Salzungen had surrendered to the peasant bands. Castles, monasteries, and convents were being confiscated. Luther's protector, Frederick the Wise, Elector of Saxony, who was now fatally ill, continued to hold forth hope for a peacefully negotiated peace. At Nordhausen, where Martin Luther attempted to preach "the word of God" to the peasants, hecklers interrupted his sermon, severely offending the doctor. In this already very tense situation, Luther returned to Wittenberg and unleashed his tract "Against the Robbing and Murdering Hordes of Peasants," not merely legitimating but boldly encouraging the slaughter of the peasants in the name of maintaining the imperial political order of the day.[21] In a widely circulated pamphlet, this most authoritative figure of the German Reformation wrote:

> Romans 13[:1] says, 'Let every person be subject to the governing authorities.' Since they [the peasants] are now deliberately and violently breaking this oath of obedience and setting themselves in opposition to their masters, they have forfeited body and soul, as faithless, perjured, lying, disobedient rascals and scoundrels usually do. . . . Furthermore, anyone who can be proved to be a seditious person is an outlaw before God and the emperor; and whoever is the first to put him to death does right and well. For if a man is in open rebellion, everyone is both his judge and the executioner; just as when a fire starts, the first man who can put it out is the best man to do the job.[22]

From this point it was only a matter of weeks until the politics of systemic, legalized, religiously sanctioned human slaughter were implemented full-scale.

*The politics of overt violence: war.* Led by Thomas Müntzer, the peasants fought with full assurance of at least three "facts": (1) that Scripture was on their side; (2) that they, the peasants, were on God's side, and that even with

vastly inferior weapons, humanly speaking, they would conquer through violence, resulting in the defeat of their overlords;[23] (3) that God was on their side
and would intervene, initiating the kingdom—the return of Christ, and with that,
Christ's kingdom on earth.[24] Each of these certain hopes turned out to be otherwise. The peasants lost the war, and with it as many as one hundred thousand of
them were slaughtered.[25]

Why did a movement that was basically nonviolent in its early stages turn so
savage?[26] What was the role of chiliastic apocalypticism—a certain dramatic and
violent view of history held by both Luther and the peasants—in the escalation
of events? What was the role of religion—both the acknowledged religion and
the "invisible," unacknowledged religion? Each of these questions is subsumed
under the following analysis of the Powers.

## The Powers Gone Amok

The framework for interpreting these historical events is organized around two
theses: (1) *Clifford Geertz's concept of religion*[27] *enhances Wink's understanding
of the Powers, developing a conceptualization of the Powers that is more useful for
sociopolitical analysis.* (2) *Both the economics of covert violence and the politics
of overt violence belong to the fallen Powers. The Powers, when left unattended,
go amok.*

**Thesis no. 1.** *Wink's concept of the Powers is enhanced as a theopolitical
category if taken in the context of Geertz's understanding of religion.* The "Powers," according to Walter Wink, are the functional equivalent in our day of the
"Principalities and Powers" in the New Testament. Wink refers to them as "the
actual spirituality at the center of the political, economic and cultural institutions." But more than the institutions themselves, the Powers are the ethos created by those institutions, which now sustains those same institutions and makes
individuals and societies nigh incapable of assessing them and sufficiently transcending them to offer a critique.[28]

Wink's most extensive elaboration on identifying the Powers is in his first
book of the trilogy, *Naming the Powers.*[29] The focus there is on New Testament
exegesis. This provides Wink with keys for gaining new insights into the cosmology of the first century C.E. Wink's second volume, *Unmasking the Powers*, is an
exposition of the "invisible forces that determine human existence." This attempt
to bring the world of which we are unconscious into our consciousness is Wink's
most daring, elaborate, and creative analysis of the Powers.

However, it is not until his last volume in the trilogy, *Engaging the Powers*,
that Wink makes more extensive application to contemporary events and societal
structures. He names certain of the Powers (*Kosmos*, *Aiōn*, and *Sarx*) as together
constituting the Domination System. These are categories that Wink carries over
from his previous two volumes, which focus almost exclusively on the thought and

language of the New Testament world.[30] Visible "societal modes" give embodiment to the "invisible forces"—which for Wink *are* the Powers—and together these constitute the Domination System. These societal modes consist of a rather wide spectrum of nonparallel phenomena. They include politics, economics, and religion—but also such disparate categories as logic, the role of the ego, sexual responsibility, and eschatology.[31] In the following paragraphs, economics and religion are examined at some greater depth and presented not merely as societal modes but as Powers.

Central to Wink's entire project in the Powers trilogy and central to the concerns of this chapter is the commitment to construct an integral worldview (cosmology) in which the Powers are perceived as *real* and operative in our contemporary Western society.[32] In a most succinct and penetrating analysis, Wink makes the following observation: "In reaction to materialism, Christian theologians invented the supernatural realm. . . . Acknowledging that this supersensible realm could not be known by the senses, they conceded earthly reality to modern science and preserved a privileged 'spiritual' realm immune to confirmation or refutation—at the cost of an integral view of reality." Wink continues this observation, noting that "this view of the religious realm as hermeneutically sealed and immune to challenge from the sciences has been held not only by the Christian center and right, but by most of theological liberalism and neo-orthodoxy."[33]

We may expand Wink's project to overcome the dualisms of modernity by drawing on Clifford Geertz's description of religion. Geertz defines religion as

1. a system of symbols that acts to
2. establish powerful, pervasive, and long-lasting moods and motivations in individuals and society
3. by formulating concepts of a general form of existence
4. and clothing these concepts with an aura of facticity
5. so that the moods and motivations seem uniquely realistic.[34]

Both phenomena—Geertzian religion and the Winkian Powers—are built upon complex systems of symbols. Both phenomena "establish powerful, pervasive and long-lasting moods and motivations" in the subconscious reality of individuals and societies. Wink refers to these moods as an "ethos"—a "thick" and determinative social atmosphere that permeates deeply into the psyche (soul) of the individual and, in Geertz's terms, clothes these perceptions "with an aura of facticity" so that "the moods and motivations seem uniquely realistic."

Wink, working within a Jungian framework, looks inward when probing further. An underlying theme throughout Wink's trilogy, but particularly emphasized in *Engaging the Powers*, is his desire to overcome the Modernist materialistic, reductionistic worldview. He does this by offering an interiority of spirituality as an integral aspect of the empirical exteriority, together constituting a "single reality."[35] Geertz, as anthropologist, thinks relationally (within society and culture), examining the thicker contours of long-term social devolutions. He refers to religious belief and "long-lasting moods" (religious factuality) as emerging not from rational deductions of everyday experience but "a priori acceptance of authority which transforms that experience" into an invisible and unexamined Power.[36] This thick, nonmaterial reality can most fittingly be designated as an "ethos" that enshrouds our collective faculties of perception and constitutes the controlling force of society. All this, I believe, correlates well with Wink's functional description of the Powers—"the invisible forces that determine human existence."[37]

By including the *intra-social ethos that enshrouds us*,[38] which Geertz defines under the rubric of religion, we are able to conceptualize a more robust understanding of the Powers, without positing an inner/outer dichotomy and locating the reality of the Powers as the interiority. This more robustly embodied, integrated understanding of the Powers (à la Geertz) remains compatible (and functionally complementary) with Wink's understanding of the Powers. But with Geertz's definition, the sociality of institutions, specifically the sociality of economics and war, is taken more seriously, with less susceptibility to being construed as yet another dualism that allows us to subconsciously deny or "block out" the hard reality of politics and social structures.

**Thesis no. 2.** *The economics of oppression and the politics of violence belong to the "fallen Powers"—that is, to the Powers gone amok.* Economics constituted a significant strand of the religion of both the commoners (mostly peasants) and officialdom as represented by Luther and the princes.[39] For the Establishment as represented by Luther and the princes, it functioned as a religious system—albeit an unrecognized, invisible religion, distinguished from their "traditional" visible religion.[40] Luther, not recognizing "invisible non-traditional religion," dealt with the "secular," of which economics is a part, by developing his two-kingdom theory and placing it outside the domain of Scripture and visible religion.[41]

The commoners needed no new theology; their experience let them "know" that the gospel addressed economics as an integral part of the faith. This is why Thomas Müntzer gained such a rapid hearing among the peasants. He verbalized what they already knew intuitively and in so doing lent legitimacy to their cause. The restoration of fishing and hunting rights and of common pastures was as much a part of their faith as was the ability to select their own parish leadership.[42] Scripture, and most especially the teachings of Jesus, as perceived by the commoners, made no Sunday/Monday or sacred/secular distinctions.

After seeing the correlation of Geertz's understanding of religion and Wink's use of the Powers, we should begin to suspect that the fallen Powers *always* function as *invisible religion*. Wink refers to these as "the actual spirituality at the center of the political, economic and cultural institutions" that we have created but that now dominate us.[43] The focus in this chapter is on *both* that which lies prior to or "beneath" traditional ethics *and* those sociocultural institutions (beyond visible religion) that create "powerful, pervasive and long-lasting moods and motivations," that is, a controlling *ethos*,[44] a phenomenon that makes religion (both visible and invisible) one of the Powers.[45]

Much of the conflict we see in the Twelve Articles results from (1) the *privatization* and *commodification* of common holdings (e.g., grazing lands and fishing and hunting rights) and (2) the *usurpation of community rights* for the "divine rights" of rulers (now termed "multinational corporations" and the World Trade Organization). We do well to remember that free-market capitalism is a devolutionary outgrowth of this more benign capitalism in its nascent stages in early sixteenth-century Europe.[46] The discipline of economics, that is, what economists do and produce, is to money and the society that pays allegiance to money, what the theologian is to God and the society that makes "God" its principle focus of allegiance. In that society, then, in which money is the functional equivalent of God, the economist becomes the functional equivalent of a theologian.[47] Economics—the fiduciary theories regarding monetary systems—should then be recognized as the "theology" of the religion of material value.[48]

*"Invisible religion" today.* We can perhaps understand the sixteenth century better by drawing comparisons with the present, and vice versa. What the cathedral in the center of the medieval village symbolized—the point in society from which life flowed and to which the populace regularly returned for sustenance—the shopping malls and banks represent in contemporary society. The consumers are the worshipers. The process of shopping is central to the liturgy, with the purchase, of course, serving a function similar to that of the Eucharist—an act of consumption. The advertising agencies—those who make consumption a virtuous necessity for the "full life"—are the evangelists, packaging the gospel in persuasive sound-bite homilies.

The Powers, left unattended, go amok. They dominate us, oppress us, and bring us into their service. They make us into oppressors. More than the institutions qua institutions, the Powers are the ethos created by those institutions, which ethos now sustains those same institutions and makes individuals and societies nigh incapable of assessing them and sufficiently transcending them to offer a critique. Even less are we capable of freeing ourselves. These are not merely *inward* "invisible forces." They are external invisible structures, invisible to us because, having become enmeshed in them, we are unable to distance ourselves from them sufficiently so as to get them into our focus. Therefore, though initially created to serve us and to sustain our lives, the Powers "determine our existence" and, left unattended—that is, without being analyzed, tamed, and brought into the service of justice for all—they become death-dealing gods of oppression.[49] Those who would undo the Powers using the strategies of violence, whether covert or overt, whether under the jurisdiction of the state or through market forces, unwittingly join the Powers. Co-opted by the Powers, they are, metaphysically, of one essence with them.

Let us ask again: How does this understanding of capitalism as religion that constitutes one of the Powers relate to the Peasants' War of 1525 and the early sixteenth-century Anabaptist movement? The Twelve Articles offer a basic framework for understanding the religion of the peasants. Thomas Müntzer burst on this scene with his message against the gods of the Establishment, which legitimated the commoners' movement and their goals.[50] The accumulation of private property, Müntzer believed, was the outcome of human greed and selfishness resulting from the fall of Adam and Eve. Society's preoccupation with material things was, for Müntzer, the most prominent symptom of disturbed relationships among God, humans, and creatures (the natural environment).[51] The Establishment, in spiritualizing the meaning of property and ownership and in rejecting the peasants' understanding of their biblically based demands, was countering the "heresy" of the peasants—not their traditional Christian (metaphysical) doctrine but their fundamental religious values, demonstrated by their refusal to pay taxes and their refusal to pledge the oath of allegiance to the civil authorities. All this clashed with the religion of nascent capitalism![52]

The princes and their armies "knew" that God was on their side and that every rebellious peasant done away with was as though slaughtered by the hand of God. It was, after all, Luther who in a feverish pitch of fear admonished the princes, saying: "Let everyone who can, smite, slay and stab, secretly or openly, remembering that nothing can be more poisonous, hurtful or devilish than a rebel. It is just as when one must kill a mad dog; if you do not strike him, he will strike you, and a whole land with you."[53]

The religion of capitalism, given no restraints, turns to oppress the poor and destroy the rich.[54] Capitalism, like all other religion that becomes an end in itself, is a Power that enslaves its practitioners.

## The Powers Can Be Redeemed: A Paradigm Shift

The Powers of capitalism and the Powers of violence, like all Powers, can be transformed by the socially embodied legacy of Jesus. "The Jesus who died at the hands of the Powers died every bit as much for the Powers as he died for people."[55] That legacy, as the postwar peasants discovered, is the way of nonviolent resistance in the context of a shared community.[56]

The German Peasants' War of 1525 and the structural linkage with the origins of the Anabaptist movement—which is one of the most extended alternative nonviolent movements in the history of the church—make the study of the Powers a fertile field of analysis because of its significance in the current construction of theological ethics of nonviolence in a postmodern era.

The "veterans of the Peasants' War provided the major leadership and probably most of the rank and file of the earliest Anabaptist movement" that emerged in the years immediately following.[57] Acts 4 became a guiding, legitimating authority—all should give of their abundance (i.e., that which they did not need) so that there would be no needy among them.

What happened in the aftermath of the Peasants' War, I believe, can most adequately be described as a paradigm shift:[58] (1) in economics, from coercive, unjust competition to cooperative sharing, that is, the formation of communities of goods; and (2) in politics, from the perception of power as violence (the power to crucify) to the perception of power as corporate nonviolence (postcrucifixion, resurrection power).

By using the concept of a "paradigm," we begin to get a visual grasp of our subconscious mechanisms of perception. A paradigm is like a windowed wall through which we see the world beyond us. This wall is the cultural and anthropological framework that determines what is open to our perception and what is hidden from it. We see the world beyond us, unaware of this perceptual framework and the limitations this places upon our understanding of what is "real." A paradigm shift involves relocating ourselves as perceivers and enlarging the windows. It is never the total removal of the cultural-anthropological framework. Thomas Kuhn, who first popularized the term "paradigm shift," explains it as follows:

> When paradigms change, the world itself changes with them. Led by a new paradigm, scientists [and theologians, politicians, and commoners] adopt new instruments and look in new places. Even more important, during revolutions scientists [and theologians, politicians and commoners] see new and different things when looking with familiar instruments in places they have looked before. It is rather as if a professional community [and a bunch of townspeople] had been suddenly transported to another planet where familiar objects are seen in a different light and joined by unfamiliar ones as well.[59]

"Of course," adds Kuhn, "nothing of quite that sort does occur: there is no geographical transportation; outside the laboratory [or the League, or the community of sisters and brothers] everyday affairs usually continue as before"—meaning there is much mop-up work that needs to be done.[60] Or, to extend the use of the visual metaphor, there is much refocusing and repositioning that needs to be done.

To paraphrase Kuhn: Long before experiencing such a dramatic shift, we (whether this be peasants or Kuhn's peers in the laboratory) are led into a series of puzzlements and anomalies in which things don't make sense! The peasants, for example, began to doubt that which they had in previous times "known" as fact. And, finally, when the anomalies could not be solved but only became larger, a crisis overtook them. A crisis convulses because of outward circumstances (e.g., the peasants' military defeat) or because the burden of an inward struggle can no longer be borne (e.g., the collapse of a belief system) or, as is usually the case, because of a combination of causes.[61] Paradigm shifts are not brought about simply by adding a bit more information to that which we have

already accumulated. Paradigm changes, specifically at the worldview or cosmological level, occur only when the framework for "knowing," for "packaging our
perceptions," no longer works. We see things that don't add up. And when we try
to place the individual pieces into a coherent picture, the components don't jibe.
In all of this, the human species, both individually and collectively, has immense
capacity to ignore and to subconsciously block out what after the shift is obvious
and at a later point may even be taken for granted.[62]

*An inversion of political power—from violence to nonviolence.*
What, then, did it mean for the commoners who survived the devastation of
military defeat and death to experience a paradigm shift in their understanding
of power? Violence had let the peasants down. The God of the battle, the God
of violence, had failed them. God as their theologians and church doctrine had
trained them and conditioned them to think, this God had let them down.[63] And
"Christ," their Christ, had betrayed them, for Jesus did not make his return as
their prophets had predicted.[64]

When seen from this perspective, the social, psychological, and spiritual
impact of this event is difficult to grasp and can hardly be overestimated. What
began to happen to the peasants was an inversion of power—violence had been
an anomaly. But it was legitimated with the use of chiliastic apocalypticism. Now
it led them into the crisis of defeat and death. Who God is and how God works
in history had now to be reconceptualized.

Nothing could bring into question the peasants' faith in the God of war and
the evil of the war itself more clearly than the overwhelming evidence that violence had failed. Power, whatever that meant, was not to be found in violence.[65]
This called for a series of dramatic shifts—from Luther, who sacralized the state
and its violence,[66] to Müntzer, who trusted in the mystical vision and took as his
models for action the warrior men of the Old Testament, to *seeing Jesus as the
center of their paradigm for the Christian's life.*[67]

The "transformation mode" of the Domination System, according to Wink,
is violence, force, and war.[68] It was within this system that both the peasants and
the princes had gone to war. But power as "military force" didn't fit the larger
puzzle; it didn't positively transform the society. Whether from the perspective
of the peasants or the princes, neither peace nor justice nor the kingdom had
emerged. In fact, to many these hoped-for realities seemed to have retreated, to
have snuffed out the hope of the Reformation.

A key first step in transforming the Powers is to unmask them. Wink astutely
perceives that "exposing the delusional system is the central . . . task in our discernment of the Powers. For the Powers are never more powerful than when they
can act from concealment. To . . . masquerade as the permanent furniture of
the universe, they make the highly contingent structures of current oppression
appear to be of divine construction."[69] Nothing could crack the masquerading
face of the Power of violence and expose its impotence and destruction more
decisively for the peasants than their defeat in war. With the shattering of the

masquerading face of violence, the model of Jesus, the nonviolent teacher and healer of the poor, was seen again for the first time. "During revolutions . . . [commoners] see new and different things when looking with familiar instruments in places they have looked before."[70] We are reminded again of Wink's statement: "The Jesus who died at the hands of the Powers died every bit as much for the Powers as he died for people."[71]

*An inversion of economics—from capitalism to a community of goods.* What the peasants experienced with war was matched only by their experience in economics. It was, after all, the oppressive economics of nascent capitalism that was a root cause of this revolution. A paradigmatic shift in the perception of economics came about—a dramatic shift in perception and hence in reality itself—from the economics of competition and greed to the economics of community and sharing.

The following steps begin to outline what happened in the process of their becoming a communally oriented, nonviolent people:

1. In the thought of all persons involved—whether nobility, mainline Reformers, proto-Anabaptist peasants, or later Anabaptists—economics and community were intricately linked. Therefore, in retrospect we realize that the mere concept (not its realization) of covenant community (*Bund*) already prior to the war supported an alternative vision and brought with it the possibility to perceive a new economic order.

2. Economics—whether the economics of capitalism or the economics of community—*is religious.* And religion,[72] even if "invisible" (i.e., not officially recognized or even seen as belonging to the *secular* realm),[73] as we have seen from Geertz, is a Power. Common ownership of property—even the concept of common ownership—was therefore a threatening heresy to the Establishment. Just as nonviolence is threatening to the Power of violence, so communal ownership of property is threatening to capitalism, whether nascent or of the "free-market globalism" type.[74] It need not be recognized as religion—but its function is nevertheless that of religion, that is, one of the Powers.

3. The "community of goods," as taught and practiced by the Anabaptists, was based on Acts 2 and 4 from its very beginnings.[75] The paradigm shift of the commoners was not limited to a renunciation of overt, state-sponsored, religiously sanctioned violence. It was also an alternative mode of living that renounced the covert violence of the emergent competitive capitalist system.

Sometimes in an effort to sustain the old paradigm, the logic shifts. Here the example of Ulrich Zwingli, the Establishment's reformer in Zurich most closely associated with the early leaders of Swiss Anabaptism (whose members in the economic struggle for justice, were not directly involved in the Peasants' War), is most informing. In 1522 (approximately three years prior to the Peasants' War), Zwingli wrote, "[Among true Christians,] no one calls any possession his own; all things are held in common."[76] By June of 1525 (two months after the Peasants' War), he wrote, "The greater part of devout, quiet Christians will find no pleasure in the Anabaptist cause because they see at once that the Anabaptists are aiming at community of goods and the abolition of government."[77]

The established state-church had let the peasants down—first the Establishment of the Catholic Roman system, but now also the Establishment of the Protestant German/Swiss system. Believers' church—a community of faith not defined by the boundaries of the state-church and the protection of the princes— now took on a new level of viability. The Anabaptists in neighboring territories more influenced by pacifist humanism undoubtedly served as critical social facilitators, midwives in birthing the paradigm shift[78]—but a transformation that for many could not (and did not) occur without the instrumentation of the defeat of violence.

The transformation of economics begins with what appears to be the simple acts of *naming* and *unmasking*—to which Wink dedicates two volumes. But unmasking is not a simple act. More is at stake. The Powers are too tenacious to surrender and flee at first exposure. Furthermore, what is unmasked for one (the prophet in our midst) is not yet perceived by the many. The paradigm, as Kuhn describes it, "stands for the entire constellation of beliefs, values, [and] techniques . . . *shared by the members of a given community*." The paradigm also "denotes one sort of element in that constellation" that serves as the concrete piece in the solution of a larger puzzle and "can replace explicit rules [and belief systems] in the solution of the remaining puzzles."[79] This is descriptive of what, in the crisis of the Peasants' War, happened to those who became Anabaptists. And, as Kuhn notes, "though the world does not change with a change of paradigm, the scientist [and the theologian and the follower of Jesus] works in a different world."[80]

Much clean-up work (adjusting to the new understanding, applying the reorientation to areas of life not immediately affected) needed to be done in the aftermath of the paradigm shift. In Kuhn's words, "When paradigms change there are usually significant shifts in the criteria determining the legitimacy" of the reality being investigated. "No paradigm ever solves all the problems it defines."[81]

This is evidenced nowhere more clearly than in the crises and transformation of one of Thomas Müntzer's followers, Hans Hut. Hut was with Müntzer on that fateful day in Frankenhausen when both Müntzer and Hut were captured. Müntzer, the fiery chiliastic leader, was executed shortly after; Hut escaped to become the baptizer of several thousand communal, pacifist-oriented Anabaptists. For the rest of Hut's short life—he died, either by execution or through suffocation, in December 1528—he had several significant "mop-up" experiences. Among the most significant were Hut's experiences in the city of Nikolsburg, where, as a fleeing Anabaptist, he was befriended by communally oriented, pacifist refugees from

Switzerland; in Schleitheim in February 1527, where the question of violence was central to the debate; and in the Augsburg Synod of August 1528, as the Anabaptists continued to struggle with the issues of violence.[82]

We should not underestimate the significance that individuals, not merely the masses, play in the birthing of paradigm shifts in which the Powers are transformed and in the long mop-up work that needs to follow. It was in the wake of Hut's baptisms among precisely those same people who had shared the defeat of economics and war that we have the strongest nonviolent communities of goods emerging.[83] They were seeing "new and different things when looking with familiar instruments in places they [had] . . . looked before."[84]

*An invasion of the theological paradigm.* My goals in this chapter have been both methodological and constructive. The two go hand in hand. Methodologically I have worked on two fronts: First, I have worked to establish a more cultural and institutional understanding (à la Geertz) of the Powers than Wink's analysis suggests—one that is deeply woven into the fabric of our own national ethos and shapes our *being* as a people. Second, I offer a cultural/anthropological framework or worldview (à la Kuhn's "paradigm shift") in which to understand the *dynamics* of how the Powers may be transformed—a framework that, without minimizing the role of the charismatic prophet or seer, emphasizes the unmasking of corporate and societal structures as paramount to sustained transformation of the Powers.

From a constructive perspective, by analyzing the economically driven Peasants' War and the emergence of nonviolent communities, I provide a historical case study for a communal ethic of corporate culture. The gist of my second objective is to respond to the question, how is the transformation of the Power of economic greed to come about? This query reaches its most acute point when focused on the Powers that embody violence, whether the covert violence of capitalism or the overt violence of war. As recapitulation, I will list a few constructive components that have emerged:

1. The Powers are more deceptively controlling and determinative than we have been led to believe. Their invisibility is as much one of exteriority as of one interiority. Their deception is as much one of outer structure as one of inner spirit. The astonishing thing is not that Luther was taken captive by them. A man of his day, he was never freed from the Powers gone amok—violence and economic oppression. In the crucial time of testing, he responded as the Powers of the day dictated.[85] The truly astonishing aspect is the "conversion," the paradigm shift—among some called Anabaptists—from violence to nonviolence, implemented and sustained not by individual competition but through community commitment in sufficient numbers so as to create a "sustainable new ethos"—that is, Powers that were redeemed.

2. Dramatic economic episodes of humanly inflicted violence and cataclysmic political horrors can become the occasion for epiphanies of justice, grace,

life, and hope. This chapter is in the style of a trajectory and is in itself not a definitive argument, but nevertheless it is hoped that the tools (social and intellectual) for the *transformation of the Powers through a "paradigm shift" that unmasks an entire ethos* will be further developed. Although questions about the adequacies of the paradigm shift remain, such queries are peripheral to a far greater danger today, namely, that we remain bound by the Powers gone amok—the Powers of violence and deceit (war and economic greed) in the garb of democracy and freedom, which function as two strains of an invisible death trap—culture-religion.[86]

3. The birthing of paradigm shifts (and the transformation of the Powers) calls for *communal models* that embody life-giving relationships. Cataclysmic events alone are not sufficient. And individual models—noble, heroic, and prophetic as these may be—seldom present us with a reality that is sufficiently robust to birth a communal and cultural paradigm shift.[87] Where such models exist, they have not been an end but in fact another beginning. They have consistently, and without exception, brought about a paradigm shift only after building a countervailing "unmasking community" that itself is but the *harbinger* of the Powers redeemed—the new society Jesus envisioned and for which he gave his life in the hope of creating it. We cannot presume to do better than did the Master. Ours is the task of participating in that community that is now, while engaging in the transformation of the Powers. Ours is also the ongoing challenge of envisioning what lies ahead—creating a community and a culture that are not yet.

# Part Three

# Engaging the Powers

# Chapter 9

# JESUS' WAY OF TRANSFORMING INITIATIVES AND JUST PEACEMAKING THEORY

## GLEN STASSEN

Walter Wink is well known for his exegesis of Matt 5:38-48 as "Jesus' third way"—a strategy of nonviolent initiatives in response to domination and violence. I intend here to specify the nature of the third way—transforming initiatives that change our way of relating to the enemy and that hope to change the enemy's way of relating to us.

## JESUS' "THIRD WAY" IN MATTHEW 5

Wink argues that the Greek word we usually translate "do not resist" (Matt 5:39) means "do not resist violently and revengefully."[1] N. T. Wright and Donald Hagner—outstanding New Testament scholars—agree.[2] Furthermore, as Clarence Jordan points out, Greek grammar says that the Greek word translated "evil" in Matthew 5:39 (*ponēros*) can equally as well be translated instrumentally "by evil means."[3] The decision according to Greek grammar between translating it as an object, "evil," or instrumentally as "by evil means," must come from the context.

*Nonviolence as resistance.* Jesus did not practice evil means—of hate, violence, revenge, domination, or self-righteous exclusion. He rejected a violent self-defense near the end of his life. But Jesus did repeatedly confront and resist evil by nonviolent means—it got him crucified. Therefore, the context clearly favors "do not resist revengefully or violently, by evil means." Hagner supports this also, and Willard Swartley has told me he finds it persuasive.[4] This translation is confirmed by Rom 12:14-21, where Paul gives us Jesus' teaching as "Never avenge yourselves. . . . Do not be overcome by evil, but overcome evil by good."

Willard Swartley's chapter in this volume argues that the word means "do not retaliate," and his argument is confirmed by the fact that this understanding echoes throughout the New Testament—in Luke 6:27-36; 1 Thess 5:15; and Didache 1:4-5; a somewhat similar teaching occurs in 1 Pet 2:21-23. Not one of these refers to an evil person. Not one of these speaks of not resisting evil. Not one of these speaks of renouncing rights in a law court. All teach not retaliating by evil means but instead taking transforming initiatives of returning good and not evil, using good means and not evil means.

Luke and the Didache give almost the same four transforming initiatives (cheek, coat, mile, begging). In 1 Thess 5:15, Paul writes, "See that none of you repays evil for evil, but always seek to do good to one another and to all." The emphasis in interpretation should not be on renouncing rights in a law court but on not retaliating by evil or violent means, and on understanding the meaning of the transforming initiatives—in that social context and in ours—and practicing them.

**Transforming initiatives.** Wink has rightly emphasized the four transforming initiatives in Matt 5:38-48: turning the other cheek, giving the coat, going the second mile, and giving to the one who begs. The teaching is not only about what not to do but about what positive initiatives you *do* do while you are *not* doing what you don't do. I call these "transforming initiatives." Wink has written of his search for a descriptive label and indicates that he did think of the word "transforming." He certainly describes them as "initiatives," but it did not occur to him to call them "transforming initiatives," so he settled on "Jesus' third way."

We may specify the nature of the third way as *transforming initiatives that change our own way of relating to the enemy and that hope to change the enemy's way of relating to us*. These transforming initiatives are nonviolent confrontations of hostile or oppressive ways of relating that recognize the dignity of the other and assert our own dignity and that offer the chance to transform the relationship into peacemaking and justice.

I want to add my bit of independent confirmation of Wink's interpretation of Matt 5:38-48 and then extend beyond it to a transforming-initiative interpretation of the whole central section of the Sermon on the Mount and to just peacemaking theory. We both developed the "transforming initiative" or "Jesus' third way" interpretation of Matt 5:38-48 independently of each other.[5] The interpretive clue that I am especially eager to bring to light is that not only Matt 5:38-48 but the whole central section of the Sermon on the Mount, Matt 5:21–7:12, has a transforming-initiative structure. This gives a structural and systematic confirmation of what we are both saying about 5:38-48. The biggest emphasis is not on what we do not do but on the transforming initiatives that we take in regard to an enemy. It also gives a major clue for interpreting the other teachings of the Sermon on the Mount.

I have shown elsewhere that the structure of Matt 5:21–7:12 is fourteen triads or threefold teachings. Throughout these teachings, the first member of each teaching is a traditional piety; the second member is the diagnosis of a vicious cycle; and the third member, where the emphasis falls, is a transforming initiative. This is well illustrated by Matt 5:38-48.

The structure of Matt 5:38-48 begins with a *traditional piety*, "an eye for an eye." Second comes the diagnosis of a *vicious cycle*, "to retaliate by violent or evil means." Third come the *transforming initiatives*, turn the cheek, give the cloak, go the second mile, give to the beggar. That threefold structure, with its climax in the third member—the transforming initiative—characterizes each of the teachings from 5:21–7:12.[6] The third member in a biblical triad is the climax. Each third member is a transforming initiative, not a negative prohibition. In each of the teachings, the imperatives (in the Greek) come in the third member, thus confirming that the emphasis should be on the transforming initiatives. It means that Jesus' emphasis is not only what we are not to do (retaliate) but on the transforming initiatives of peacemaking that he teaches. The pattern is so consistent in Matt 5:21–7:12 that it strongly confirms this emphasis throughout the teachings, including in 5:38.

***Jesus' third way of peacemaking.*** Thus, the emphasis in 5:38 is Jesus' third way of peacemaking, taking transforming initiatives of peacemaking, as Wink has helped us all see. The consistent pattern throughout the fourteen teachings gives strong support to active initiatives of peacemaking. This supports the trend toward emphasizing the creative, surprising, transforming initiatives of peacemaking in this teaching, as in Betz, Garland, Grundmann, Hagner, Jordan, Lapide, Luz, Wink, and myself, among others, rather than interpretations that key primarily on what is renounced.

I want to be clear: I do believe that Matt 5:38-48 teaches renunciation of violence or retaliation; but I believe the main emphasis is on the imperatives in the third part, on taking transforming initiatives of peacemaking.

For example, Jesus' teaching on the second mile has its meaning in the context of being compelled by a Roman soldier to carry his pack one mile. Jesus does not emphasize what we are not to do, such as pull out a knife and kill him or comply sullenly, breathing resentment all the way, although renouncing those courses of action is implied. Nor does he say we should give in and carry the pack one mile without complaining. Rather, he emphasizes the transforming initiative of carrying it a second mile, and, if it is combined with Matt 5:23ff., making peace while going on the way. Similarly, Jesus' teaching on the left cheek has its meaning in the context of being a person in that shame-and-honor culture is slapped with a demeaning, backhanded slap on the *right* cheek. Turning the *left* cheek is a nonviolent confrontation of the wrong; this action says, "No more," and asserts dignity, while raising the possibility of peacemaking. Jesus' implicit emphasis is on a nonviolent direct action of confrontation and peacemaking. The same is true of the teaching on the shirt and on giving to the one who begs: each is an initiative that moves the relationship toward dignity and peacemaking.[7]

In *The Politics of Jesus*, John Howard Yoder reports two cases of collective nonviolent direct action that were successful in changing Roman policy toward Israel. These events happened shortly before and after Jesus' ministry, all within the same ten-year span.[8] John Dominic Crossan reports seven nonviolent demonstrations by Jews against Roman policies.[9] "All those demonstrations were nonviolent, all had very specific objectives, and four out of the seven achieved those objectives without loss of life." The practice of transforming initiatives is not an invention in our time; it was practiced in Jesus' time.

Two practices of peacemaking have emerged in our time that implement this practice of taking transforming initiatives toward an enemy, one well known and the other not so well known: *nonviolent direct action* and the strategy of *independent initiatives*. Both deserve to be widely known, widely supported, and widely practiced.

## NONVIOLENT DIRECT ACTION AND INDEPENDENT INITIATIVES

*Nonviolent direct action* is spreading around the world—practiced in India by Gandhi and in the United States by Martin Luther King Jr. and Cesar Chavez; in Poland, East Germany, and Czechoslovakia; in the Philippines and even in Iran; throughout Latin America and in Kosovo until the forces of violence thought they had a better strategy.[10] It is achieving change for justice and avoiding the violence and war that would otherwise boil up from the conditions of injustice and oppression.

The strategy of *independent initiatives* is less well known. But it has been the key to getting rid of the most destabilizing nuclear weapons of all, the weapons most likely to start a nuclear war, the medium-range and shorter-range nuclear weapons—and to getting rapid actions and agreements from the United States and Russia to remove nuclear weapons from surface ships and to reduce the number of long-range nuclear weapons from 17,000 on each side to 3,500. We must take the next step, reducing to 1,000 each and heading toward zero. The strategy works like this:

1. Take an initiative that decreases distrust and threat perception by the other side, by decreasing some offensive threat, but not significantly reducing defensive capability. Examples are a halt to testing of nuclear weapons, or Gorbachev's removing half the Soviet tanks from west of the Ural Mountains, or Ehud Barak's finally handing over the Palestinian and Lebanese territory that had been promised and was long overdue.
2. Announce the initiative in advance, clearly explaining that you are hoping for some reciprocal initiative, and that if it works, you will take more initiatives, because you want to shift the context from escalation toward de-escalation.
3. Be sure to take the initiative on schedule, even if some hostile words or events occur; the aim is to decrease distrust so that the other side can take some initiatives.

4. Make the initiative clearly visible and verifiable by the other side.
5. Take the initiative independent of waiting for the slow process of negotiations; afterward it can be worked into a treaty.
6. Take initiatives in a series; it will take more than one to overcome deep distrust.
7. If the other side reciprocates, reward them with additional significant initiatives; if they do not, keep the door open by continuing with a series of small initiatives.

This is a good expression of what Jesus meant by turning the other cheek, going the second mile, giving the cloak. Both nonviolent direct action and independent initiatives implement Jesus' practice of transforming initiatives:

1. They affirm that the enemy is a member of God's community, loved by God, with some valid interests, even while confronting unjust actions of the enemy.
2. They are proactive initiatives of grace and peacemaking, not simply passive resignation.
3. They confront the other nonviolently, with an invitation to make peace that includes justice.
4. They are historically embodied practices, not merely ideals.
5. They acknowledge the log in our own eyes and take responsibility for peacemaking rather than simply judging the other.

## TEN PRACTICES OF PEACEMAKING

Recently, twenty-three interdisciplinary scholars, including both just-war theorists and pacifists, noted that these practices of peacemaking—and several others—have developed within current practice since World War II and that they are spreading, making peace, and preventing war in many places around the world. This group believes that the whole world needs to know about these practices, and it wants to add its support to them. So these scholars joined together to develop a just peacemaking theory. It took five years, but the group, of which I was a part, reached unanimous consensus in *Just Peacemaking: Ten Practices to Abolish War*.[11]

We named and described ten practices (see figure 9.1) that have developed since the world realized we must not have another world war like World War II and we must not have a nuclear war. My purpose in what follows is to name these ten practices of peacemaking and to show how they are expressions of the transforming initiatives, the practices of peacemaking, that Jesus teaches in the Sermon on the Mount. *Nonviolent direct action* and *independent initiatives* are the first two practices. The third practice is *conflict resolution*.

---

### FIGURE 9.1. THE TEN PRACTICES OF JUST PEACEMAKING

#### PEACEMAKING INITIATIVES

1. Support nonviolent direct action.
2. Take independent initiatives to reduce hostility and threat.
3. Use cooperative conflict resolution.
4. Acknowledge responsibility for conflict and injustice; seek repentance and forgiveness.

#### JUSTICE

5. Advance democracy, human rights, and religious liberty.
6. Foster just and sustainable economic development.

#### COMMUNITY

7. Recognize emerging cooperative forces in the international system and work with them.
8. Strengthen the United Nations and international efforts for cooperation and human rights.
9. Reduce offensive weapons and weapons trade.
10. Encourage grassroots peacemaking groups and voluntary associations.

From Glen Stassen, ed., *Just Peacemaking: Ten Practices for Abolishing War* (Cleveland: Pilgrim Press, 1998).

---

***Practice conflict resolution.*** This well-known peacemaking practice is the command of Jesus in Matthew 18, as John Howard Yoder shows.[12] It is also commanded by Jesus in Matthew 5:21ff., in the Sermon on the Mount. First comes the traditional teaching, "You shall not murder." Second comes the vicious cycle: continuing in anger or calling your brother a fool. This is not a command in the Greek, but rather it is a participle: it is a diagnosis of a vicious cycle that leads to judgment and destruction.

Third, we encounter five commands, and this is where the emphasis lies: on reconciliation (Matt. 5:23-26); self denial (29-30); the prohibition of divorce (32) and of oaths (34-37); non-retaliation and the love of enemies (38-42, 44-48). It is the grace-based way of deliverance, the transforming initiative: Go, make peace with your brother and with your accuser. This is the way of grace that God has taken toward us in Christ. God had something against us for our disobedience and enmity, so God took a grace-based transforming initiative and came to us in Christ and made peace. When we go to our brother or our enemy and talk things through and make peace, we are participating in the way of grace that God shows us in Christ. And this is not optional. It is an imperative, a command. It is not, "If you think the one you are angry at, or who is angry at you, is good enough, deserving enough, open-minded enough." It is a command from Jesus: "Go, make peace." There is no guarantee of success, but there is the clear direction in which we are to go.

Skills for how to talk with someone when there is enmity are developed in the practice of conflict resolution, taught by John Paul Lederach and others at Eastern Mennonite University.[13] This practice of just peacemaking is making a difference. Former president Jimmy Carter saw that UN forces were about to make a violent invasion of Haiti, so he rushed to Haiti and practiced conflict resolution as he had done at Camp David, talking with the despots ruling Haiti and persuading them to leave nonviolently. The result: the invasion took place without a shot being fired.

Similarly, President Clinton sent former senator George Mitchell to Ireland to practice conflict resolution in that age-old, historically intransigent, hate-filled conflict, and we may yet have peace in Northern Ireland. President Carter had brought Anwar Sadat of Egypt and Menachem Begin of Israel to Camp David for conflict resolution, and now Israel has peace with Egypt, peace with Jordan, and one agreement with the Palestinians—and may or may not find the way to peace with Palestine and Syria. We all need to pray. And we need to applaud those who help such conflict resolution to happen. It was not tried before the Gulf War and before the bombing of Kosovo, and the results have been tragic for millions of people.[14]

*Acknowledge responsibility for conflict and injustice and seek repentance and forgiveness.* The next practice hardly needs justification as a key part of the way of Jesus Christ. Jesus clearly taught forgiveness in the Lord's Prayer. He also taught acknowledging our own responsibility when he named the log in our own eyes, as well as in all the vicious cycles that he named, from anger through divorce, hating enemies, practicing righteousness to be seen by others, hoarding money, and judging others.

Donald Shriver points to five regular practices that Jesus taught and modeled. Each built forgiveness into the practice of the community. These are (1) healings that brought outcasts into community membership; (2) the practice of eating with outcasts, which similarly brought outcasts into community; (3) the practice of restorative justice that he taught the community; (4) prayer that not only emphasized forgiveness but that he taught would not be effective if those praying did not forgive those who offended them; and (5) the community practice of forgiving enemies like Zacchaeus and other tax collectors, Roman soldiers, and those who executed him, and, later, those who executed Stephen.[15]

It has been understood by realists for centuries that rulers of nations do not repent or give forgiveness because they would lose face and it would weaken them in their competition for power. So wars are fought over unconfessed injustices that still fester from as long ago as the Serbs' struggle with the Ottoman Empire and the Battle of Kosovo in 1389.

However, a new practice has arisen out of Dietrich Bonhoeffer's writing of a confession of his and Germany's guilt during the Nazi period. Churches in Germany started making confession on Germany's behalf, not without criticism, chagrin, and offense. Christian conscientious objectors to war volunteered to do their alternative service in other nations that Germany had injured; three Action-Reconciliation volunteers have lived in our home during their times of service. The churches plowed the ground and planted the seeds, and then political leaders who were committed to peacemaking got to work.

Willy Brandt, Germany's chancellor, went to the Warsaw Ghetto in Poland and presented a wreath in memory of Jews and Poles slaughtered by Germans there. Deeply moved, he sank to his knees in tearful prayer. Poland was moved; the world was moved. Brandt announced that Germany would accept the diminished border of Germany at the Oder Neisse River and would never try to get formerly German territory back from Poland. Then German president Richard von Weizsäcker delivered an eloquent address in the German parliament specifically naming German sins during the Nazi period and expressing German repentance for its sin. The words are powerful; Shriver quotes them at length. The outcome has been repentance and forgiveness between Germany and many of its former enemies and a present-day Germany that has been transformed into a force for peacemaking.

The prime minister of Japan has finally apologized concretely and in writing to Korea for Japan's atrocities against Koreans, and Korean president Kim Dae Jung responded that an apology is what Korea had been waiting for and that now cultural and social exchanges may finally take place. President George H. W. Bush finally led Congress to pay reparations to American citizens of Japanese descent unjustly imprisoned and deprived of their property and homes during World War II. President Clinton traveled to Guatemala and to Africa to declare repentance on behalf of the United States and worked to express repentance toward African Americans.

Acknowledging complicity and seeking or giving forgiveness is a remarkable new practice of peacemaking that can lance festering boils that threaten to erupt into violence and war. Croatian-American theologian Miroslav Volf describes it brilliantly in his *Exclusion and Embrace*.[16] The practice of repentance and forgiveness, so clearly taught and practiced by Jesus, is now spreading among nations and is healing resentments that cause wars.

The next two practices are practices of justice. My other chapter in this volume is titled "The Kind of Justice Jesus Cares About," and I point to the expression of this in the next two practices of peacemaking.

***Promote democracy, human rights, and religious liberty.*** Jimmy Carter, a faithful Baptist, was determined to express his faith in his presidency in a way that could also be translated into public language shared by others, and he initiated a strong and consistent emphasis on human rights. He had already stood courageously for human rights in Georgia's struggle to overcome racial discrimination and segregation. He announced that U.S. foreign policy would examine the human rights records of other countries and that our foreign aid would be contingent on these records. This policy has continued ever since. Of course it was mixed in with considerations of power and interest, but it has had a significant influence for justice.

Furthermore, the Roman Catholic Church committed itself to work for human rights, especially during the time of Pope John XXIII and when the Second Vatican Council did its work in 1963, and it has continued, though again in the mixed forms that any church or government policy assumes in the struggle between the old and the new. Other denominations also pushed for human rights around the world, including American and Southern Baptists.

Partly as a result of these forces, and because of other indigenous forces pushing for justice, Latin America, which used to be mostly military dictatorships, is now made up of all democracies with human rights—or at least is officially moving in that direction, in spite of the power of elites and militaries. And democracy is spreading in many former dictatorships behind the former Iron Curtain, and in South Korea, Taiwan, and Indonesia, as has long been true of India. Many African countries are struggling in that direction.

When we participate in churches that encourage this spread and join human rights groups such as Amnesty International or Witness for Peace, we undergird this trend. And here is the zinger: not one democracy with human rights fought a shooting war against another democracy with human rights in the whole twentieth century. When we push for human rights, we strengthen the force that is creating zones of peace. Some question this sweeping claim, but the data from the study of international relations are laid out in *Just Peacemaking*. But this is not a reason for self-congratulation on the part of the United States. The power of money is so corrupting in the election process in the United States that we are close to becoming a plutocracy rather than a democracy. This corruption shows in the influence of the military-industrial complex over the budget and policy and in the funding of the Contras against a properly elected democracy in Nicaragua.[17]

***Pursue just and sustainable economic development.*** The data also tell us that just and sustainable economic development that focuses on building communities is crucial for peacemaking. I think of Carl Ryther, a Baptist agricultural missionary, whose methods were crucial in transforming Bangladesh, one of the poorest nations in the world, into becoming self-sufficient in food production. I think of Musheshe and the Uganda Rural Development Project, which he leads and which I have visited, transforming the lives of rural Ugandans in the western part of the country, and I pray that the war in the Congo is not destroying it. I think of Bread for the World and of Ron Sider's book *Rich Christians in an Age of Hunger.*

The final four practices foster community. Jesus' understanding of justice recognized the crucial importance of being included in community and of not being cast out. We think of the poignant story of the cripple at the Pool of Bethsaida, who had no one to move him into the water when it was stirred up. Lacking community, he was powerless. Jesus healed him and restored him to community.

In the Sermon on the Mount, the climax of the first six teachings is Jesus' teaching that we are to love our enemies. Here Jesus is expanding the community to include not only friends, as in Leviticus, but also enemies. Love in the New Testament is not only an attitude—it is actions, and it concerns the question, who belongs to the community? As God gives rain and sunshine to the unjust as well as the just, so we participate in God's gracious love and are God's children when we include enemies in community. This means peacemaking must organize networks in which enemy nations come into regular relationship so that they will develop ways for taking cooperative actions with one another. An expression of this central theme of Jesus' teachings is the growing international networks of cooperative action.

**Recognize emerging cooperative forces in the international system and work with them.** Paul Schroeder is a leading historian of international relations. In the *Just Peacemaking* book, Schroeder applies the wisdom that comes from the breadth of his historical knowledge. He argues that four kinds of emerging cooperative forces in the international system are steadily bringing enemies into community in a way that is historically new, and that we are called to work with these cooperative forces in order to prevent wars. Schroeder observes the following cooperative forces:

1. All of us can see the dramatic increase in the volume, density, and spread of international travel, communication, exchange, and transactions of all kinds and the organization of these into international networks. All of this international exchange is binding us together into an international society. The empirical evidence is clear: nations that participate extensively in this international exchange are less likely to engage in war.

2. All of us can see the rise of the trading state. No longer is it profitable to try to extend national power and interest by making war; the way to fame and fortune is through international trade. Surely much is unjust in the way international trade and finance are organized by wealthy interests. Our book says, "The question of how we can make global corporations ethically and legally responsible in each country where they operate, despite their enormous power and their ability to leave any country, is one of the most crucial ethical questions for the next decades" (27). Nevertheless, we all recognize the reality of this enormous force, and it does tend to shift momentum from war to trade competition.

3. The spread of democracy, described above, creates zones of peace.
4. The decline in the utility of war makes war less likely. The power of other nations to retaliate with devastating force is so great that war does not pay. The cost of investing in the technology of war making is great, and nations that avoid such heavy investment do better economically.

These four cooperative forces in the international system tend to bind nations together into an international society that includes enemies as well as friends. These forces mean that the international system is no longer an anarchy but an anarchic society, with complex interdependence. It is becoming a society, with growing ties among nations and among the people and organizations that have power in those nations.[18] These forces increase the ability of the next practice of just peacemaking to thrive.

**Strengthen the United Nations and other international efforts for cooperation and human rights.** Political science data show that the higher the involvement of a country in international government organizations, the less likely it is to engage in military disputes.[19] The United Nations is engaged in meeting the health needs of children and the less wealthy throughout the world in ways that rarely make the news but that are critical for millions of people. The United Nations is engaged in supporting and helping enforce peace agreements and truces in many areas of tension throughout the world. The United Nations connects representatives from the many nations in mutual learning, mutual restraint, and mutual peacemaking in ways that would otherwise be unlikely to take place.

Yet nationalistic political forces in the U.S. Congress have been working to deny the United Nations the money that the United States owes and that is crucial for its peacemaking work. These forces have been pressing for unilateral action by the U.S. military and for the bypassing of the United Nations. We are truly in a battle with the powers and authorities of nationalistic, unilateral, redemptive violence over the ability of the United Nations to do its peacemaking work. The seriousness of the struggle, and the degree of the danger, is not common enough knowledge. "Confronting the Powers," in Walter Wink's sense, means we are called to confront these Powers with a clear commitment to peacemaking, a clear vision of the fallenness of the Powers, and an accurate awareness of what is happening. Only by joining in the work of church peacemaking groups and the work of networks like UN-USA can we be well informed and effective in our witness to the body politic and to one another.

**Reduce offensive weapons and weapons trade.** The peacemaking practice of pushing governments to reduce offensive weapons and the weapons trade works in sync with what international relations scholars call the empirical reality that war is so destructive that it does not pay.

It also fits Jesus' command in the Garden of Gethsemane: "Put up your sword." It fits his prophetically symbolic act of entering Jerusalem on a colt, the foal of a donkey, in fulfillment of the prophecy of Zech 9:9ff. that the Messiah would come as a prince of peace and would abolish war. It fits his central call to love our enemies. It fits his consistent opposition to the strategy of the insurrectionists, who wanted to make war against the Roman soldiers, as John Yoder makes clear in *The Politics of Jesus.* N. T. Wright concludes:

> Jesus consistently and continuously warned his contemporaries that unless Israel repented— . . . i.e., gave up her military confrontation with Rome and followed his radical alternative vision of the kingdom—then her time was up. Wrath would come upon her, in the form not so much of fire and brimstone from heaven, as of Roman swords and falling stonework. In particular, Jerusalem herself, and especially the Temple and its hierarchy, had become hopelessly corrupt, and was as ripe for judgment as it had been in the days of Jeremiah. In this coming judgment, the true people of YHWH—Jesus' followers—would be vindicated.[20]

In the *Just Peacemaking* book, we point out that because of the cooperative forces we have identified, the developing world's imports of military weapons dropped from $60 billion in 1988 down to $15 billion in 1996—just one-fourth what it had been seven years previously. We tell of steps that have been taken to reduce nuclear weapons and of the next steps that can be taken and need to be taken. We tell of groups like Peace Action, Union of Concerned Scientists, and the Campaign to Abolish Nuclear Weapons, as well as denominational peace fellowships, that invite us to participate in pushing for these reductions. This brings us to the tenth practice of just peacemaking.

**Join grassroots peacemaking groups and voluntary associations.** These are the groups that prod the governments to engage in the practices of just peacemaking. N. T. Wright tells of Jesus' strategy of establishing groups of followers in the different villages, and Paul continued that strategy. By their adoption of Jesus' praxis, these groups were distinctive in their local communities. Like followers of John the Baptist, or of the Pharisees or the Essenes, Jesus' followers joined together in a distinctive praxis that he gave them in the Sermon on the Mount.

John Howard Yoder called the attention of individualistic Protestants to the church as alternative community, to the biblical emphasis on visible community sharing practices commanded by Jesus. Yoder's influence is spreading among New Testament scholars, theologians, and ethicists. Yoder writes of the praxis of servanthood authority, forgiving debts, sharing meals, welcoming outcasts, granting forgiveness, practicing nonviolence, and showing love. Like the Essenes, the disciples believed themselves in some sense to be the true Israel. They sharply criticized the temple and its cover-up of injustice and exclusion of foreigners. They found their primary community in the fellowship of Jesus' followers instead of in the temple. This fellowship was a surrogate family—see Mark 3:31-35, which has five parallels in the Gospels. "Whoever does the will of God is my brother and sister and mother."

So we are to join in groups in churches that do the will of God as revealed by Jesus. Churches are to follow Jesus, and small groups in those churches are to lead them in following Jesus. Some will join in peacemaking groups outside churches where we can witness by our distinctive praxis of Jesus' way. We are called to follow Jesus not as loners but as parts of groups that carry out his way.

## THE WITNESS OF NONVIOLENCE TO THE STATE

We have arrived at an important conclusion. Jesus' way, the way of the Sermon on the Mount, is not only about what we are to avoid doing but also about the transforming initiatives of positive peacemaking. This means that the shape of the life of faithful discipleship is marked not only by refusing to do violence but also by engaging in the practices that make peace.

Furthermore, we have begun to see that Jesus' practices of peacemaking have analogous expressions in practices of peacemaking groups and governments that are effectively preventing many wars. The ten practices of just peacemaking have all emerged in practice in the period following World War II. During that time, church leaders, political leaders, business leaders, military leaders, and many people throughout the world have come to see that war is too destructive and that we must together search for practices that are effective in preventing war.

These ten practices are not mere ideals; they are all being practiced in many places throughout the world. As John Howard Yoder observed, the normative Christian practices that Jesus taught are not mysterious and invisible but could be observed by a sociologist and have their expression in the world,[21] so these ten practices are being practiced effectively in the world and are being observed by political scientists. They are in fact preventing the misery and sin of violence and war in many places. And they can spread. We can help that spread as we make our witness.

Sometimes people who are committed to nonviolence, and to following Jesus, have not seen how they could make their witness to the state that seems committed to do violence. Sometimes they have not seen how the Sermon on the Mount and the other teachings of Jesus are God's will for all humankind. Sometimes they have been shy about proclaiming their witness so all can hear. They have thought that they were committed to nonviolence but that the government was not, so they have succumbed to a dualism in which Jesus' teachings were for the church but were not God's will for the government.

Here, in an understanding of Jesus' third way as transforming initiatives of peacemaking and in the ten practices of just peacemaking theory, we have a way to overcome that dualism. Surely we cannot assume that governments are based on Christian faith. Surely they are not—even though some leaders may be persons of faith. But in a time of nuclear, chemical, and biological weapons, a time of the enormous costliness of war, a time when avenues other than war are far more promising, the witness to the way of nonviolence is increasingly appealing to people of other faiths and no stated faith.

Our witness makes increasing sense in surprising places. And in a time when we are learning practices of peacemaking that express Jesus' teaching and seeing those practices being effective in preventing many wars, our witness makes sense even to people who do not share our faith. Seeing the Sermon on the Mount as transforming initiatives and seeing its expression in just peacemaking theory enables us to see how we can make our witness to the state and to our neighbors who do not share our faith—yet.

# Chapter 10

# RESISTANCE AND NONRESISTANCE
## WHEN AND HOW?

## WILLARD M. SWARTLEY

Over the years I have pondered just what the Christian response is to evil. The traditional Mennonite view emphasized nonresistance and also a dual view of government. I remember hearing a sermon at my home church in Doylestown, Pennsylvania, one Sunday that emphasized our need to be submissive or obedient to government because it is ordained of God and therefore good. On another Sunday, we were encouraged not to comply with certain government policies, especially military conscription, because government is under the power of the evil one. Both emphases, in fact, stressed New Testament truths. I note at least three views in the New Testament of the nature or status of government powers (see figure 10.1).

What I *did not* hear in those days was an emphasis on Jesus' having vanquished the Principalities and Powers and on the fact that we believers are freed therefore from the power of the Powers. The term "nonviolent resistance" was

---

FIGURE 10.1. NEW TESTAMENT VIEWS OF GOVERNMENT

NEGATIVE

Matt 4:8-10 (Luke 4:6-8): Satan over kingdoms
Eph 6:11-12: world rulers of present darkness
Revelation 13: "beast," servant of the dragon (12:9)
1 Cor 2:6-8: rulers ignorant of Jesus
1 Cor 6:4: least esteemed by the church
Mark 10:42: rulers of this world "lord it over"
Luke 13:1-3: Pilate's massacre
Luke 13:31-33: Herod the fox
Mark 13:9-13: persecution of Christians, martyrdom of apostles

---

---

### POSITIVE

Rom 13:1-7: ordained/ordered by God; servant of God's wrath; rewards
    good, punishes evil
1 Tim 2:1-4: prayers for kings and for peace abound; enables gospel to
    spread
Titus 3:1: be submissive and obedient, ready for every good work
1 Pet 2:13-17: be subject to and honor the emperor
In all of the above, Christians are to be subject to the authorities. Further,
    Roman law is congenial to Paul (Acts 18:12-17, 22:22-29, 25:23-27,
    26:32).

### NORMATIVE

Col 2:15: God in Jesus disarmed, made public display of, and triumphed
    over the Powers
Eph 1:19-23: by resurrection power, Jesus reigns over every rule,
    authority, power, and dominion
Eph 3:10: the church witnesses to the Powers
1 Pet 3:22: Powers under the feet of the exalted Jesus
1 Cor 15:24-26: Powers disempowered and destroyed
Rom 8:35-39: no power can separate us from the love of God in Jesus
    Christ
Eph 6:12-20: resist the Powers
Col 2:10: Christ is head over all rule and authority

---

not in our vocabulary. There was also suspicion of the word "pacifism," because liberal Christians were pacifists and they based their arguments more on pragmatic factors than on simple obedience to Scripture.

Times have changed drastically in Mennonite communities. I expect many of us could count on one hand the number of sermons we have heard on nonresistance since 1970. What has happened in this period of transition?

## TRENDS IN MENNONITE PEACEMAKING

Leo Driedger and Donald Kraybill refer to this change as moving "from quietism to activism" in the subtitle of their book, *Mennonite Peacemaking*. And they helpfully describe the shifts in emphasis in Mennonite peacemaking over the last century (see figure 10.2). To this list we may add "Peacemaking, Mediation, Conflict Transformation, 1990–2000."[1]

But is the subtitle of Driedger and Kraybill's book—"From Quietism to Activism"—really an accurate description? Were Mennonites simply quietistic

FIGURE 10.2.                                    MENNONITE
PEACEMAKING, 1890–1990

| DOMINANT THEMES | TIME PERIOD |
| --- | --- |
| The Doctrine of Nonresistance | 1890–1920 |
| The Principles of Peace | 1920–1940 |
| Biblical Nonresistance | 1940–1950 |
| The Way of Love | 1950–1960 |
| Witness to the State | 1960–1968 |
| Nonviolent Resistance | 1968–1976 |
| Peace and Justice | 1976–1983 |
| Peacemaking | 1983–1990 |

in the earlier era? And are they really now activists? Or is the situation more complex? Figure 10.3, adapted from their book, correlates degrees of modernization among Mennonites with degrees of three different dimensions of peacemaking.

From Driedger and Kraybill's data, we discover that support for peacemaking (the composite score) actually rises, from 27 to 34 percent, as Mennonites move from farms to large cities. This contradicts the notion that urbanization weakens peacemaking convictions. Support for nonresistance, however, declines 10 percent for urban Mennonites. The data show that urbanization, high socioeconomic status, high individualism, and high materialism correlate with significantly lower scores in nonresistance, but only urbanization and socioeconomic status correlate with a significantly higher score in activism. High individualism and high materialism scores show significantly lower scores in activism as well. In the education factor, graduate school correlates with decreases in nonresistance, but there are not significant increases in activism. This analysis indicates that, in the Mennonite grassroots, nonresistance is certainly alive. Quite significantly, the modernization factor of education shows a markedly higher score in witness to government: from 6 percent for those with only elementary school education to 38 percent for those with graduate education.[2]

Over the past several years, Walter Wink has asked me whether the Mennonite position is that of nonresistance or of a more active nonviolent resistance. I have never clearly answered his question because no single position exists among Mennonites. Article 22 in *Confession of Faith in a Mennonite Perspective* (adopted 1995)[3] has a section titled "Peace, Justice, and Nonresistance," which, according to Driedger and Kraybill, "calls on believers to do justice and practice nonresistance and nonviolence in the face of violence and warfare." The commentary for this section, they say, notes that "nonresistance and nonviolence, rightly understood, contribute to justice." Moreover, nonresistance can mean a

Figure 10.3. Correlation of Modernization with Peacemaking Dimensions

| ASPECTS OF MODERNIZATION EXPERIENCED BY MENNONITES | ENDORSEMENT OF THREE DIMENSIONS OF PEACEMAKING | | | COMPOSITE "PEACEMAKING SCORE" |
|---|---|---|---|---|
| | Nonresistance | Witness | Activism | |
| Urbanization | | | | |
| Rural | 25* | 16 | 26 | 27 |
| Large City | 15 | 30 | 38 | 34 |
| | (r) (-.10) | (.16) | (.12) | (.04) |
| Socioeconomic Status (SES) | | | | |
| Lower | 23 | 14 | 24 | 24 |
| Upper | 21 | 39 | 38 | 40 |
| | (r) (-.04) | (.28) | (.06) | (.08) |
| Education | | | | |
| Elementary | 33 | 6 | 37 | 31 |
| Graduate school | 25 | 38 | 39 | 43 |
| | (r) (-.05) | (.36) | (.04) | (.09) |
| Individualism | | | | |
| Low | 37 | 35 | 35 | 44 |
| High | 11 | 14 | 32 | 23 |
| | (r) (-.25) | (-.18) | (.01) | (-.15) |
| Materialism | | | | |
| Low | 33 | 28 | 40 | 42 |
| High | 13 | 19 | 28 | 23 |
| | (r) (-.21) | (-.09) | (-.09) | (-.17) |

*25 percent of those living in rural areas scored high on the nonresistance scale.

r = Pearson correlation coefficient with a range of -1.0 to +1.0

Source: Leo Driedger and Donald B. Kraybill, *Mennonite Peacemaking: From Quietism to Activism* (Scottdale, Pa.: Herald Press, 1994).

"nonviolent confronting of offenders with the effects of their behavior." Although the term "nonresistance" is retained in the draft of the new confession, its meaning is interpreted in a more active sense.[4]

In the specific practices of nonresistance—refusing military service, refusing war-promoting activities, not suing in court, and not holding political office—a great variation exists among the five Mennonite groups included in the Mennonite profile survey conducted in 1989. Members of the Mennonite Conference scored a high of 80 percent on refusing military service; members of the Evangelical Mennonite Conference scored a low of 2 percent on not holding political office.[5]

Driedger and Kraybill's comments require analysis, however. The *Confession* as adopted in 1995 does not contain in the commentary or articles the sentence

"Nonresistance and nonviolence, rightly understood, contribute to justice." This line comes from the "First Draft of 1992," which Driedger and Kraybill consulted but which disappeared in the intervening revisions. The noun form "nonviolence" is not used in the final draft.[6] Rather, the complete statement speaks of nonresistance in three paragraphs but only once uses the term "a nonviolent way of confronting wrongdoers" and once "nonviolent resolution."[7]

The first use of "nonresistance" is in a sentence that speaks of "practicing nonresistance even in the face of violence and warfare."[8] The second and third uses occur in the *Commentary* where, in the first case, nonresistance is correlated with nonviolence: "Nonresistance means 'not resisting.' Our example is Jesus . . . who confronted in a nonviolent way that shows us how to overcome evil with good."[9] The third occurrence expands the traditional emphasis of refusal to participate in war: "We affirm that nonparticipation in warfare involves conscientious objection to military service and a nonresistant response to violence."[10]

Following from my own work on this topic, I note a major lacuna in the Mennonite emphases generally. Why hasn't the Mennonite Church used the word "nonretaliation"? The more pervasive New Testament emphasis falls on "do not return evil for evil." This command (oft repeated) is best expressed with the word "nonretaliation." But it occurs rarely in Mennonite literature or in Christian literature more generally.

The complement to "do not return evil for evil" is "overcome evil with good." I believe that this two-sided command should be what we emphasize, and then we should allow other terms—"nonresistance," "nonviolent resistance," or "pacifism"—to dangle. Each expresses one part of what nonretaliation and overcoming evil with good might mean in actual life situations. Thus, both nonresistance and resistance are essential to the Christian response to evil.

Scripture is clear that believers are to resist the devil (1 Pet 5:8-9, James 4:7). Moreover, Eph 6:11-12 uses the word "resist," calling believers to stand against the wiles or strategies of the devil, with the fight defined as against "the principalities and powers, the world rulers of this present darkness, the spiritual hosts of wickedness in the heavenly places." In verse 13, the term *anthistēnai* is used for *resisting* "in the evil day." As Wink points out, a similar Greek term is used in Matt 5:39 (*anthistēmi*). But Matthew says "do not" whereas Ephesians says "do."

Hence, I discuss, first, the rightful place of resistance to evil. The Christian term for this is "spiritual warfare," or "Christian warfare" (see below). Second, I more carefully consider nonresistance. Third, I reflect on the paradox of how resistance and nonresistance may function simultaneously to appropriate fully Jesus Christ's victory over the Powers.

## SPIRITUAL WARFARE: PAUL'S MARTIAL IMAGERY AND THE ETHIC OF NONRETALIATION

The martial imagery and conflict between good and evil in Pauline writings is the logical extension of Jesus' confrontation of the demonic power in the Gospels, portions that make up about one-third of the narrative text of Mark and Luke. Wink's study of "Power" language and reality in volume 2 of his trilogy points in the direction of considering all this as one whole.[11] The personal, systemic, structural aspects are present in both sets of literature.

Indeed, if peace with God (Rom 5:1-11) and among believers achieved by the cross (Eph 2:1-23) is to be maintained, spiritual warfare must be considered an essential feature of the Christian life. For while Christ disarmed or "depotentiated" the Powers, they are not abolished. The term *katargeō* in 1 Cor 15:24 cannot be translated "abolished," according to Wink, and I agree.[12] It is essential to stand against the idolatrous presumptions of the Powers, whenever and wherever they manifest themselves.

The well-known call to Christian warfare in Eph 6:10-18[13] emphasizes this point. The spiritual armor listed here is derived mostly from Isaiah, where it earlier described God's battle against chaos and evil. The list is as follows:

| | |
|---|---|
| belt of truth around waist | Isa 11:5 |
| breastplate of righteousness/helmet of salvation | Isa 59:17 |
| feet shod with the equipment of the gospel of peace | Isa 52:7 |
| shield of faith | Isa 7:9b |
| sword of the Spirit | Isa 11:4 |
| Word of God | Isa 49:2 |

Clinton Arnold identifies all parts of the armor except the sword of the Spirit as defensive. The sword, the Word of God, is offensive, since it is the means of evangelism, of rescuing people from the bondage of evil and gathering them into Christ's kingdom.[14] But this is too facile an analysis. All the weapons have an offensive and defensive side to them. Truth, righteousness, salvation, the gospel of peace, and faith are powerful in confronting and disarming the enemy. In actuality, in the Christian life, the offensive and the defensive blend together. This is an important learning in spiritual warfare.

Not only must we remember the importance of prayer and reliance on the armor that God gives, but we must know also the nature of our weapons to be able to stand against the evil one. Paul states clearly the nature of the Christian's weapons: "For though we live in the world we are not carrying on a worldly war, for the weapons of our warfare are not worldly but have divine power to destroy strongholds. We destroy arguments and every proud obstacle to the knowledge of God, and take every thought captive to obey Christ, being ready to punish every disobedience, when your obedience is complete" (2 Cor 10:3-6 RSV). This raises the issue of how we must guard against spiritual warfare's sliding into messianic imperialism that does not accord with the nonviolence of the cross. Spiritual warfare cannot become an excuse to resort to violence to overcome evil.

Adolf von Harnack describes well Paul's warfare texts:

> We encounter immediately with Paul a number of warlike-sounding admonitions and images (1 Thess. 5:8; 2 Cor. 6:7; Rom. 6:13-14, 23; 13:12; Eph. 6:10-18), and we see that they have their origin in the images of the Old Testament prophets. This is particularly clear with the most extended allegory of this kind (Eph. 6:10-18). But even its detailed execution shows at once that virtually everything, the weaponry and the battle, is meant in a spiritual sense. It states expressly that it is concerned with the "gospel of peace." So the whole presentation is given the character of a lofty paradox, and the military element is neutralized.[15]

The use of warfare language is an issue that cannot be glossed over. Miroslav Volf, in his brilliant *Exclusion and Embrace*, deals most responsibly and helpfully with this issue:

> Is not the language of "struggle" and "combat" inappropriate, however? Does it not run at cross-purposes with nonviolence? Consider the fact that Jesus' public ministry—his proclamation and enactment of the reign of God as the reign of God's truth and God's justice—was not a drama played out on an empty stage, vacated by other voices and actors. An empty stage was unavailable to him, as it is unavailable to us. It was there only in the beginning, before the dawn of creation. On the empty stage of nonexistence, God enacted the drama of creation—and the world came into being. Every subsequent drama is performed on an occupied stage: all spectators are performers. Especially in a creation infested with sin, the proclamation and enactment of the kingdom of truth and justice is never an act of pure positing, but always already a transgression into spaces occupied by others. Active opposition to the kingdom of Satan, the kingdom of deception and oppression, is therefore inseparable from the proclamation of the kingdom of God. It is this opposition that brought Jesus Christ to the cross; and it is this opposition that gave meaning to his nonviolence. It takes the struggle against deception and oppression to transform nonviolence from barren negativity into a creative possibility, from a quicksand into a foundation of a new world.[16]

Numerous texts show that the use of warfare imagery does not negate the ethic of nonretaliation and love of enemy. In fact, the battle against the spiritual powers is the possibility for not retaliating and for not using violence to resist the enemy. Analogous to the theology of divine warfare in the Old Testament, God as Warrior makes possible the negation of human warfare. The people are called to trust in God's protection and provision.[17] Spiritual warfare may be understood then as the best antidote to waging military warfare, as the early church of the first three centuries so clearly understood.

Rom 16:20 exhibits a startling blend of war and peace imagery: "The God of peace will shortly crush Satan under your feet." Similarly, Eph 6:10-18 set beside 2:11-22 features just as striking a blending of the language of peacemaking and warfare-resistance. Another similar complementary set of images occurs in Rom 12:17-21 and 2 Cor 10:3-4.

Thomas Yoder Neufeld contends that in Ephesians 6 God's work as Divine Warrior is "democratized" so that the church—the saints—participate with God in the battle against evil. Clinton Arnold puts the spiritual warfare into the context of the Ephesian believers' past religious allegiances to the Artemis cult, with its various forms of magic and astrology, and to other mystery cults, in all of which great fear of demonic powers played a major role. Hence, Christ's victory is a conquest of the Powers; the believers are called to stand against them with the divine armor: "Victory over the 'Powers' is not assured apart from the appropriation of the power of God. Failure to resist allows the devil to reassert his dominion."[18] Ragnar Leivestad in *Christ the Conqueror* treats Ephesians 6, together with numerous other "victory" texts (like Eph 4:8-10), and the New Testament as a whole.[19] His work shows a strong stratum of unity in New Testament thought, and especially among the seven letters of Paul and Ephesians and Colossians.

At the same time that Paul employs a wealth of martial imagery to describe the believers' resistance to the powers of evil, he fully affirms both commands of Jesus, to love the enemy and not to retaliate. The key text here is Rom 12:14-21, which has striking similarities to 1 Peter 2–4. The command not to retaliate occurs also in 1 Thess 5:13b, 15.

Gordon Zerbe cites more than thirty texts that witness to some form of non-retaliation, including not cursing, not litigating, forbearing, enduring, and being at peace.[20] Further, in Eph 3:9-10, the church as a body is the demonstration of the manifold wisdom of God to the Powers. This surely refers to the unified humanity described in chapters 1–2 and rehearsed in Paul's apostolic mission (3:1-8). Here the Pax Christi becomes a model for the Pax Romana. It demonstrates that the wall of hostility has been broken. A new community is born.

This community knows its identity as having been buried with Christ and raised with Christ and co-seated in its authority with Christ at God's right hand. Thus, it has its own kingdom mission and agenda. It neither courts nor condemns Rome and the contemporary nations of this world. Nor does it give its main energies to aid or block the imperialistic pacification programs, of which the Pax Romana was a grand model. Rather, the new humanity of Christ's body seeks out people everywhere who will identify with the new creation reality. It welcomes them to become "children of peace," freed from the tyranny of the Powers in whatever personal, national, socioeconomic, political, or ideological guise they manifest themselves.[21]

## THE TIME AND MEANS OF NONRESISTANCE

In the 1940s, two influential publications on nonresistance were prepared for guiding Mennonite thinking: one, the oft-reprinted book by Guy Hershberger, *War, Peace, and Nonresistance*, and the other, a thirty-five-page study pamphlet by John E. Lapp, "Studies in Nonresistance: An Outline for Study and Reference."[22]

What is striking in this earlier period is not only the dominance of the nonresistance tradition but the almost total lack of attention to justice. It is God's business and prerogative to take vengeance and judge justly against evil. Hence, the shift in Mennonite emphases is not a slight turn but in fact is at least a ninety-degree turn from earlier emphases and teaching. Mennonite college and seminary courses on war, peace, and nonresistance became courses on war, peace, and revolution.[23]

Another important shift between the earlier and later emphases was a loss of corporate belief to more individual stances. It was expected that the Mennonite Church would stand corporately against participation in war, and the entire peoplehood would support young people adhering to that stance and discipline those not adhering. This corporate dimension has been weakened in the later emphases on justice and nonviolent resistance. This observation correlates with the Driedger and Kraybill data that the dimension of Individualism decreases adherence to belief in Nonresistance. Some current voices, such as Stanley Hauerwas, call us again to corporate commitment to stand against the American captivity of the Bible:

> I maintain that the Sermon on the Mount presupposes the existence of a community constituted by the practice of nonviolence, and it is unintelligible divorced from such a community. . . . [I] suggest that the Sermon on the Mount constitutes and is constituted by a community that has learned that to live in the manner described in the Sermon requires learning to trust in others to help me so live. In other words, the object of the Sermon on the Mount is to create dependence; it is to force us to need one another.[24]

But there have always been individuals who stand sturdily against the prevailing order, both in church and in world. The absolutist stance of Leo Tolstoy on nonresistance seems almost startling to us:

> Non-resistance to evil is the commandment that unifies the whole teaching [of Jesus], but not if it is a mere saying, only if it is a rule that is obligatory for everyone, a law. . . . To see this commandment as a mere saying, a saying that

cannot be followed without supernatural help, is to destroy the whole of the teaching [of Jesus]. . . . To unbelievers it seems simply ridiculous, and it cannot appear otherwise. We have installed an engine, heated up the boiler, set it in motion, but not attached the transmission belt—this is what we have done to the teaching of Christ by saying that it is possible to be a Christian without fulfilling the commandment of non-resistance to evil.[25]

Tolstoy gave up his aristocratic way of life, became a poor peasant, and sought to carry out the teachings of Jesus literally.

In reflecting upon the recent Mennonite history, the impact of the Vietnam era—when Mennonite voices joined other Christian and secular voices to end the war—was a major factor in the shift in emphasis. More analysis and critical reflection needs to be done. Analysis of the entries in chapter 4, "The Bible, Peace and War," of the massive *Annotated Bibliography of Mennonites on War and Peace*[26] attests to this shift. But further analysis in other chapters of the ten thousand entries needs to be done in order to document more fully the shift and the nuances in between. The issue of paying taxes used for war received major attention in the 1970s[27] and seems to have been a "bridge" issue, appealing to both sets of theological convictions—the earlier emphasis on nonresistance and the later emphasis on seeking justice through political priorities.

What does all this mean as we seek to fulfill God's call to faithfulness in this time? How, specifically, is nonresistance related to resistance?

## THE PARADOXICAL WITNESS OF SCRIPTURE

The relationship of the church to the empire is significant, as Klaus Wengst notes in describing the relation between the Pax Romana and the peace of Jesus Christ:

> The loyalty which Paul requires towards the power of the state is the loyalty of the one who is alien to the world and a "citizen of heaven," not the loyalty of the person who is assimilated but that of the one who is not. He and his personal experiences are an impressive example of that. The loyalty to which he admonishes his readers cannot therefore be total; there is the possibility of specific refusal.[28]

As does Wengst, we may link Romans 13 with Phil 3:20, which states: "But our citizenship is in heaven, and it is from there that we are expecting a Savior, the Lord Jesus Christ." This Savior is the one to whom we give our allegiance, the one to whom we give our devotion and worship. None of the Caesars of this world, none of the empires' monarchs, none of the presidents of the world's democracies are worthy to receive this honor, power, and glory. We can be subject to them, because our Liberator, whom we acclaim as mighty Lord, is in heaven. He is the Lord of hosts, Lord of the Powers.

## "RENDERING TO CAESAR":
## LUISE SCHOTTROFF'S CONTRIBUTION

In my judgment, the best theological statement on the paradoxical and necessary relationship has been developed by Luise Schottroff, in an article published in English in *Love of Enemy*.[29] Her perception is profound, as selected quotes show:

> Matthew 5:38-41 . . . commands the refusal to retaliate as well as prophetic judgment of violent persons. . . . As imitators of God, Christians are supposed to confront the enemies of God with his mercies. . . . Loving one's enemy is the attempt to change the violent person into a child of God through a confrontation with the love of God. That is, love of one's enemy can be concretely presented as the prophetic proclamation of the approaching sovereignty of God.[30]

Schottroff then takes up the topic "Make Room for God's Wrath: Romans 12:14-21." She identifies a sevenfold paranesis:

> Do not curse (12:14).
> Repay no one evil for evil (12:17).
> Never avenge yourselves (12:19).
> Do not be overcome by evil, but overcome evil with good (12:21).
> Leave it to the wrath of God (12:19).
> Vengeance is mine (12:19).
> If your enemy is hungry, feed him . . . for by so doing you will heap burning
>     coals upon his head (12:20).

She then contends that this behavior breaks the spiral of violence and grows out of "the assurance that God's judgment is just."[31] She summarizes her thesis by referring to a threefold behavioral ensemble: "This behavioral ensemble consisting of refusal to pay retribution, expecting prophetic judgment, and loving the enemy has its reason or its goal in the justice of God or in the sovereignty of God."[32] Schottroff then takes up Rom 13:1-7.[33] She argues that Rom 12:2 and 13:2 present a normative pattern that determines the interpretation of 13:1-7. In 12:2, the believer is called "to resist": "do not be conformed" to this age/world. In 13:2, on the other hand, the command is "do not resist." The same Greek word noted earlier in Matt 5:39 and Eph 6:13, *anthistēmi*, is used. The resistance in view, Schottroff says, is against Satan and the world. In principle, the believer does not resist the powers that God ordained. But living out the former command often puts Christians in collision with the state powers, because in them the very Satan that Christians must resist is at work. Christians did not desire conflict with the empire, and even at times sought to avoid it, but their faithfulness to the command to "resist" brought them into conflict. "The root of the problem was their resistance against Satan and sin as the true rulers of this world."[34] Further, she contends that the "resistance of Christians against Satan is not the resistance of the powerless. God's power is on their side."[35] Living through this paradox is what gave the early Christians their freedom for everyday service to God, even in an uncongenial or hostile environment.

## ROM 13:1-7: A CLOSER LOOK

More than Schottroff apparently does, I understand Romans to be Paul's response to a specific historical situation. Expelled from Rome, together with Jews, in 49 C.E. by Claudius's edict (Acts 18:1-2), Jewish Christians returned to Rome during the years 54–56 C.E.; at this time a tax revolt was also brewing against the emperor Nero. The likely issue behind Romans 12–13 was how the Christians should respond to the government and to the evil manifest in the tax problem, the evil of injustice and the evil of revolt. The *major* theme of Rom 12:9 — 13:10 is how to respond to *evil* (recurring eight times — 12:9, 17 (two times), 21 (two times); 13:3, 4, 10). To that question, Paul's answer is unmistakably clear:

1. Hate [stay clear of] evil [*to ponēron*]
   but hold fast to the good [*tō agathō*] (12:9).
2. Bless those who persecute you,
   bless and do not curse (12:14).
3. Repay no one evil [*kakon*] for evil [*kakou*]
   but focus on good [*kala*]
   and making peace [*eirēneuontes*] (12:17-18).
4. Do not be conquered by evil [*kakou*]
   but conquer evil [*kakon*] with good [*agathō*] (12:21).
5. Be subject to the authority[ies], who is [to be]
   a terror to evil [*kakō*],
   not to good [*agathō*];
   he is God's servant to you (13:3)
   unto the good [*agathon*].
   If you do evil [*kakon*], fear,
   for the servant avenges God's wrath [*orgēn*] against evil
   [*kakon*] (13:4).
   Be subject therefore not only to avoid wrath [*orgēn*]
   but also for the sake of [keeping a good] conscience (13:5).

6. Pay what is owed [*opheilas*];
owe [*opheilete*] no one anything but love [*agapan*] (13:7-8).
7. Whoever loves [*ho agapōn* ] fulfills the law[!];
whoever loves [*ho agapōn*] the neighbor
does not advance [promote] evil [*kakon*].
Love [*agapē*], therefore, is a fulfillment of the law (13:8).

Note also the contrast between the works of darkness and the armor of light (13:12).

Peacemaking, doing the good, and loving the neighbor (enemy) are the Christian responses to evil; avenging evil is forbidden to Christians, for vengeance (*ekdikos*, used three times, 12:17, 19; 13:4) belongs to God and the servant of wrath (*orgē*, used three times, 12:19; 13:4, 5).

## ANOTHER WITNESS: 1 PETER 3

The first letter of Peter sounds a similar theme,[36] as Mary Schertz has recently demonstrated. I wish to reinforce her case by mentioning an additional aspect of literary analysis, the repetition of key terms in this passage.[37] Significantly, the terms "evil" and "good" (with variants of doing evil or good) occur in partial or complete parallelism a dozen times here. The list is as follows:

Maintain *good* conduct so when you are accused of evil-doing they will see your *good works* (2:12).
Governors are to punish *evil-doers* and praise *good-doers*; by being subject and *doing good*, you put to shame the *ignorance of foolish humans* (same word as in v. 13 to describe the *human* institution) (2:14-15).
God approves enduring suffering for *doing good* but not for *sinning* (2:20). (Note v. 23 as a parallel thought, but with the terms *not reviling* when reviled and *not threatening* when suffering.)
Wives are to be *good doers* and not be *terrified*, presumably by *evil* treatment (3:6).
Do not return *evil for evil*—but rather *bless* (3:9).
He who sees *good* days keeps his lips from speaking *evil* (3:10).
Turn away from *evil* and do *good* (3:11).
The Lord regards the *righteous* but is against those doing *evil* (3:12).
Who is there to do *evil* against you if you are zealous for the *good* (3:13)?
If you keep a clear conscience when abused, those who *revile* you for *good* in Christ are shamed (3:16). It is better to suffer for doing *good* than for doing *evil* (3:17).

The sprinkling of this "good" (*agathon*) and "evil" (*kakon*) vocabulary throughout the segment quite clearly indicates that good and evil are the dominant themes of this particular text. The fact that the terminology occurs in each of the five subunits indicates also the author's intention, namely, that a particular kind of conduct, that is, *doing good*, is called for in situations in which others do *evil* to us. The text focuses not on any of the institutions per se, however, but in the way in which the institutions and relationships express themselves. The situation envisioned by the epistle is that of believers experiencing evil in each of the circumstances: believers at the hands of the authorities, slaves at the hands of masters, and wives at the hands of husbands. The central unit provides the model for Christian response and the last a general warranting summary.

## THE NATURE OF CHRISTIAN RESISTANCE (AND NONRESISTANCE)

Drawing in part on Schottroff's work, which I regard as the best Mennonite theological statement by a non-Mennonite, I understand the point of Rom 13:1-7 to be that both nonresistance and resistance, of whatever type, must be a way to witness to Jesus' lordship over all, a way to overcome evil with good.[38] As we have just seen, the same message sounds forth from 1 Peter. The response to which we are called is a way to owe no one anything but love. It is at once a sign of our subjection to, and freedom from, the Powers, because we know our citizenship is in heaven. This response is not motivated by disrespect for the Powers or refusal to recognize their authority. And it has the surprising dimension of the folly of the cross—the defeat of evil by extending genuine, unlimited love that stands for truth, justice, and shalom precisely where evil seeks to reign.

If through this means God has revealed divine justice for all humanity, so in this way of loving we seek to extend God's justice in the relationships among humans and the nations of this world. We fight no wars of our own; we rather witness in life and word to God's victory over evil. We bear witness to Jesus Christ's confrontation of and victory over the Powers. God's justice, not ours, is the cause of our witness.

## Chapter 11

# THE KIND OF JUSTICE JESUS CARES ABOUT

## GLEN STASSEN

The New Testament provides overwhelming evidence that Jesus cared about covenant justice in the same way that the prophets of Israel did. My purpose here is to present some of that evidence and to ask what the dimensions of that justice were that Jesus not only taught about but acted on and was crucified for. What kind of justice did Jesus care about?

I want to show that from various directions New Testament scholarship is pointing to that question of justice as central for understanding Jesus. There is a surprise in store for us, however: it is hard to find a New Testament scholar who pays attention to what Jesus might have meant by justice, what kind of justice is involved in his teaching and his actions, and how his understanding of justice was or was not continuous with the prophets in whose tradition he stood.

### RECENT DEBATES

Willard Swartley edited a book, *The Love of Enemy and Nonretaliation in the New Testament*,[1] in which Walter Wink and Richard Horsley debate one another. In his contribution to that volume, Horsley makes a strange split between what he apparently thinks of as two hermetically sealed spheres. He claims that Jesus' peacemaking relates only to the sphere of "interpersonal relations in Galilean villages" and does not relate to "the sphere of imperial political-economic relations." He argues that Wink is wrong in saying that Jesus teaches nonviolence in relating to the Roman Empire. Yet he admits that Matthew doesn't divide them that way (compare this with the "second mile," which is surely in the imperial context, as are other relations to Roman soldiers and tax collectors). This split seems contrary to Horsley's historically realist method; ironically, it abstracts Jesus from historically real conflict with the imperial structure, a conflict that his book *Jesus and the Spiral of Violence* makes clear is quite real.

I think this split is explained by Horsley's reaction against Martin Hengel and what he calls other "hostile German Lutheran idealist interpreters."[2] First, Hengel interprets in the context of imperial political-economic relations; second, he argues that Jesus was not a (violent) revolutionist; and, third, he concludes therefore that Jesus was a quietist—quietism being the other alternative perceived by a wealthy German Lutheran scholar who splits the world and the Bible into two realms, the public and the private.[3] So Horsley, reacting against Hengel, (1) wants Jesus interpreted in the village context, not in the imperial context; (2) agrees that Jesus was not a violent revolutionary; but (3) holds instead that Jesus was a peacemaker concerned especially with economic conflict in the village.

John Howard Yoder and Wink have provided more compelling interpretations on this point. Historically understood, (1) Jesus was surely in the imperial context also, where conflicts between Jews and Romans were boiling up again and again; and (2) Jesus was not a violent revolutionary, nor a quietist, but (3) an advocate of a clear strategy of active peacemaking in relation to the Roman Empire (a peacemaking of transforming initiatives, in my terminology) and very critical of the Domination System.

Wink clearly gets the best of this debate. The problem is that Horsley is opposing pacifism as if it were quietism that neglects economic oppression, and he wants economic and political revolution. Where has Horsley gotten the impression that pacifism entails quietism that neglects economic injustice? Where has he gotten the impression that Wink's form of pacifism does not care about economic injustice? Well, it is true that Wink does not write much about justice and injustice.

But Wink does write a great deal about the Domination System, and its violence and hierarchical inequality, and that surely implies injustice. But biblically and realistically, to counter the unchecked power of a Domination System we need structures of justice that work to curtail domination by unchecked power. I would like to see Wink write about that.

Horsley adds to Wink an insightful analysis of economic conflict in the village and also economic oppression by the imperial power structure[4]—and peacemaking initiatives to correct economic injustice. I would like Wink to emphasize this point more, as Yoder does with his emphasis on Jubilee.[5] Wink does agree with this point explicitly on p. 112 of *Love of Enemy*. Horsley says he himself has been a pacifist since his mid-teens but is not sure Jesus taught a nonviolent strategy. He does not support this with evidence, and Wink makes a strong case for Jesus' nonviolence based on clear evidence.[6]

Wink replies to Horsley: "We are both wary of pacifism, especially that form of pacifism which is more concerned with the purity of the pacifist than winning justice for the oppressed. Neither of us is disposed to take Jesus' teachings as a law that says a follower 'cannot' engage in violence, though neither of us can really get away from Jesus' nonviolence as in some sense normative." He is saying that they agree on the social context. They differ on the teachings. "On Horsley's read-ing, two of the most distinctive aspects of Jesus' ministry—loving and forgiving enemies and fellowshipping with outcasts—bite the dust."[7]

N. T. Wright has objected that Horsley would need to claim that there was no serious movement of violent revolution in Jesus' lifetime in order to sustain the thesis that Jesus fits exactly into the category of peasant movement, which Horsley adopted from Eric Hobsbawm, and further that Jesus supported the peas-ants in their attitude of protest without it implying violence. Wright shows that Horsley's is a false claim: "It is seriously misleading, as I have already shown, to imagine that serious violent revolution was not on the agenda in the 20s of the first century A.D."[8] Horsley maintains that Jesus did not flout the peasant move-ments by welcoming tax collectors and prostitutes, which is surely mistaken.

John Dominic Crossan has offered another criticism of Horsley's discussion. Although Crossan adopts Horsley's theory that an organized insurrection group called the Zealots did not arise until after Jesus' time, he writes that

> neither do I think that all was peaceful until the decades immediately preced-ing the revolt. [To the contrary,] Palestine moved from a century of turmoil, first to a period of conspiracy in the mid-fifties with the Sicarii, and then into internal war by 65 C.E., with all classes involved in open rebellion. . . . Gurr's pattern of turmoil, conspiracy, and war helps us understand that the events of 66 C.E. cast their shadow back over the entire preceding century. . . . The tra-jectories of those four different types of peasant turmoil . . . indicate recurrent trouble in almost every decade of the preceding century.[9]

Crossan cites extensive and numerous uprisings before, during, and after Jesus' ministry: "The Palestinian peasantry was in a state of political turmoil—rel-atively spontaneous, unorganized, with substantial popular participation, includ-ing violent political strikes, riots, political clashes, and localized rebellions"—and including nonviolent protests.[10]

In *Engaging the Powers*,[11] Wink does mention Jesus' advocacy of economic equality in the context of peasant society, but he has admitted he is a little thin here. He points to no practice of economic equality except a mention of the com-mon purse. In this chapter, I suggest that Wink's side of the debate can be much helped by developing Jesus' advocacy of justice. Surely our practices of peace-making and faithfulness to Jesus in the context of the domination of the global-izing economic powers and authorities can be much helped.

I write mindful of my brilliant Mennonite Ph.D. student Paulus Widjaja. Paulus is from Indonesia, and he will return to Indonesia to teach. In his country, the injustice and the lack of a government that has a reputation for justice and the legitimacy needed to quell anarchy are causing angry reaction that is erupt-ing into terrible violence. I also think of my Ph.D. student Jerry Nwonye, from

Nigeria. There injustice on the part of the government is causing repeated violence. And I think of Kosovo, where injustice caused war by Serbs, by Albanians, and by NATO, which in turn has caused lasting bitterness that erupts into more violence. Finally, I am thinking of the prophets of Israel, who proclaimed the word of the Lord: injustice brings the judgment and destruction of war; repent and practice justice, and peace will follow.

## POWER, DOMINATION, AND A JESUS WHO CARES ABOUT JUSTICE

In chapter 3, Dan Leichty shows that the power-drive of people fearing death is irrationally strong, and it causes injustice, exclusion, and violence. Similarly, in chapter 2, Nancey Murphy argues that MacIntyre needs an answer to Michel Foucault's demonstration that the power-drive penetrates and distorts all positions. In order to practice nonviolence, we need to support the kind of justice that limits the domination of power. Murphy shows that MacIntyre does not have an answer. We need a remedy to curb and redirect the will to power. Her point is supported powerfully by Wink's analysis of the Domination System. To curb the power-drive, she advocates pacifism, revolutionary subordination, free-church polity, and simple lifestyle.

I think Murphy's discussion is brilliant. I praise it, and I agree with it. I think we need to go one step further, to the kind of justice that limits the domination of concentrated power. As Wink's analysis has made clear, power comes to us not only as the power of an individual but also as Domination Systems with their spiritual justifications, ideologies, and drives. The answer needs to include justice that puts limits on power and domination. Maybe the answer is simply an extension of the practice of free-church polity, which tames authoritarian power and tames "self-interested individuals." The free-church contribution includes democracy, procedures of justice, and a sense of the common good or covenant, designed to curb and redirect the will to power.

Furthermore, the free-church tradition that we advocate points to Jesus, and Jesus calls for justice. Murphy and I agree that this is not a universal, rationalistic, foundationalist understanding of justice. I want to be clear that I reject that kind of understanding, too. I begin not with allegedly "universal" reason but with Jesus in the context of Jesus' roots in the traditions of the Hebrew Scriptures.

## JESUS DOES CARE ABOUT JUSTICE

Gerd Theissen, New Testament scholar at the University of Heidelberg under whom I have studied, shows that in the first decades of the twentieth century, 80 percent of German pastors and most theologians opposed the democratic Weimar Republic. They mostly favored the conservative German Nationalistic

Peoples' Party. Accordingly, they systematically neutralized Jesus' social criticisms. They handed down to us an individualistic and otherworldly picture of Jesus that does violence to the evidence and to the scholarly methods they claimed to be following. Their biblical interpretation claimed objectivity, but their consistent omission of Jesus' criticisms of injustice showed that it was historically relative.[12]

I do not mean to imply that present-day New Testament scholars have the same ideology that those scholars had. I am asking, however, whether we still feel an unconscious hangover from their influence, or whether our present-day social locations blind us to the contours of Jesus' critique of injustice.

A major step forward in the "third quest of the historical Jesus," advancing it beyond the old quest and the new quest, is its focus not first on Jesus' teachings but on Jesus' actions. Certain of Jesus' actions are historically firm and certain. They establish firm guidelines for understanding what the historical Jesus was doing—and in what narrative context—that are convincing even for highly skeptical scholars.

What follows will draw from insights of the brilliant and I think the most accurate and best study of the historical Jesus, *Jesus and the Victory of God*, by N. T. Wright.[13] Wright lists actions and practices that scholars widely agree were characteristic of the historical Jesus: Jesus went from village to village with an itinerant ministry. Jesus traveled around calling on people to repent. Jesus went around effecting remarkable cures, including exorcisms. Furthermore, Jesus called a group of close disciples, of whom twelve were given special status.

Wright points out that Jesus was often praying. "He ate with 'sinners' and kept company with people normally on or beyond the borders of respectable society." This eating with outcasts "caused regular offence to some of the pious." Jesus took the dramatically symbolic action of attacking the temple. Wright concludes: "The best initial model for understanding this praxis is that of a prophet . . . bearing an urgent eschatological, and indeed apocalyptic, message for Israel," announcing the kingdom of the God of Israel. On the strength of these observations, I suggest we must talk more specifically about the Domination System but also of the prophetic actions and teaching of Jesus and of the specific character of the kingdom of God.

***Jesus' attack on the temple system.*** New Testament scholars are paying new attention to Jesus' attack on the temple system. William Telford, Ched Myers, David Garland, Richard Horsley, E. P. Sanders, N. T. Wright, John Dominic Crossan, and Marcus Borg, among others, are focusing new attention here.[14] They are seeing this as a major clue to why he was crucified and to his understanding of his mission. They are seeing that it was not merely a "cleansing" of the temple but indeed a prophetic and symbolic attack on the whole temple system for practicing a cover-up of injustice as described in Jeremiah 7. This is one pointer to the justice Jesus cared about.

N. T. Wright points out that in six different passages Jesus prophesied the destruction of the temple: Mark 13; 14:58; 15:29-30; John 2:9; Acts 6:14; Thomas 71. He often disagrees with Crossan, but here he says that Crossan comes very close to the right answer on what caused Jesus to be crucified:

> Crossan thinks, and I fully agree with him, that Jesus' action in the temple was a symbolic destruction; that some words of Jesus about this destruction are original; and that these words and this action followed with a close logic from the rest of Jesus' agenda, the program enacted in healings and meal-sharings. . . . I think . . . that at this point we are on very firm historical ground indeed.[15]

David Garland writes that Jesus' action at the temple was neither an act of violent revolution nor merely a "cleansing" or reform of the temple but a symbolic prophetic action of protest against injustice and its cover-up. Why would Jesus merely try to cleanse the temple when he predicts it will soon be destroyed? "If sacrificial animals cannot be purchased, then sacrifice must end. If no vessel can be carried though the temple, then all cultic activity must cease." And if money cannot be made, then the financial support for the temple and the priests will be gone. "Jesus does not seek to purify current temple worship but symbolically attacks the very function of the temple and heralds its destruction." His hostility to the temple emerges as a charge at his trial (14:58) and as a taunt at the cross (15:29).[16]

Jesus cited two passages from the prophets as he carried out this prophetic action. Isaiah 56:7, "My house shall be called a house of prayer for all peoples," is part of the declaration in Isa 56:1-8 that God's purpose is to bless all who are being excluded, the foreigners, the eunuchs, and the outcasts. "During his entire ministry Jesus has been gathering in the impure outcasts and the physically maimed, and has even reached out to Gentiles. He expects the temple to embody this inclusive love. . . . In Jesus' day the temple had become a nationalistic symbol that served only to divide Israel from the nations."[17]

Jeremiah 7 says we should not keep claiming we have the temple of the Lord when we need to amend our ways and truly execute justice with each other, not oppress the alien, the orphan, or the widow or shed innocent blood and go after other gods. The temple is functioning as a cover-up for injustice, what Bonhoeffer called "cheap grace," that does not call for changing our ways and our loyalties. If we continue to practice injustice and claim God is on our side because we have the temple of the Lord (or we have the church), God will destroy the temple (or the church) and cast us out of God's sight. By quoting from Jeremiah 7, Jesus

> denounces the false security that the sacrificial cult breeds. . . . The den is the place where robbers retreat after having committed their crimes. It is their

hideout, a place of security and refuge. Calling the temple a robbers' den is therefore not a cry of outrage against any dishonest business practices in the temple. Jesus indirectly attacks them for allowing the temple to degenerate into a safe hiding place where people think that they find forgiveness and fellowship with God no matter how they act on the outside. Jesus' prophetic action and words attack a false trust in the efficacy of the temple sacrificial system. The leaders of the people think that they can rob widows' houses (Mark 12:40) and then perform the prescribed sacrifices according to the pre-scribed patterns at the prescribed times in the prescribed purity in the pre-scribed sacred space and then be safe and secure from all alarms. They are wrong. . . . The fig tree incident brackets the temple action and interprets it. It reveals more clearly that Jesus does not intend to cleanse the temple. Instead, his actions visually announce its disqualification. The fig tree that has not borne fruit is cursed, not reformed or cleansed. The parable of the tenants of the vineyard (12:1-11) makes the same point. As Jesus seeks fruit from the fig tree, so God, the owner of the vineyard, seeks fruit from the vineyard. When no fruit is to be found or when it is withheld, destruction follows.[18]

When we pay attention to the prophetic teachings that Jesus cites—Jeremiah 7 and Isaiah 56—we see that Jesus' dramatic prophetic action is an attack on the cover-up of four kinds of injustice: (1) exclusion of outcasts; (2) deprivation of the powerless; (3) domination by the political/priestly/economic powers and authori-ties; and (4) the violence of bloodshed. It is based in the prophets' understanding of justice. And, like the prophets, it is also attacking idolatry, unfaithfulness to God's way. I shall argue that these are four key dimensions of Jesus' understand-ing of justice and that Jesus ties faithfulness to God very tightly to the practice of justice. The opposite is injustice and unfaithfulness.

***Jesus stood in the tradition of the prophets.*** N. T. Wright begins his study of the historical Jesus with the thesis that has emerged out of his massive study: "I shall argue, first, that Jesus' public persona within first-century Judaism was that of a prophet, and [second] that the content of his prophetic proclama-tion was the 'kingdom' of Israel's God."[19] "The prophetic aspect of Jesus' work is often surprisingly ignored." Wright gives a synopsis of the verses that describe Jesus as a prophet mighty in word and deed.[20] "This portrait of Jesus as a prophet seems the most secure point at which to ground our study of Jesus' public career, and in particular of his characteristic praxis. Equally impressive are the strong hints, throughout the Gospels, that Jesus was modeling his ministry not on one figure alone, but on a range of prophets from the Old Testament. . . . Above all, Jesus adopts the style of, and consciously seems to imitate, Elijah."[21]

Jesus was proclaiming a message from the covenant god, and living it out with symbolic actions. He was confronting the people with the folly of their ways, summoning them to a different way, and expecting to take the consequences of doing so. We are here, historically speaking, on certain ground. . . . Elijah had stood alone against the prophets of Baal, and against the wickedness of King Ahab. Jeremiah had announced the doom of the Temple and the nation, in the face of royalty, priests and official prophets. . . . all were accused of troubling the status quo. When people "saw" Jesus as a prophet, this was the kind of model they had in mind.[22]

What we all surely know is that a central theme for the prophets of Israel was their announcing that God wills justice to the powerless—the orphans, the widows, the poor, and the foreigners (or immigrants). The two Hebrew and two Greek words for "justice" occur 1,060 times in the Bible. Hardly any other word is repeated so often. We are often handicapped in recognizing this if we do not read Hebrew and Greek, because the two Hebrew words are often translated "righteousness/integrity" and "judgment" in various versions, and these do not convey the kind of delivering, community-restoring justice that the Hebrew intends. The Hebrew means *the kind of justice that delivers the powerless from their oppression and bondage into covenant community with provisions sensitive to the cries of the weak, in the way YHWH hears the cries of the weak and acts to deliver them and bring them into covenant community.*[23] They point to a drama—the drama of YHWH's action of deliverance and creation of the community. This is the tradition with which Jesus identified.

***Jesus proclaimed the reign of God—God's presence, salvation, peace, and justice.*** The kingdom of God has suffered misunderstanding as well. Whether we are ordinary Christians or New Testament scholars, we have learned to focus our discussions of the kingdom of God on the question of whether it is future or present—or some combination of present, like mustard seeds, and future, like the whole mustard bush.

Dot and I were married in Charlottesville, Virginia, on a Saturday. We started off on our honeymoon, driving toward the Smoky Mountains of North Carolina, down the Blue Ridge Parkway. We stopped overnight near Natural Bridge. On Sunday morning, we worshiped in the nearest Baptist church we could find. The church was in the midst of a revival. The revival preacher had covered the whole front of the sanctuary with a huge map of the sequence of events in the coming end of the world, in brilliant colors of orange, green, purple, blue, brown, black, red, and fuchsia. He spent the first half of his sermon reviewing the first half of the map, whose meaning he had described in more detail the previous week; the second half was a preview of what he would disclose in the coming week. It was a portentous and symbolically pregnant beginning for our marriage.

But Jesus says no one knows the time or season;[24] the point is to be ready. Yet how can you be ready if you do not know what kind of ethics fits the reign of God, what kind of ethics is practiced by those who are ready? The important question on which we should be focusing our research is, what are the marks and the practices of the kingdom so we can act in ways that prepare for it and participate in it, and so we can notice it when it comes?

Think of *Waiting for Godot*. At the end of the play, two boy-angels tell us that one act of the play was about the sheep who did the deeds of the kingdom when Godot came and that the other act was about the goats who did not do the deeds of the kingdom. That means Godot came in both acts, in the form of Jesus, even though the two bums who are the antiheroes of the play failed to recognize Godot when he came (he came in the form of Lucky). And in one act, they did minister to him and his sidekick. Not only did the two bums fail to recognize Godot when he did come right into their absurd lives, in both acts—although they crucified him in the first act and ministered to him and his sidekick in the second act—but the play's readers and audiences also usually fail to recognize what is happening. I guess the message of the play is that we are all bums who don't have a clue how to recognize Godot when Godot comes. We are too busy asking, when will the kingdom come?

The other focus of usual Protestant discussion is whether the kingdom is brought completely by God's grace or whether it demands faithfulness and obedience from us. This question comes from Protestant theology, not from what made most sense in Jesus' context. N. T. Wright argues that the kingdom of God was well understood in Jesus' Jewish context: it was about Israel's covenant with God, God becoming king, and the world at last being put to rights. I think Wright is correct. God "would administer justice for Israel and judgment on the nations." It "meant the coming vindication of Israel, victory over the pagans, the eventual gift of peace, justice and prosperity."[25] It meant the reign of God as the prophets prophesied: not the end of the space-time universe, not the "cosmic meltdown." The debates about the kingdom have not focused on the heart of the matter and are anachronistic. The crucial question is not so much that of the kingdom's timing as of its content.[26]

***Jesus, justice, and Judaism.*** What were Jesus' aims? Wright agrees with John Meier and E. P. Sanders that he sought the restoration of Israel to God's will, beginning with his highly symbolic call of twelve disciples, and so of course intended to leave behind a community of disciples.[27] And here is the pointer to justice: Israel's hope for the kingdom focused clearly on God's will for justice. One of the big advances of the third quest for the historical Jesus is rooting Jesus solidly in Judaism. The old quest, the Bultmannian school and to a significant extent the Jesus Seminar, attempted to single out how Jesus differed from Judaism, and thus they airbrushed out most of what was concrete and got a very thin Jesus, too thin to resist their efforts to make him conform to their own idealistic or less-than-idealistic wishes and interests. Israel had a strong focus on God's will for justice. The old quest airbrushed that out also. Will we?

Here I am modifying Wright just a bit. I am agreeing with all he says about Jesus' announcing the kingdom, about the restoration of Israel, about Jesus' being in line with the prophets, and about the twelve disciples as a community that restores God's will for Israel and as spreading communities or cells that do that. Jesus is bypassing the temple system altogether, claiming to admit all, as Wright says Crossan writes about so movingly.[28] "Jesus is claiming to be ushering in Israel's long-awaited new world; and he is doing it, apparently, in all the wrong ways" as fulfillment of the whole line of the Hebrew Scriptures. "He is making a claim to be the one in and through whom Israel's God is restoring his people. The claim . . . points, within his own teaching, to a final clash with the authorities, who will wish him dead and act on that wish." I am convinced that this is accurate. But Wright takes the parable of the prodigal son as his key to interpreting the nature of the kingdom of God. He sees the prodigal son as Israel gone into exile, wishing the Father dead. And the kingdom of God means a new exodus for Israel, a return to the covenant relation with YHWH in the land. This is the place where Wright has not found agreement among a number of scholars, and I am not following him on his special interpretation of the parable of the prodigal son and the specific language of a new exodus. Of course, if I did, it would also point to justice as central: the exodus was very much about deliverance from the injustice of Pharaoh into the covenant community where the delivering justice of YHWH was to be followed.

W. D. Davies taught me to understand the meaning of the kingdom of God by looking at the prophecies of the kingdom by the prophets of Israel. If you look at the prophetic predictions of the time when God will become king, one set of characteristics is foreigners not governing Judaea, the temple being rebuilt, the Messiah arriving, Israel observing the Torah properly, the pagans being defeated and/or flocking to Zion for instruction. The question is, in what sense did Jesus affirm this meaning?[29]

It seems clear that Jesus did not affirm the meaning that Israel will rule over the nations. But Jesus clearly affirmed and enacted the other four marks of the kingdom of God: (1) God will be present like the light of day; (2) God will save us, deliver us, forgive us; (3) God will bring peace; and (4) God will bring justice. Look at passages like Isa 9:6-7; 52:7; 60; 61; Zech 9:9ff.; and Psalm 37. Again and again you will see the four marks: God's presence, salvation, peace, and justice. Yet this points again to Jesus caring about justice. N. T. Wright argues that

> Crossan and the great majority of NT scholars have misunderstood the nature of apocalyptic. Just as Crossan "reads" Jesus' healings, and his open table-fellowship, as indicating a profoundly subversive intent within the world of his day, so I have argued that "apocalyptic" writings, and Daniel in particular, were read in the first century as describing not "the darkening scenario of an imminent end to the world" but the radical subversion of the present world order. . . . "Apocalyptic"

is not about a god doing something and humans merely spectating. It invests human political and social action with its full theological significance.[30]

Throughout the Gospels, Jesus sees himself in the tradition of the prophets, who called for repentance as he did, who proclaimed God's reign as he did, and who called for justice. The marks of the reign of God are God's presence, salvation, peace, and justice. I wish I had the space to look further at some of the prophetic passages describing the coming reign of God to see the kind of justice that they are talking about.[31] Wright concludes that "once we understand 'apocalyptic' writings and sayings in their proper historical context . . . the element of sharp and often quizzical social critique . . . is not only retained but enhanced."[32]

## JESUS IN THE SYNOPTIC GOSPELS
## TEACHES FOURFOLD JUSTICE

I am looking at Jesus from two angles and thereby getting a stereoscopic view. I am taking a bilingual approach, listening stereophonically, because each language can hear what the other might miss, and each can correct the other. Thus far I have been looking with the third quest of the historical Jesus. The other angle is the canonical Gospels as we have them, as authoritative for Christians and Christian churches. Richard Hays argues that "we have a better chance of holding our own predispositions in abeyance—and thus allowing our communities to be shaped by Scripture—if we follow the procedure . . . of treating each Gospel individually and attending to its narrative logic, its representation of the figure of Jesus, and its consequent moral world." Nevertheless, "intellectual integrity demands some investigation of what can be known historically about Jesus."[33]

From the angle of the canonical Gospels, and using the criterion of multiple attestation (I do not have time or space here to exegete each Gospel and verse individually), I count forty-eight times in the Synoptic Gospels, not including parallels, when Jesus confronts the aristocracy for their injustice. One hears people, who are apparently influenced by modern individualism or a static two-realms dualism between private and public or some kind of quietism, say that Jesus taught only love for individuals and not justice in relation to political authorities. Perhaps these people forget that state and church were not separated but were in very close proximity on the same hill and in the same temple, and that Rome allowed the Jewish authorities to do most of the daily ruling. By "the aristocracy" Jesus confronted, I mean the Sadducees and the chief priests or representatives of the temple hierarchy, who were the day-to-day political/religious/economic authorities, plus the wealthy, who had great power, and the Pharisees, who were authorities Jews regularly encountered,[34] plus Herod, Pilate, and the Roman rulers. I see four themes running through Jesus' confrontations over injustice—four dimensions of the justice that Jesus emphasized.

*Jesus' mission is nonviolent.* I count twenty-one times—not counting parallels—when Jesus confronts the authorities for the injustice of violence and makes clear that his mission is nonviolent. For example, Matt 23:31ff. (RSV): "You are sons of those who murdered the prophets. . . . Therefore I send you prophets and wise men and scribes, some of whom you will kill and crucify, and some you will scourge in your synagogues and persecute from town to town, that upon you may come all the righteous blood shed on earth." In Luke 13:31ff., the Pharisees warn Jesus that Herod wants to kill him. Jesus says: "Go and tell that fox, 'Behold, I cast out demons and perform cures today and tomorrow, and the third day I finish my course. Nevertheless I must go on, . . . for it cannot be that a prophet should perish away from Jerusalem'" (RSV). In Matt 23:37ff., Jesus mourns, "O Jerusalem, Jerusalem, killing the prophets and stoning those who are sent to you! How often would I have gathered your children together as a hen gathers her brood under her wings, and you would not!" (RSV). I am also including passages like Matt 5:43ff., where Jesus calls on us to love our enemies and include them in community, and the parable of the compassionate Samaritan, which teaches peace between Jews and Samaritans.[35] N. T. Wright sees this nonviolence as central for Jesus' narrative, message, actions, and ethics.[36] This supports and broadens the base for Yoder's argument for nonviolence in his seminal book, *The Politics of Jesus*, and for his pointing to the practice of binding and loosing extended into conflict resolution in *Body Politics*.[37]

*Jesus confronts the wealthy.* I also count eighteen passages in which Jesus, in the tradition of the prophets, confronts the wealthy—and the religious/political powers and authorities who were in cahoots with the wealthy—for cheating the poor and hoarding for themselves and committing injustice against the poor and calls for justice for the poor. For example, Mark 7:9ff.: "You have a fine way of rejecting the commandment of God in order to keep your tradition! For Moses said, 'Honor your father and your mother. . . .' But you say that if anyone tells father or mother, 'Whatever support you might have had from me is Corban' . . . then you no longer permit doing anything for a father or mother." Luke 12:21 speaks of the rich man who builds bigger barns to hoard all his grain and his goods: "So is he who lays up treasure for himself, and is not rich toward God" (RSV) And Luke 16:14f.: "The Pharisees, who were lovers of money, . . . scoffed at him. But he said to them, 'You are those who justify yourselves before men, but God knows your hearts'" (RSV). Mark 10:21 says to "go, sell what you own, and give the money to the poor." Mark 10:25 tells us that "it is easier for a camel to go through the eye of a needle than for someone who is rich to enter the kingdom of God." And Mark 12:38-40: "Beware of the scribes, who. . . devour widows' houses and for the sake of appearance say long prayers. They will receive the greater condemnation." In Matt 23:25 we find: "Woe to you, scribes and Pharisees, hypocrites! For you clean the outside of the cup and of the plate, but inside they are full of greed and self-indulgence." In Luke 7:24-30, Jesus praised John the Baptist as God's prophet to warn them and said, by contrast, that "those who put on fine clothing and live in luxury are in royal palaces. . . . All the people who heard this . . . acknowledged the justice of God, because they had been baptized with John's baptism."[38] This connects with Yoder's argument for the practice of breaking bread together and its extension into sharing economically.[39] And it connects with practicing Jubilee in *The Politics of Jesus*. But it has a broader base in Jesus' affirmation of the covenant in the Torah, and of delivering justice in the prophets.[40]

*Jesus repeatedly confronts those who dominate others.* Some teachings fit in more than one category; I count nineteen passages in this category of domination and lording it over others: (Mark 10:42-43 RSV): "Those who are supposed to rule over the Gentiles lord it over them, and their great men exercise authority over them. But . . . whoever would be great among you must be your servant." In Luke 6:9ff., Jesus asks the scribes and Pharisees if it is lawful on the Sabbath to do good or to do harm, to save life or to destroy it, and he heals the man with the withered arm: "But they were filled with fury and discussed with one another what they might do to Jesus." (Matt 5:11): "Blessed are you when people revile you and persecute you and utter all kinds of evil against you falsely on my account. . . . For in the same way they persecuted the prophets who were before you." Matt 23:2ff. (RSV): "The scribes and the Pharisees [Luke 20 says lawyers] . . . preach, but do not practice. They bind heavy burdens, hard to bear, and lay them on [people's] shoulders; but they themselves will not move them with their finger. . . . And they love the place of honor at feasts." Mark 12:38-40: "Beware of the scribes, who like to walk around in long robes, and to be greeted with respect in the marketplaces, and to have the best seats in the synagogues and places of honor at banquets! They devour widows' houses and for the sake of appearance say long prayers."[41] This connects with Yoder's advocacy of servanthood authority in *The Politics of Jesus* and elsewhere, and with the practice of "the rule of Paul" and "the fullness of Christ" or affirming that every member brings important gifts.[42]

*Jesus included the outcast.* Finally, Jesus' understanding of justice included the crucial importance of being included in community and not being cast out. We think of the poignant story of the cripple at the Pool of Bethsaida, who had no one to move him into the water when it was stirred up. He lacked community and so was powerless. Jesus healed him and restored him to community. Often Jesus healed outcasts and brought them back into society by touching those whom no one else in that society would touch. Jesus touched lepers and a woman with a flow of blood and the dead, or they touched him, and he regularly instructed the healed person to submit to the priests, so as to be certified as ready to be included in community or to go back to their community.[43] Furthermore, he connected healing and forgiveness (Mark 2:5-9), where forgiveness meant not only wiping out past sins but embracing in community. Wright argues that, for a first-century Jew, most if not all of the works of healing, which form the bulk of Jesus' mighty works, could be seen as the restoration to membership in Israel of those who, through sickness or whatever, had been excluded as ritually unclean. The healings thus function in exact parallel with the welcome of sinners, and this, we may be quite sure, was what Jesus himself intended. He never performed mighty works simply to impress. He saw them as part of the inauguration of the sovereign and healing rule of Israel's covenant God.[44]

He further writes:

> We have, in the last forty years, "discovered" that Matthew, Mark, Luke, and John—and even, according to some—Q and Thomas—had a great interest in "community." It ought to be just as clear, if not clearer, that Jesus himself was deeply concerned about the social and corporate effects of his kingdom-announcement. . . . A good deal of evidence indicates that Jesus fully intended his stories to generate a new form of community.[45]

And almost all agree that Jesus revolutionized the understanding of who is to be included in community. God gives sunshine and rain to friends and enemies alike, and we are to participate in God's grace, including our enemies in our community of love (Matt 5:43ff.). This is symbolized so clearly in the fact of his including Zealots and a tax collector in his community of disciples. He practiced a justice that clearly went beyond the justice of the Pharisees and even of the prophets. He died to save his enemies—and us.

This connects with Yoder's understanding of alternative community in *The Politics of Jesus* and the practice of baptism as breaking down racial and other walls of division, as well as the practice of the fullness of Christ, in *The Body Politics*.[46]

## TOWARD A PUBLIC ETHIC OF FOURFOLD JUSTICE

As Yoder argues in *Christian Witness to the State*, *Body Politics*, and *For the Nations*, the key practices ordained by the New Testament, like feeding the hungry, have analogous meaning for public ethics in multicultural society. The Lord's Supper in 1 Corinthians 11 is about "discerning the body," which means discerning that Jesus gave his body for others, and that the church, as faithful to Jesus, is for others. The food available in the church supper needs to be for the poor who come to church hungry even if they cannot arrive early while the food is plentiful. And since this is God's will revealed in Christ, it is God's will for the society outside the church as well, just as Jesus fed the five thousand in the crowd. Community-restoring justice is God's will for all.

We are finding ourselves in a society that is truly multicultural—not only multiethnic but also multifaith. We see many being hurt by injustice—racial injustice, community disorganization, inadequately supported schools, violent culture, increasing gap between concentrated wealth and widespread poverty, and domination by concentrated power. This hurts people. It also infiltrates the culture of Christians, shaping our perceptions in distorted and unfaithful ways. It hurts the character of the oppressed, and it hurts the character of the comfortable. Christians and non-Christians are among both the oppressed and the comfortable.

So we need a public ethic of justice if we are to make our witness. We need to be able to speak a language that communicates in multicultural, multiethnic, multifaith society. Otherwise our witness is not heard. And otherwise our heads get infected by secular ideologies for which we have no antibodies.

But there is only one Lord, Jesus Christ; we have no other Lord. Therefore, the norm for our public ethic of justice needs to translate Jesus' care for justice as faithfully as possible into public language and needs to check back again and again to see if it is faithful to Jesus, in the tradition of the prophets of Israel. Our principle here as elsewhere is this: Let the church be faithful to Jesus.

Yoder advocates making ad hoc alliances with those who can help. We could seek help from the public ethic of justice developed by numerous theorists: Habermas, Benhabib, Fraser, Rawls, Bounds, Sen, Young, Walzer, and others. I suggest that our criteria as we select our ad hoc partners need to come first from Jesus, in the tradition of the prophets of Israel. Judging by these criteria, I find Michael Walzer, along with Amartya Sen and Elizabeth Bounds, to be most helpful.

## MICHAEL WALZER'S GROUNDS FOR A THEORY OF JUSTICE

Walzer, like Nancey Murphy, argues persuasively that we should not try to base our theory of justice on a universal, rationally necessary foundation for the following reasons: First, our postmodern world is multicultural; it lacks agreement on a universal, rationally necessary foundation. Second, any effort to reduce truth or justice to what can be agreed by all the different traditions reduces it to so thin a claim as to say very little and move people very little. Third, in fact, people learn their understanding of justice by deducing it not from a thin, universal proposition but from the thick, historically complex, particular traditions in which they are formed. We are shaped by our thick, particular history. Christians are shaped by narratives of Israel and Jesus and also by the particular narratives of the societies in which they have been shaped, not first of all by Kant's principle of universalizability. These are what move us. Fourth, enlightenment rationalism undercuts and opposes particular faith and particular community. And, finally,

Enlightenment rationalism teaches us to claim we think and act on the basis of universal rationality, and this blinds us to our traditions, worldviews, mortality-denying powers and authorities, and ideologies, which in fact shape our perceptions. These need to be named, unmasked, and criticized.

So Walzer argues we get our understandings of justice from our thick traditions, not from thin universals. He presents historical narratives: U.S. history, medieval Jewish history, tensions in India over the caste system and in Australia over racism, and the prophet Amos and the tradition of the prophets. He explicitly makes room for, and listens to, narratives like our stories of faith and unfaithfulness, persecution and witness.

Walzer's own faith is Judaism, and although he writes a public theory of justice that seeks to appeal to many, he claims this faith as his own thick tradition.[47] I asked him, "What tradition of political philosophy do you work in?" He replied, "Well, I am editing a series of volumes on Judaism. That is my tradition." Like Anabaptism, this is a tradition that knows persecution for its faith. He knows we need a public ethic of justice to guard us and others from being persecuted. Yoder wrote similarly, not long before he died, in *Journal of Religious Ethics* that historically we have done better in liberal democracy, and we have a stake in supporting a kind of justice that guards against injustice[48]

**Walzer's method.** Walzer's method is inductive, beginning with a particular experience, rather than deductive from a universal principle, and so in that sense is Aristotelian rather than Platonic. His is a narrative method. Reiteration is a key step in his method: he expects that if the narrative of the Exodus is so formative for us, and truthful, then Palestinians probably have a narrative of their own that has some analogous truth in it. He wrote *Exodus and Revolution* to show how the narrative of the Exodus gets reiterated in different ways in great varieties of different traditions—not as a thin principle but as a thick narrative. Walzer emphasizes that we all live in several traditions; we need a way to understand and communicate (witness) in more than our own, home tradition.

Years ago I took an overnight Greyhound bus from Harrisonburg to Chicago. As I was getting on the bus, I spotted an old-order Mennonite young man, sitting alone. I immediately sat down next to him. We soon established rapport—so much so that we talked the whole night through. It was during the Vietnam War, and he was on his way to spend his alternative service. He told me much about his community that I was eager to learn. And I could tell him much about sixteenth-century Anabaptism that he did not know. Very early in the conversation, as I asked him about his community, he smiled happily and reached up on the luggage rack for his bag, fetching a scrapbook that he had just been given by his church youth group. Each page was filled with handwritten poems or prayers, handmade copies of hymns, hand-drawn pictures of the youth group. The message on each page was clear and strong: "We know you are going out into the world of temptation. But we will be with you. We will pray for you, daily. We will be thinking of you the whole time. Take this scrapbook and look at it regularly, remembering that you are not alone. We are with you. Be strong. Do not give into the temptations of the world. Be faithful. We are praying for you."

The world of temptation to which he was going was a Mennonite old-folks home in Michigan. To my admittedly somewhat fallen Baptist perspective, that did not seem like the most temptation-filled part of the world. But from the perspective of his strong community, that place was outside the community; it was another culture. As he said to me, sitting there in his plain clothes with his wonderful, beautiful scrapbook, once you drive a car, what is there left to distinguish you from the world?

This is a parable for all of us. We are all in more than one tradition. Unless our intracommunity ethic includes standards of justice that can guide us meaningfully as we travel in other traditions in the public world, we are likely to have our minds and hearts infiltrated by idolatrous ideologies. Unless our Christian ethic can be translated in a way that enables us to know what is temptation versus what is being a Jew to the Jews and a Greek to the Greeks, and to know how to make our witness understandably in our multicultural world, we are not likely to be faithful to the living God who is already there in Michigan, including already there in Detroit and in the suburbs, caring for people who are suffering from all four kinds of injustice that Jesus witnessed against.

Michael Walzer's theory of justice is set out in his book *Spheres of Justice.*[49] His method is guided by mutual respect. This means he shows respect for the thick narratives of community told by people of diverse perspectives. There is great breadth of listening and great sensitivity in Walzer's inductive, historical approach. He expects to see some truth, some awareness of justice, in people who have been created in the image of God, even though it has been distorted by various interests and conflicts. His interpretation of the truth that he sees there is implicitly guided by his own prophetic tradition. Perhaps this is why it is so close to the fourfold justice Jesus taught and embodied in his own tradition—that of the prophets of Israel.

Walzer's understanding of justice has antidomination as a central theme. He is especially worried about the domination of concentrated economic power, spilling over into domination over political office and policy, domination by men over women, domination over minority races, and domination over the eleven spheres of life that he highlights. And he is worried by other forms of domination—race, gender, national membership, and favoritism of various kinds. So his justice builds barriers against domination. This is analogous to Jesus' opposition to the injustice of domination.

***Walzer's emphasis on rights.*** Walzer's spelling out of the meaning of justice in the eleven spheres he discusses depends not only on mutual respect and antidomination but also on three sets of rights. These are based not on Enlightenment rationalism but on particularist interpretation, shaped in part by his own

Jewish tradition and by his attention to the early Puritans' struggle for democracy (a struggle much influenced by ideas borrowed from Anabaptists). This means his ethic gives us a way to work on the basis of our particular history, to develop a public ethic that has a modest, mutually respectful, transcultural intent, thus not having the weaknesses of a fideism or closed kind of communitarianism with only a conventional ethic that lacks transcultural applicability.[50]

First is *the right to community*. Walzer's emphasis on community, as well as his emphasis on thick narrative, distinguishes him from Enlightenment individualism. He argues that community is the most basic right. Without community, we will not survive. Without community, we will be without culture and without power. Without community, we will lose our identity: remember the bus trip to Michigan and the scrapbook. Our public ethic must include the need for community. Walzer emphasizes both the negative right not to be excluded from community membership and the positive right of particular communities to the support that can enable them to survive and not be persecuted or undercut by the powers and authorities. This correlates with Jesus' emphasis on justice as restoration to community and as the restoration of the community of Israel.

Second is *the right to liberty*. This is the right not to be dominated and oppressed. It correlates with Jesus' justice that opposes domination. Our history—Anabaptist, Baptist, free-church, and believers-church—is a history of having been persecuted for our faith, having pioneered in developing the concepts and practices of religious liberty, and needing to emigrate in order to find religious liberty. I worry about the kind of communitarianism that expects homogeneity and dislikes difference. I cherish Walzer's provisions guarding minority rights, religious liberty, and other liberties against domination.

Walzer's liberty is not mere individual autonomy; it includes carefully defined obligations to participate in community.[51] And Walzer's community is "participative community" rather than "integrative community." It encourages all to participate in shaping community and supports that right, and not only for those who agree with the leaders or the powerful. So Walzer advocates liberty also as the positive right to participate in shaping community decisions. This correlates with Yoder's advocacy of "the rule of Paul," in which everyone has a gift, everyone may speak, and all are obligated to listen, and the whole community participates in discerning the guidance of the Spirit.

The third right is *the right to life*. This means nonviolence, in the negative sense of the right not to be killed. Walzer actively participated in and intellectually supported anti–Vietnam War protests. He wrote *Just and Unjust Wars* to give people opposing that war an articulate and widely persuasive basis for their criticism of the war. Like nearly all political philosophers, Walzer does use and affirm just-war theory. This does not mean that pacifists committed to nonviolence cannot learn from his writings on justice. Furthermore, he bases his version of just-war theory on the right to life and a commitment against violence that attacks the right to life, liberty, and community. This makes just-war theory more honest than some versions, and more useful in criticizing war than other versions.

John Howard Yoder wrote *When War Is Unjust* and was known for understanding just-war theory and pushing it to be honest. Walter Wink sees a use for just-war theory if its goals are seen as violence reduction.[52] I am committed to the way of nonviolence myself. In my teaching of students from multiple traditions, I teach both nonviolence as the way of Jesus and just-war theory of a particular kind, so that if my students are not committed to nonviolence, at least they have some ethic other than supporting whatever bombing the government engages in. This is what John Yoder encouraged me to do, knowing I would be teaching many nonpacifists.

The right to life also has the positive sense of the right to develop one's life-calling, with education, housing, food, work, health care, and so on. Walzer writes extensively on this right. It correlates well with Jesus' emphasis on justice for the poor.

I have only begun to point to the richness of Walzer's theory of justice. I commend it for careful study and for guidance in our public witness. I believe it is a public ethic of justice that fits most appropriately with the way of Jesus Christ. In our polymorphous world, we need a language of justice that can help tame and limit the enormous buildups of concentrated power that threaten all. Walzer can help us to participate in that struggle and to make articulate witness.

# SELECTED WRITINGS
## OF WALTER WINK

2003. *Jesus and Nonviolence: A Third Way*. Minneapolis: Fortress Press.

2002. *The Human Being: Jesus and the Enigma of the Son of the Man*. Minneapolis: Fortress Press.

2000. *Peace Is the Way: Writings on Nonviolence from the Fellowship of Reconciliation* (editor). Maryknoll, NY: Orbis Books.

1999. *Homosexuality and Christian Faith: Questions of Conscience for the Churches* (editor). Minneapolis: Fortress Press.

1998. *The Powers That Be: Theology for a New Millennium*. New York: Doubleday.

1998. *When the Powers Fall: Reconciliation in the Healing of the Nations*. Minneapolis: Fortress Press.

1993. *Cracking the Gnostic Code: The Powers in Gnosticism*. Atlanta: Scholars Press.

1992. *Engaging the Powers: Discernment and Resistance in a World of Domination*. Minneapolis: Fortress Press.

1989. *Transforming Bible Study: A Leader's Guide*, 2nd ed. Nashville: Abingdon Press. [1st ed., 1980.]

1987. *Violence and Nonviolence in South Africa: Jesus' Third Way*. Philadelphia: New Society Publishers.

1986. *Unmasking the Powers: The Invisible Forces That Determine Human Existence*. Minneapolis: Fortress Press.

1984. *Naming the Powers: The Language of Power in the New Testament*. Minneapolis: Fortress Press.

1973. *The Bible in Human Transformation: Towards a New Paradigm for Biblical Study*. Philadelphia: Fortress Press.

1968. *John the Baptist in the Gospel Tradition*. New York: Cambridge University Press. [2001, reprint, Eugene, OR: Wipf and Stock Publishers.]

## Articles

2004. "Beyond Just War and Pacifism: Jesus' Nonviolent Way." Pp. 53–76 in *Contemporary Views on Spirituality and Violence*. Edited by J. Harold Ellens. Vol. 4 of *The Destructive Power of Religion*. Westport, CT: Praeger.

2004. "The Myth of Redemptive Violence." Pp. 265–86 in *Models and Cases of Violence in History*. Edited by J. Harold Ellens. Vol. 3 of *The Destructive Power of Religion*. Westport, CT: Praeger.

Winter 2002. "Can Love Save the World?" *Yes!* no. 20.

October 17, 2001. "Apocalypse Now? Threats to Survival." *Christian Century* 118, no. 28: 16–19.

March 21, 2001. "Guns R Us? Myths of a Gun-Toting People." *Christian Century* 118, no. 10: 21–29.

1997. "The Apocalyptic Beast: The Culture of Violence." Pp. 71–77 in *The Return of the Plague*. Edited by Jose Oscar Beozzo. Maryknoll, NY: Orbis Books.

1996. "Beyond Just War and Pacifism." Pp. 102–21 in *War and Its Discontents: Pacifism and Quietism in the Abrahamic Traditions*. Edited by J. Patout Burns. Washington, DC: Georgetown University Press.

1995. "Stringfellow on the Powers." Pp. 17–30 in *Radical Christian and Exemplary Lawyer: Honoring William Stringfellow*. Edited by Andrew W. McThenia. Grand Rapids, MI: Eerdmans.

November 1, 1995. "The Powers Made Us Do It." *Christian Century* 112: 1017–18.

Summer 1995. "William Stringfellow, Theologian of the Next Millennium: A Review Essay." *Cross Currents* 45, no. 2: 205–16.

May/June 1995. "Principalities and Powers: A Different Worldview." *Church and Society* 85: 18–28.

January/February 1995. "The Kingdom: God's Domination-Free Order." *Weavings* 10: 6–15.

May/June 1994. "Write What You See: An Odyssey." *Fourth R* 7, no. 3.

January 1993. "EcoBible: The Bible and Ecojustice." *Theology Today* 49, no. 4: 465–77.

1992. "Bible Study and Movement for Human Transformation." Pp. 120–32 in *Body and Bible: Interpreting and Experiencing Biblical Narratives*. Edited by Björn Krondorfer. Philadelphia: Trinity Press International.

1992. "Neither Passivity nor Violence: Jesus' Third Way." Pp. 102–25 in *The Love of Enemy and Nonretaliation in the New Testament*. Edited by Willard M. Swartley. Louisville: Westminster/John Knox Press. With response by Richard A. Horsley, 126–32, and counter-response by Walter Wink, 133–36.

Fall 1992. "Demons and DMins: The Church's Response to the Demonic." *Review and Expositor* 89: 503–13.

Spring 1992. "Beyond Just War and Pacifism: Jesus' Nonviolent Way." *Review and Expositor* 89: 197–214.

1991. "Jesus and the Domination System." *Society of Biblical Literature Seminar Papers* 30: 265–86.

1990. "The Hymn of the Cosmic Christ." Pp. 235–45 in *The Conversation Continues: Studies in Paul and John in Honor of J. Louis Martyn*. Edited by Robert T. Fortna and Beverly Roberts Gaventa. Nashville: Abingdon Press.

Spring 1988. "The Education of the Apostles: Mark's View of Human Transformation." *Religious Education* 83: 277–90.

Spring 1979. "The Parable of the Compassionate Samaritan: A Communal Exegesis Approach." *Review and Expositor* 76: 199–217.

Spring 1978. "The 'Elements of the Universe' in Biblical and Scientific Perspective." *Zygon: Journal of Religion and Science* 13, no. 3: 225–48.

# Notes

## Introduction. Engaging Walter Wink

1. Walter Wink's book *John the Baptist in the Gospel Tradition* (Cambridge, MA: Cambridge University Press, 1968) recently returned to print in a paperback edition by Wipf and Stock Publishers.

2. Walter Wink, *The Bible in Human Transformation: Towards a New Paradigm for Biblical Study* (Philadelphia: Fortress Press, 1980).

3. Walter Wink, *Transforming Bible Study: A Leader's Guide* (2nd ed.; Nashville: Abingdon, 1989).

4. Walter Wink, *Naming the Powers: The Language of Power in the New Testament* (Minneapolis: Fortress Press, 1984), 5.

5. Walter Wink, *Engaging the Powers: Discernment and Resistance in a World of Domination* (Minneapolis: Fortress Press, 1992), 10.

6. Wink, *Naming the Powers*, 7.

7. Wink, *Engaging the Powers*, 10.

8. Ibid., 10.

9. Wink, *Naming the Powers*, 10.

10. Ibid., 104–5.

11. Ibid., 100.

12. Walter Wink, *Unmasking the Powers: The Invisible Forces That Determine Human Existence* (Minneapolis: Fortress Press, 1986), 5.

13. Ibid., 7.

## Chapter 1. The New Worldview

1. James H. Olthuis, "On Worldviews," in *Stained Glass: Worldviews and Social Science* (ed. Paul A. Marshall, Sander Griffioen, and Richard J. Mouw; Lanham, Pa.: University Press of America, 1989), 32.

2. There has been a great deal of confusion about the definition of worldviews. In *The Transforming Vision* (ed. Brian J. Walsh and J. Richard Middleton; Downers Grove, Ill.: InterVarsity Press, 1984), the various authors identify the following as "worldviews":

(1) "A Christian worldview" (there is no such thing—Christianity simply adopted the Traditional Worldview of the ancient world); (2) a "culture" (but a culture is simply a part of the social "furniture" unique to every group); (3) "answers who am I" (no, myths do that); (4) "where am I" (yes, worldviews locate heaven and earth and the visible and invisible and provide time and space orientation); (5) "what's wrong" (no, myths do that); (6) "what is the remedy" (ditto). Finally, on p. 177, we get a good definition: "A worldview is a pretheoretical view of the totality of reality."

Not much more helpful is Olthuis, "On Worldviews," in *Stained Glass*. He picks up the last definition from Walsh and Middleton, *The Transforming Vision*, and develops it further: worldviews "are pre-theoretical visions that function much like religious convictions" (p. 9). But Griffioen wonders if there are as many worlds as there are worldviews. This renders the term meaningless. He confuses worldviews with theologies. Others confuse the term with ethics, myth, and faith. I think it essential that we hold to a single, noncomplex definition: worldviews are preconscious presuppositions on which all other cognitive functions are based.

3. Charles H. Kraft concurs that there is no "biblical worldview" (*Christianity with Power* [Ann Arbor: Vine Books, 1989], 103–4).

4. Socrates reveals his roots in dualistic Orphism when he says, "We ought to try to escape from earth to the dwelling of the gods as quickly as we can; and to escape is to become like God" (Theaetetus 176B, Loeb Classical Library).

5. David Ray Griffin, *Religion and Scientific Naturalism* (SUNY Series in Constructive Postmodern Thought, ed. David Ray Griffin; Albany: State University of New York Press, 2000), 14.

6. Steven Weinberg, *The First Three Minutes* (New York: Basic Books, 1977), 154.

7. Jacques Monod, *Chance and Necessity* (New York: Vintage Books, 1972), 173.

8. Richard Dawkins, cited by Nicolas Wade, "Double Helixes, Chickens and Eggs," *New York Times Magazine*, January 29, 1995, 20. Thanks to David Ray Griffin for the substance of this paragraph (*The Reenchantment of Science* [SUNY Series in Constructive Postmodern Thought, ed. David Ray Griffin; Albany: State University of New York Press, 1988]).

9. "Scientism" is defined by physicist Gerald Holton as "the overenthusiastic importation of 'scientific' models into nonscientific fields" ("The Antiscience Problem," *Skeptical Inquirer* 18 [Spring 1994]: 264). David Steindl-Rast comments, "The clashes of the past were never between science and dogma . . . but between scientism and dogmatism. Scientism, which restricts man's whole worldview to the limited perspective of science, and dogmatism, which makes the world image of a certain period in history an absolute—these two must clash" ("Views of the Cosmos," *Parabola* 2 [1977]: 13). I have especially benefited from David Ray Griffin's brilliant critique of scientism in a number of his books, including *Religion and Scientific Naturalism*; *Parapsychology, Philosophy, and Spirituality: A Postmodern Exploration* (Albany: State University of New York Press, 1996; *Reenchantment without Supernaturalism: A Process Philosophy* (Ithaca: Cornell University Press, 2000); and *The Reenchantment of Science*.

10. Bruce Bradshaw, *Bridging the Gap* (Monrovia, Calif.: MARC, 1993), 57.

11. Mary Coelho, lecture at Kirkridge Retreat Center, Bangor, Pa.

12. Guy Murchie, *The Seven Mysteries of Life* (Boston: Houghton Mifflin, 1978), 320.

13. Erwin Schrödinger, cited by Menos Kafatos and Robert Nadeau, *The Conscious Universe: Part and Whole in Modern Physical Theory* (New York: Springer Verlag, 1990), 188.

14. "Science and Secrecy," *New York Times Book Review*, October 2, 1994.

15. Larry Dossey, *Recovering the Soul* (New York: Bantam Books, 1989), 180.

16. Personal correspondence.

17. Morris Berman, *The Reenchantment of the World* (Toronto: Bantam Books, 1984); Mary Evelyn Tucker and John A. Grim, eds., *Worldviews and Ecology* (Maryknoll, N.Y.: Orbis Books, 1994).

18. Fritjof Capra, *The Web of Life* (New York: Doubleday, 1996), 30.

19. Brian Swimme and Thomas Berry, *The Universe Story* (HarperSanFrancisco, 1992), 132–34, 242.

## Chapter 2. Social Science, Ethics, and the Powers

1. Chapter 6 in this volume.

2. Walter Wink, *Naming the Powers: The Language of Power in the New Testament* (Minneapolis: Fortress Press, 1984), 102.

3. Ibid, 92f.

4. Of course this is an oversimplification: physics itself is now many-layered, and atoms as understood by chemists are no longer "atoms" in the philosophical sense of being the most basic constituents of matter.

5. My account here is from Ian G. Barbour, *Issues in Science and Religion* (New York: Harper & Row, 1966), 324–27. See Hans Driesch, *Science and Philosophy of the Organism* (2nd ed.; London: G. Allen & Unwin, 1930).

6. The most helpful of these, as well as one of the earliest analyses, is Donald T. Campbell, "'Downward Causation' in Hierarchically Organised Biological Systems," in *Studies in the Philosophy of Biology: Reduction and Related Problems* (ed. F. J. Ayala and T. Dobzhansky; Berkeley: University of California Press, 1974), 179–86.

7. For an overview of the problem and an approach to its solution, see Nancey Murphy, "Supervenience and the Downward Efficacy of the Mental: A Nonreductive Physicalist Account of Human Action," in *Neuroscience and the Person: Scientific Perspectives on Divine Action* (ed. Robert J. Russell et al.; Vatican City State and Berkeley, Calif.: Vatican Observatory and Center for Theology and the Natural Sciences, 1999), 147–64.

8. Walter Wink, *Unmasking the Powers: The Invisible Forces That Determine Human Existence* (Minneapolis: Fortress Press, 1986), 143.

9. Ibid., 142.

10. Ibid., 143; quoting Clement of Alexandria.

11. See, for example, Edward O. Wilson, *Consilience: The Unity of Knowledge* (New York: Knopf, 1998).

12. Wink, *Unmasking the Powers*, 158–59.

13. Ibid., 159.

14. Nancey Murphy and George F. R. Ellis, *On the Moral Nature of the Universe: Theology, Cosmology, and Ethics* (Minneapolis: Fortress Press, 1996).

15. James O'Toole, *The Executive's Compass: Business and the Good Society* (New York: Oxford University Press, 1993), 35–36.

16. Reinhold Niebuhr, *Moral Man and Immoral Society* (New York: Scribner's, 1932).

17. John Milbank, *Theology and Social Theory* (Cambridge: Basil Blackwell, 1990), 1, 3.

18. Walter Wink, *Engaging the Powers: Discernment and Resistance in a World of Domination* (Minneapolis: Fortress Press, 1992).

19. Milbank, *Theology and Social Theory*, 4.

20. Wink, *Engaging the Powers*, ch. 2.

21. For a complementary view, see the account of the development of the modern sense of nature in Louis Dupré, *Passage to Modernity* (New Haven: Yale University Press, 1993).

22. For a critique of the association of culture with the artificial, over against the natural, see Bruno Latour, *We Have Never Been Modern* (trans. Catherine Porter; Cambridge, MA: Harvard University Press, 1993).

23. Milbank, *Theology and Social Theory*, 12. The following parenthetical page references are to this source.

24. Alasdair MacIntyre, *After Virtue* (2nd ed.; Notre Dame, IN.: University of Notre Dame Press, 1984).

## Chapter 3. Principalities and Powers

1. John Howard Yoder, *The Politics of Jesus: Vicit Agnus Noster* (Grand Rapids, Mich.: Eerdmans, 1972).

2. Hendrikus Berkhof, *Christ and the Powers* (Scottdale, Pa.: Herald Press, 1962).

3. Yoder, *Politics of Jesus*, 145.

4. My acquaintance with Wink's work comes through his well-known trilogy on the Powers, and also from his summary statement, *The Powers That Be: Theology for a New Millennium* (New York: Doubleday, 1998).

5. This summary is taken especially from Walter Wink, *Engaging the Powers: Discernment and Resistance in a World of Domination* (Minneapolis: Fortress Press, 1992).

6. Ernest Becker, *The Birth and Death of Meaning: An Interdisciplinary Perspective on the Problem of Man* (New York: Free Press, 1971); *The Denial of Death* (New York: Free Press, 1973); and *Escape from Evil* (New York: Free Press, 1975).

7. It is, of course, an anthropomorphism to speak of an evolutionary process such as natural selection as having "endowed" anything at all to any species, since this imputes volition to an impersonal process. Speaking from the strictly social-scientific point of view, therefore, nothing more is implied in the use of this language than the tautology that if a species has survived, it must possess the means of having survived. Yet it is difficult to speak of this in the absence of language that imputes some elements of volition and personality to that which is conceived as an impersonal process. The fact that it is so difficult to speak of these things without anthropomorphic and reifying terms is a significant point of connection for dialogue between theology and the sciences, but that is far beyond the scope of this essay.

8. Each of these theories of human psychological motivation has a certain common-sense plausibility to it. We do have times in our lives when we feel sexual and aggressive urges welling up from within. We are aware of being moved to accumulate or to imitate those whom we envy or respect. We know how strongly the desire for power can be as a motivating force. We could add here other current theories of human motivation, such as self-esteem maintenance or the sociometric hypothesis. What places the theory of generative death on a different level of theorizing, however, is its ability to *contain* the intuitive truth of each of these other theories as limiting cases, approximately valid under specific conditions, within the larger framework of generative death anxiety.

9. Further exploration of this treatment of mental health, with special emphasis on human spirituality, can be found in Daniel Liechty, *Transference and Transcendence: Ernest Becker's Contribution to Psychotherapy* (Northvale, N.J.: Jason Aronson, 1995). See also Daniel Liechty, "Reaction to Mortality: An Interdisciplinary Organizing Principle for the Human Sciences," *Zygon: Journal of Religion and Science* 33, no. 1 (March 1998): 45–58.

10. Becker, *Escape from Evil*, 63ff.

11. This is one of the enduring insights of those sociologists and social theorists associated with the concept of the *social construction of reality*, a tradition in which Becker firmly stands for his own work. See here especially Karl Mannheim, *Ideology and Utopia: An Introduction to the Sociology of Knowledge* (New York: Harcourt, Brace & World, 1953); Peter Berger and Thomas Luckmann, *The Social Construction of Reality: A Treatise on the Sociology of Knowledge* (New York: Anchor/Doubleday, 1967); Burkart Holzner, *Reality*

*Construction in Society* (Cambridge, MA: Schenkman Publishing Company, 1967); John Searle, *The Construction of Social Reality* (New York: Free Press, 1995).

12. This work, known as Terror Management Theory in the specialized literature, was founded by social psychologists Jeff Greenberg (University of Arizona), Tom Pyszczynski (University of Colorado), and Sheldon Solomon (Skidmore College). It has now extended to their students and their students' students. Results have been tested and confirmed across the age and socioeconomic spectra and in at least four countries (United States, Canada, Germany, and Israel). The bibliography of publications reporting on this work runs well over one hundred items and is growing. I here cite only the most easily accessible summary material. Jeff Greenberg, Tom Pyszczynski, and Sheldon Solomon, "The Causes and Consequences of a Need for Self-Esteem: A Terror Management Theory," in *Public and Private Self* (ed. Roy F. Baumeister; New York: Springer Verlag, 1986), 189–207; A. Rosenblatt et al., "Evidence for Terror Management Theory I: The Effects of Mortality Salience on Reactions to Those Who Violate or Uphold Cultural Values," *Journal of Personality and Social Psychology* 57 (1989): 681–90; Jeff Greenberg et al., "Evidence for Terror Management Theory II: The Effects of Mortality Salience on Reactions to Those Who Threaten or Bolster the Cultural Worldview," *Journal of Personality and Social Psychology* 58 (1990): 308–18; Sheldon Solomon et al., "A Terror Management Theory of Social Behavior: The Psychological Functions of Self-Esteem and Cultural Worldviews," in *Advances in Experimental Social Psychology*, vol. 24 (ed. M. Zanna; San Diego: Academic Press, 1991), 93–159; Sheldon Solomon et al., "Tales from the Crypt: On the Role of Death in Life," *Zygon: Journal of Religion and Science* 33, no. 1 (March 1998): 9–44; Jeff Greenberg et al., "Why Do People Need Self-Esteem? Converging Evidence That Self-Esteem Serves an Anxiety-Buffering Function," in *The Self in Social Psychology* (ed. Roy F. Baumeister; Philadelphia: Taylor and Francis, 1999), 105–18.

13. Becker, *Escape from Evil*, 96.

14. See here, especially, Sam Keen, *Faces of the Enemy: The Psychology of Enmity* (San Francisco: Harper & Row, 1986); Richard Stivers, *Evil in Modern Myth and Ritual* (Athens: University of Georgia Press, 1982); Paul Carus, *The History of the Devil and the Idea of Evil from the Earliest Times to the Present Day* (New York: Bell, 1969); Jeffrey Burton Russell, *The Devil: Perceptions of Evil from Antiquity to Primitive Christianity* (Ithaca: Cornell University Press, 1987); Jeffrey Burton Russell, *Prince of Darkness: Radical Evil and the Power of Good in History* (Ithaca: Cornell University Press, 1992).

15. As Roger Shattuck demonstrates in his masterly book, *Forbidden Knowledge: From Prometheus to Pornography* (New York: St. Martin's, 1996), 227–99, even the Marquis de Sade was totally dependent on a firmly held social distinction of virtue and sin for his sexual criminality to have any effective shock value. In the absence of such social distinction, all of his imagined adventures just appear pathetically exhausting.

16. Still an extremely useful and very informative collection are the essays gathered by Nevitt Sanford and Craig Comstock, *Sanctions for Evil: Sources for Social Destructiveness* (Boston: Beacon, 1971). Although published thirty years ago, many of these essays are still fresh and have been receiving subsequent validation through further research. Especially to the point being made here is the chapter by Troy Duster, "Conditions for a Guilt-Free Massacre," 25–36.

17. Becker, *Escape from Evil*, 150, 153.

18. There are significant differences, however. At the point in Wink's phenomenology where one would expect him to turn from observation to established social-scientific theory to interpret the data, he turns instead to exegesis of mythology. Likewise, when

seeking to explicate the real observation about spiraling violence, Wink turns not to established social-scientific theory but to further literary musings of the Girardian type. It is clear that Wink intends this move from social phenomenology to literature to be a convincing method of driving his point home more completely, but it can only leave a social scientist confusedly scratching his or her brow.

19. An extremely cogent thesis concerning the human fascination with weapons and war is found in Barbara Ehrenreich, *Blood Rites: Origins and History of the Passions of War* (New York: Metropolitan Books/Henry Holt, 1997). Ehrenreich challenges the traditional picture of protohumans as conquering hunters, logically suggesting that, given our physical limitations, protohumans were much more likely to have been a prey species until relatively very recently in our history. It was only as the brain developed to the point that protohumans were able to invent weapons (a few-score thousand years ago) that the transition was made from prey to predator. Ehrenreich suggests that our almost magical attraction to weaponry is rooted in this transition. This thesis complements nicely the theory of generative death anxiety, pointing toward another aspect of significant mental shifting that took place relatively recently in the species history due to the developing computational power of the human brain.

20. Dave Grossman, *On Killing: The Psychological Cost of Learning to Kill in War and Society* (Boston: Little, Brown, 1995).

21. Peter L. Berger, *Pyramids of Sacrifice: Political Ethics and Social Change* (New York: Anchor/Doubleday, 1976).

22. One thinks here of Antonio Gramsci's analysis of what he called the "hegemony of common sense" in society. Antonio Gramsci, *The Modern Prince and Other Writings* (New York: International Publishers, 1957).

23. This concept of the inner gnawing hunger as "lack of Being" I picked up from David Loy, *Lack and Transcendence: The Problem of Death and Life in Psychotherapy, Existentialism and Buddhism* (Atlantic Highland, N.J.: Humanities Press, 1996).

24. In his controlled group work with incarcerated violent criminals, social theorist C. Fred Alford reports this same language of inner gnawing and an inchoate feeling of dread on the part of subjects, who would strike out toward others in violent acts to mask and quell this inner gnawing. See C. Fred Alford, *What Evil Means to Us* (Ithaca: Cornell University Press, 1997).

25. Wink, *Powers That Be*, 112ff.

## Chapter 4. A Pacifist Critique of the Modern Worldview

1. Walter Wink, *The Bible in Human Transformation: Towards a New Paradigm for Biblical Study* (Philadelphia: Fortress Press, 1973).

2. John Howard Yoder, *The Politics of Jesus* (Grand Rapids, Mich.: Eerdmans, 1972).

3. Walter Wink, *Naming the Powers: The Language of Power in the New Testament* (Minneapolis: Fortress Press, 1984).

4. Walter Wink, *Unmasking the Powers: The Invisible Forces That Determine Human Existence* (Minneapolis: Fortress Press, 1986).

5. Walter Wink, *Engaging the Powers: Discernment and Resistance in a World of Domination* (Minneapolis: Fortress Press, 1992).

6. James C. Scott, *Seeing Like a State: How Certain Schemes to Improve the Human Condition Have Failed* (New Haven: Yale University Press, 1998), 5.

7. Ibid., 13.

8. Ibid., 15.

9. Ibid., 20.

10. Ibid., 21.

11. Wink, *Engaging the Powers*, 227. See also Walter Wink, "Can Love Save the World?" *Yes!* no. 20 (Winter 2002).

12. Albert Borgmann, *Crossing the Postmodern Divide* (Chicago: University of Chicago Press, 1991), 21–22.

13. Ibid., 22–23.

14. Richard Tarnas, *The Passion of the Western Mind: Understanding the Ideas That Have Shaped Our World View* (Boston: Ballantine Books, 1990), 285.

15. Ibid., 286.

16. Ibid., 287.

17. Ibid., 288–89.

18. Andrew Bard Schmookler, *The Parable of the Tribes: The Problem of Power in Social Evolution* (Berkeley: University of California Press, 1984), 17–18.

19. David Abram, *The Spell of the Sensuous: Perception and Language in the More-Than-Human World* (New York: Vintage Books, 1996).

20. Ibid., 131.

21. Ibid., 138–39.

22. Ibid., 31.

23. Kevin Bradt, *Story as a Way of Knowing* (Kansas City, MO: Sheed & Ward, 1997), 74.

24. Abram, *Spell of the Sensuous*, 260.

25. Ibid., 94.

26. Robert Hughes, *The Fatal Shore: The Epic of Australia's Founding* (New York: Knopf, 1987), 331–32.

27. Borgmann, *Crossing the Postmodern Divide*, 23.

28. Ibid., 27–28.

29. Ibid., 31. See also David Haward Bain, *Empire Express: Building the First Transcontinental Railroad* (New York: Viking, 1999).

30. Borgmann, *Crossing the Postmodern Divide*, 32.

31. Ibid., 34.

32. Ibid.

33. Stephen Toulmin, *Cosmopolis: The Hidden Agenda of Modernity* (New York: Free Press, 1990), 20.

34. Ibid., 104–5.

35. Scott, *Seeing Like a State*, 377.

36. Ibid., 93.

37. Ibid., 305–6.

38. Ibid., 291–92.

39. Quoted in ibid., 340.

40. Gabriel Horn, *Contemplations of a Primal Mind* (Novato, Calif.: New World Library, 1996), 28.

41. Ibid., 28–29.

42. Wendell Berry, *Life Is a Miracle: An Essay against Modern Superstition* (Washington, DC: Counterpoint, 2000), 136.

43. Ibid., 137–38.

44. Borgmann, *Crossing the Postmodern Divide*, 110–47.

45. Tarnas, *Passion of the Western Mind*, 432.

46. Martin Buber, *I and Thou* (New York: Scribner's, 1970), 143.

47. Gordon D. Kaufman, *In Face of Mystery: A Constructive Theology* (Cambridge, MA: Harvard University Press, 1993), 338–39.

## Chapter 5. Providence and the Powers

1. Nicolai Berdyaev, *Slavery and Freedom* (New York: Scribner's, 1944), 88.

2. Personal communication from Dale Clem.

3. The exception was the Epicureans, who rejected the notion of providence because the world was created by chance occurrences of passing atoms and not by a rational or divine power; providence destroys freedom and moral self-determinism; and most damaging of all, providence is negated by the way the good suffer evil while the wicked prosper (Jerome H. Neyrey, "The Form and Background of the Polemic in 2 Peter," *JBL* 99 [1980]: 407–31).

4. A Roman governor once asked Rabbi Akiba why God did not maintain the poor if God loved them (*B.T. Baba Bathra* 10a). This was a completely reasonable question, given Roman assumptions.

5. J. Rufus Fears, "The Theology of Victory at Rome: Approaches and Problems," *ANRW*, part 2, 17.2 (ed. H. Temporini and W. Haase; Berlin, 1981), 752. The Roman appropriation of victory from the Greeks was a datable event (296–293 B.C.E.), reflecting a dawning awareness of its destiny as an expansive empire. Victory is a god for winners. Fears traces the origin of the religious conception (might = right = divine) to the myth of the victory of Marduk over Tiamat (807).

6. M. P. Charlesworth, "Providentia and Aeternitas," *HTR* 29 (1936): 107–32. No Christian has ever outdone the pagan Aelius Aristides in his praise of providence. Living in the decline of paganism around 178 C.E. in Smyrna, he combined all the features of the most devout pietist: a totally individualistic approach to religion, complete preoccupation with his own healing, a terrific egoism muted by genuine dependence on and gratitude to the gods, and a heap of tales of synchronous events. See, in addition, Campbell Bonner, "Religious Feeling in Later Paganism," *HTR* 30 (1937): 119–40; and J. Behm and E. Würthwein, "προνοέω, πρόνοια," in Gerhard Kittel, ed., *Theological Dictionary of the New Testament* (Grand Rapids, Mich.: Eerdmans, 1967), 4:1009–17.

7. Middle Platonist philosophy was not so crass. Pseudo-Plutarch and Nemesius identified three levels of providential guidance: Primary Providence, which begets Fate and therefore somehow includes Fate; Secondary Providence, which is begotten together with Fate; and Tertiary Providence, which is begotten later than Fate and therefore is contained within Fate in the same way that free will and chance are contained within it. The first belongs to the highest gods, the second to the "young gods," the third to the daemons (who are not necessarily evil). Only the highest Providence is free from Fate. In the Nag Hammadi *Origin of the World* 109:22–25, daemonic Fate comes close to what I am calling negative providence, but remains at the level of "general" providence and is not clearly associated with evil. See Michael A. Williams, "Higher Providence, Lower Providences and Fate in Gnosticism and Middle Platonism," in *Neoplatonism and Gnosticism* (ed. Richard T. Wallis and Jay Bregman; Studies in Neoplatonism: Ancient and Modern 6; New York: International Society for Neoplatonic Studies/SUNY Press, 1991), 481–505; and Michael A. Williams, *The Immovable Race* (Leiden: E. J. Brill, 1985), 134–37, 156–57. There is one text that does depict the lower providence in a decidedly negative light, however—Pap. Ber. 125:10—126:16: "Tread down their [the Powers'] (alleged) 'providence' (*pronoia*), smash their yoke and raise up what is mine."

8. Tertullus, the Jewish orator who made a representation against Paul before Felix, the Roman governor of Judea, is depicted by Luke as perfectly conforming to the Roman notion of providence: "Your Excellency," he says to the leader of the Roman occupying power, "because of you we have long enjoyed peace, and reforms have been made for this people because of your providence [*pronoias*]. We welcome this in every way" (Acts 24:2).

9. J. Rufus Fears, "The Cult of Virtues and Roman Imperial Ideology," *ANRW*, part 2, 17.2 (ed. H. Temporini and W. Haase; Berlin, 1981), 827–948; and Harold Mattingly, "The Roman 'Virtues,'" *HTR* 30 (1937): 106–11. Jacques Monod hawks this ancient belief, under the guise of pure science, when he cites as the compelling reason for abandoning all religions for science, "its prodigious power of performance." "Modern societies are built upon science. They owe it their wealth, the power, and the certitude that tomorrow far greater wealth and power still will be ours if we so wish" (*Chance and Necessity* [New York: Alfred Knopf, 1971], 170).

10. Cited in *Frying Pan*, November 1980, 25.

11. Rudolf Steiner, *The Mission of the Individual Folk Souls* (London: Rudolf Steiner Press, [1910] 1970), 76.

12. George Gilder, *Wealth and Poverty* (New York: Basic Books, 1980), cited by Roger Starr, "A Guide to Capitalism," *New York Times Book Review*, February 1, 1981, 10.

13. The understanding of providence here is the same whether it is ascribed to Paul or to Luke.

14. Suetonius, *Nero* 56.

15. H. G. Baynes, *Germany Possessed* (London: Jonathan Cape, 1941), 227.

16. Eberhard Bethge, *Dietrich Bonhoeffer* (New York: Harper & Row, 1985), 685.

17. Walter C. Langer, *The Mind of Adolf Hitler: The Secret Wartime Report* (New York: Basic Books, 1972), 34.

18. Carl G. Jung, *Mysterium Coniunctionis* (Collected Works 14; Princeton: Princeton University Press, 1963), 464. See also the excellent study by Robert Aziz, *C. G. Jung's Psychology of Religion and Synchronicity* (Albany: State University of New York Press, 1990).

19. Carl G. Jung, *Psychology and Religion: West and East* (Collected Works 11; Princeton: Princeton University Press, 1958), 592. Coincidence is purely statistical, purely chance. Usually it has no special significance and is soon forgotten. Most improbable coincidences likely result from play of random events. The very nature of randomness assures that combing random data will yield some pattern (Bruce Martin, "Coincidences: Remarkable or Random?" *Skeptical Inquirer* 22 [September/October 1998]: 23–27; and John Allen Paulos, "Coincidences," *Skeptical Inquirer* 15 [Summer 1991]: 382–84). An example is *The Bible Code* by Michael Drosnin (New York: Simon & Schuster, 1997). Synchronicity, on the other hand, is not only improbable but meaningful. Those to whom it happens seldom forget the experience. For them it holds superordinate meaningfulness.

20. Jung, *Psychology and Religion: West and East*, 526. Jung distinguishes three types of synchronous events: (1) the coincidence of a psychic state in the observer with a simultaneous, objective, external event that corresponds to the psychic state or content (the examples below of those whose torture stopped the instant they prayed); (2) the coincidence of a psychic state with a corresponding, more or less simultaneous, external event taking place outside the observer's field of perception, that is, at a distance, and only verifiable afterward (the example below of the hot pads); (3) the coincidence of a psychic state with a corresponding not-yet-existent future event that is distant in time and can only be verified afterward (as in cases in which a dream anticipates a later event). To these we

should add the obverse of (3): (4) the coincidence of an event with a corresponding not-yet-existent future psychic state that is distant in time (as in the disciples' later recognition of the meaningfulness of the otherwise meaning-destructive crucifixion of Jesus).

21. Carl G. Jung, "Synchronicity: An Acausal Connecting Principle," in *The Structure and Dynamics of the Psyche* (Collected Works 8; Princeton: Princeton University Press, 1969), 501–2.

22. Carl G. Jung, *The Symbolic Life* (Collected Works 18; Princeton: Princeton University Press, 1950), 500.

23. George Riggan, in conversation.

24. I made an immediate record of this event and of that which follows the same day they occurred.

25. The most extensive and powerful experience of synchronicity that has occurred to me took place when I was nineteen. It is too long to detail here. It has been published in "Write What You See," *The Fourth R* 7 (May/June 1994): 3–9.

26. Jean Shinoda Bolen, *The Tao of Psychology: Synchronicity and the Self* (San Francisco: Harper & Row, 1979), 7.

27. Bill Wylie Kellermann, *Seasons of Faith and Conscience* (Maryknoll, N.Y.: Orbis Books, 1991), xix–xxiii. Similar providential aid in opposing the Powers is recounted by Dan Delany, "A Family Does Time for Peace," *Catholic Agitator*, June 1981, 4; Jim Douglass, *Lightning East to West* (Portland, Ore.: Sunburst Press, 1980), 9–10; Phil Berrigan and Elizabeth McAlister, *The Time's Discipline* (Baltimore: Fortkamp, 1989), 115–17.

28. Rhea Miller, "Canticle to Christ," *Ground Zero*, Spring 1992, 10–11.

29. Joyce Hollyday, "Tested in the Desert," *Sojourners*, June 1991, 19.

30. Viktor E. Frankl, *Man's Search for Meaning* (Boston: Beacon, 1963), 39–40.

31. Aleksandr I. Solzhenitsyn, *The Gulag Archipelago* (New York: Harper & Row, 1978), 1:484.

32. Mihajlo Mihajlov, "Mystical Experience of the Labor Camps," *Kontinent* 2 (New York: Doubleday, 1977), 105; cited by Carl Scovil, "Christian Responses to the Nazi State in Germany," *Katallagete*, Spring 1978, 39.

33. The NRSV fails to see that Jesus is addressing the *angel* of Jerusalem and turns the sentence into a statement *about* it rather than an address *to* it.

34. See the brilliant analysis of the structure of social change movements by Bill Moyer in *Doing Democracy* (Gabriola Island, Canada: New Society Press, 2001).

35. Synchronous events cannot be caused or manipulated, but they can be evoked by right-brain exercises such as painting, writing poetry, or dancing; or by the modern equivalent of the casting of lots (see Acts 1:26), in which people draw randomly from a basket the name of a partner who will do a play reading or share a lunchtime discussion of a given topic together. In the case of drawing lots, part of the assignment is to ask what is the meaningful coincidence involved in the "choice" of this dramatic role or partner.

The *I Ching* and tarot cards represent more formalized methods of divination. Tarot is unfortunately associated with gypsies and fortune-tellers, and both are subject to misuse: letting the method make one's decision rather than, like Paul, reserving the responsibility for choosing regardless of the indications; trivialization of the process by using it when there is little affect and hence too inadequate an inner preparation and concentratedness to constellate psychic energy; the submersion of the ego and abandonment to unconscious, psychoid factors, with a concomitant passivity and limpness of the will; excessive and superstitious reliance on the unconscious to the exclusion of reason and common sense. With these cautions in mind, however, these methods can be of value.

36. Goethe, cited without reference by Marion Woodman, *The Pregnant Virgin* (Toronto: Innercity Books, 1985), 72.

## Chapter 6. Traditions, Practices, and the Powers

1. René Descartes, *Meditations on First Philosophy*, in vol. 2 of *The Philosophical Writings of Descartes* (trans. John Cottingham, Robert Stoothoff, and Dugald Murdoch; Cambridge: Cambridge University Press, 1985),12.

2. René Descartes, *Discourse on Method*, in vol. 1 of *The Philosophical Writings of Descartes* (trans. John Cottingham, Robert Stoothoff, and Dugald Murdoch; Cambridge: Cambridge University Press, 1984)116.

3. Alasdair MacIntyre, *After Virtue* (2nd ed.; Notre Dame, Ind.: University of Notre Dame Press, 1984).

4. Thomas Kuhn, *The Structure of Scientific Revolutions* (2nd ed.; Chicago: University of Chicago Press, 1970).

5. Alasdair MacIntyre, "Epistemological Crises, Dramatic Narrative, and the Philosophy of Science," *Paradigms and Revolutions* (ed. Gary Gutting; Notre Dame, Ind.: University of Notre Dame Press, 1980), 54–74 (quotation p. 69). First published in 1977.

6. Alasdair MacIntyre, *Whose Justice? Which Rationality?* (Notre Dame, IN: University of Notre Dame Press, 1988).

7. Ibid., 166–67.

8. Alasdair MacIntyre, *Three Rival Versions of Moral Enquiry: Encyclopaedia, Genealogy, and Tradition* (Notre Dame, Ind.: University of Notre Dame Press, 1990).

9. I would add that it has been criticized as effectively but more constructively by recent Anglo-American philosophers.

10. MacIntyre, *After Virtue*, 187.

11. See MacIntyre, *Three Rival Versions*, 215.

12. James Wm. McClendon Jr., *Ethics: Systematic Theology, Volume 1* (Nashville, TN: Abingdon, 1986; rev. ed. 2002), 173.

13. John Howard Yoder, *The Politics of Jesus* (rev. ed.; Grand Rapids, Mich.: Eerdmans, 1994).

14. Walter Wink, *Naming the Powers: The Language of Power in the New Testament* (Minneapolis: Fortress Press, 1984).

15. McClendon, *Ethics*, 174.

16. Ibid., 176.

17. See Walter Wink, *Engaging the Powers: Discernment and Resistance in a World of Domination* (Minneapolis: Fortress Press, 1992).

18. At this point I am tempted to digress and propose an account of the spiritual aspect of the Powers not as their interiority but in terms of "supervenient" levels of description. See Nancey Murphy, "Nonreductive Physicalism: Philosophical Issues," in *Whatever Happened to the Soul? Scientific and Theological Portraits of Human Nature* (ed. Warren S. Brown, Nancey Murphy, and H. Newton Malony; Minneapolis: Fortress Press, 1998), 127–48. I believe such an account would be more congenial to contemporary understandings of individual human "interiority" and also to McClendon's "three-stranded" analysis of Christian ethics. But this would not vitiate the points of agreement among Wink, McClendon, and myself on the important role of fallen social structures in human life. That is, while the concept of the "within of things" does not make sense to me when applied to nonconscious beings, Wink's emphasis on the "within" of an organization is helpful. It is one way of emphasizing the fact that social groups have "personalities" and "moral

characters" over and above those of the individuals who make them up. So, for example, an academic institution has a character that may survive the total replacement, over time, of its administration, faculty, staff, and students. And, as Wink rightly points out, this institutional character cannot be reduced to the written rules of the institution.

19. Wink, *Engaging the Powers*, ch. 9.

20. For a more detailed account of these practices, see Nancey Murphy, *Theology in the Age of Scientific Reasoning* (Ithaca: Cornell University Press, 1990), ch. 5.

21. Wink, *Engaging the Powers*, ch. 16.

22. John Howard Yoder, *Body Politics: Five Practices of the Christian Community before the Watching World* (Scottdale, Pa.: Herald Press, 1992), ch. 5.

23. "Two Letters by Pilgram Marpeck," *Mennonite Quarterly Review* 32 (July 1958): 198.

24. Ibid., 199.

25. MacIntyre has been criticized for providing an "agonistic" account of human rationality by John Milbank in *Theology and Social Theory: Beyond Secular Reason* (Oxford: Basil Blackwell, 1990).

26. I owe many of the insights in this section to conversations with Prof. Christian Early.

27. I began working on the ideas in this chapter when I was invited to a conference on Mennonite higher education, held at the Canadian Mennonite Bible College in Winnipeg. I thank the organizers for that invitation. My remarks were published as Nancey Murphy, "A Theology of Education," in *Mennonite Education in a Post-Christian World* (ed. Harry Huebner; Winnipeg: CMBC Publications, 1998).

## CHAPTER 7. JESUS CHRIST: VICTOR OVER EVIL

1. See my earlier contributions, Willard M. Swartley, "The Christian and the Payment of Taxes Used for War" (paper distributed by Mennonite Board of Congregational Ministries and used in New Call to Peacemaking Packet, 1980), translated by Wolfgang Krauß into German and published as "Die Steuerfrage im Neuen Testament," in *Was Gehört dem Kaiser: Das Problem der Kriegssteuern* (ed. W. Krauß; Weisenheim am Berg: Agape-Verlag, 1984), 66–82. See also Willard M. Swartley and Thomas N. Finger, "Bondage and Deliverance: Biblical and Theological Perspectives," in *Essays on Spiritual Bondage and Deliverance* (ed. Willard Swartley; Occasional Papers 11; Elkhart: Institute of Mennonite Studies, 1988), 10–38.

2. Thomas McAlpine, *Facing the Powers: What Are the Options?* (Monrovia, Calif.: MARC, 1991).

3. McAlpine's description of this category is too restrictive. It should include a broader use of exorcism in the ministry of the church. Peter Wagner's theory and strategy regarding territorial powers are only one emphasis, and a disputed one among scholars and practitioners of deliverance ministry. See Clinton Arnold, *Crucial Questions about Spiritual Warfare* (Grand Rapids, Mich.: Baker Books, 1997); and Clinton Arnold, *Powers of Darkness: A Study in Principalities and Powers in Paul* (Grand Rapids, Mich.: Zondervan, 1992). See also George McClain, *Claiming All Things for God* (Nashville: Abingdon, 1998), for ritual use of exorcism to free social and political systemic power from demonic control.

4. Luke's gospel emphasizes this latter point by announcing that Jesus' coming is "peace on earth, goodwill toward humanity" (see 2:14). Jesus' public ministry is consummated with the antiphonal response from Jesus' disciples, "Peace in heaven, and glory in the highest"

(19:38). Luke uses the word "peace" (*eirene*) fourteen times, thus showing special effort to connect the establishment of God's shalom with "healing all those who were oppressed" (Acts 10:38).

5. Walter Wink, *Engaging the Powers: Discernment and Resistance in a World of Domination* (Minneapolis: Fortress Press, 1992), 134.

6. Kathleen M. Fischer and Urban C. von Wahlde, "The Miracles of Mark 4:35–5:43: Their Meaning and Function in the Gospel Framework," *BTB* 11 (1981): 15. The most thorough treatment of Jesus' combat against Satan in the Gospels is to be found in James B. Kallas's works: *The Significance of the Synoptic Miracles* (Greenwich, CT: Seabury, 1961); *Jesus and the Power of Satan* (Philadelphia: Westminster, 1968); and *The Real Satan* (Minneapolis: Augsburg, 1975). Gregory A. Boyd, *God at War: The Bible and Spiritual Conflict* (Downers Grove, Ill.: InterVarsity Press, 1997), extends Kallas's work and includes more recent literature, such as Graham Twelftree's several contributions.

7. See the many essays in Willard M. Swartley, ed., *The Love of Enemy and Nonretaliation in the New Testament* (Louisville: Westminster John Knox, 1992).

8. See my treatment and development of this claim in Willard M. Swartley, *Israel's Scripture Traditions and the Synoptic Gospels: Story Shaping Story* (Peabody, MA: Hendrickson Publishers, 1994), 134–45.

9. See Susan Garrett, *The Demise of the Devil: Magic and the Demonic in Luke-Acts* (Minneapolis: Augsburg Fortress, 1989), for a detailed study of the gospel's encounter with magic and the demonic in Luke-Acts. See also her treatment of Satan's work in many dimensions, in Mark, in *The Temptations of Jesus in Mark's Gospel* (Grand Rapids, Mich.: Eerdmans, 1998).

10. Wink has told me of his experience of witnessing a psychotherapist's use of an Episcopal exorcistic liturgy to rid a counselee (with whom she had worked for years without success) of the grip of evil upon her life. Further, his testimony about that experience is one of positive results: a change occurred in the woman that enabled the counselor to proceed quite rapidly toward healing in the woman's life. See also Wink's discussion of Satan and evil spirits in *Unmasking the Powers: The Invisible Forces That Determine Human Existence* (Minneapolis: Fortress Press, 1986), 22–68. His seven points of guidance are on pp. 58–64, and his summary paragraph on p. 68 seeks to integrate personal and collective structural possession. I would prefer use of the terms "oppression" and "obsession." I agree that the personal and systemic feed each other.

11. Walter Wink, *When the Powers Fall: Reconciliation in the Healing of the Nations* (Minneapolis: Fortress Press, 1998), 24.

12. Walter Wink, *The Powers That Be: Theology for a New Millennium* (Doubleday, 1998), 122–27.

13. See Willard M. Swartley, ed., *Violence Renounced: Rene Girard, Biblical Studies and Peacemaking* (Telford: Pandora; Scottdale, Pa.: Herald Press, 2000).

14. Erick Dinkler, "Eirene—The Early Christian Concept of Peace," in *The Meaning of Peace* (ed. Perry B. Yoder and Willard M. Swartley; rev. ed.; Elkhart, Ind.: Institute of Mennonite Studies, 2001), 95.

15. This climactic instruction on the way (*en tē hodō*), set within the "conquest" (exodus) imagery of the Old Testament, leaves no doubt that Jesus is presenting a counter model to *acquisitive desire and mimetic rivalry* for the ordering of social and political relationships. If entering and living within the kingdom are guided by this new empowering imagery, which subverts prevailing empire images, then the "way-conquest" tradition, which provided prominent imagery for this section of Mark's presentation of Jesus,

has undergone significant transformation. The Divine Warrior–Son of humanity–Messiah attains the victory, ransoming many, through suffering and death.

16. James Williams, *Bible, Violence, and the Sacred: Liberation from the Myth of Sanctioned Violence* (New York: HarperCollins, 1991), 224.

17. In the only exorcism in this section (Mark 9:14-30), Jesus sharply rebukes the disciples for their lack of faith. This story makes clear that Mark's Jesus does not avoid the fight against evil. Cross-bearing and servanthood are not substitutes for or bypasses around the task of overcoming evil.

18. This accords with atonement theories that emphasize Jesus' humiliation and death as tricking the devil (cf. 1 Cor 2:6-8).

19. René Girard, *Things Hidden Since the Foundation of the World* (Stanford: Stanford University Press, 1987), 213.

20. Luke-Acts presents a stirring account of how Christian faith spread from Jerusalem to Rome, nonviolently. A model-imitation pattern is also found in Luke-Acts, where Jesus' nonviolent conduct before authorities inspires the persecuted in their testimony to the gospel before rulers. I regard Richard Cassidy's thesis tenable: that Acts serves the cause of "strengthening allegiance to Jesus Christ and witness before political authorities." Thus, Luke's primary goals were, first, to write out of his personal allegiance to his Lord and strengthen believers in their allegiance and, second, to shape the conduct of believers, . . . specifically to provide models for their own "Christian witness . . . before Roman officials." See Richard Cassidy, *Society and Politics in Acts of the Apostles* (Maryknoll, N.Y.: Orbis Books, 1989), 159–60.

21. Compare four in Thomas N. Finger, *Christian Theology: An Eschatological Approach*, vol. 1 (Scottdale, Pa.: Herald Press, 1985), 322–33. See also Willard M. Swartley, *Covenant of Peace: The Missing Peace in New Testament Theology and Ethics* (Grand Rapids, Mich.: Eerdmans, 2006), 223–36.

22. William Klassen connects this text to the missionary proclamation of peace in Luke 10: "There is a similar juxtaposition of joy, victory, fall of Satan, and 'treading under foot snakes and scorpions and all the forces of the enemy' in the commissioning of the disciples in Luke (10:18ff.). They return having retained their identity as children of peace and this causes Jesus to become exuberant (Lk 10:21)."

Paul, like his fellow Jewish apocalyptic writers, sees peace coming through the conquest of evil, the conquest of Satan, a conquest that is intimately related to the faithfulness of the believers. But at the same time it is God, the God of peace who destroys evil (Klassen, "The God of Peace: New Testament Perspectives on God," in *Towards a Theology of Peace* (ed. S. Tunnicliffe; London: European Nuclear Disarmament, 1989), 129 [pp. 121–31 for whole article].

23. The word "real" occurs rarely in the Bible. But the word is rather at home in Greek thought. A check in concordances confirms the point that no Hebrew or Greek word is readily translated "real." Translators introduced it here in the RSV.

24. Ulrich Mauser's analysis of "the rudimentary elements of the world" (*stoicheia*) in Colossians is pertinent here. He contends that these likely refer to the four primary elements, held by the Greek philosopher Epimenides to be fire, water, air, earth (*The Gospel of Peace* [Louisville: Westminster John Knox, 1992], 143–44). In order not to offend these powers, the Colossian Christians thought it necessary to engage in various ascetic and ritual practices. By so doing, they honored these powers as gods and undermined the all-sufficiency and supremacy of Jesus.

25. For sustained description of this process, see Daniel Patte's exposition of Paul's faith convictions in Romans 1–8 (*Paul's Faith and the Power of the Gospel* [Philadelphia: Fortress Press, 1983], 261, 284–85).

26. Here the literature is vast. Key sources are Clinton Arnold, *Ephesians: Power and Magic; The Concept of Power in Ephesians in Light of Its Historical Setting* (SNTSMS 63; Cambridge: Cambridge University Press, 1989); Hendrikus Berkhof, *Christ and the Powers* (trans. J. H. Yoder; Scottdale, Pa.: Herald Press, 1962); George B. Caird, *Principalities and Powers: A Study in Pauline Theology* (Oxford: Clarendon Press, 1956); Hans von Campenhausen, "Zur Auslegung von Röm 13: Die dämonische Deutung des exousia-Begriffs," in *F. S. A. Bertholet zum 80. Geburtstag* (ed. W. Baumgartner; Tübingen: J.C.B. Mohr, 1950), 97–113; Wesley Carr, *Angels and Principalities: The Background, Meaning and Development of the Pauline Phrase hai archai kai hai exousiai* (SNTSMS 42; Cambridge: Cambridge University Press, 1981); Oscar Cullmann, *The State in the New Testament* (New York: Scribner's, 1956); Martin Dibelius, *Die Geisterwelt im Glauben des Paulus* (Göttingen: Vandenhoeck & Ruprecht, 1909); Clinton Morrison, *The Powers That Be: Earthly Rulers and Demonic Powers in Romans 13:1-7* (London: SCM Press, 1960); Peter T. O'Brien, "Principalities and Powers: Opponents of the Church," in *Biblical Interpretation and the Church* (ed. D. A. Carson; Nashville: Thomas Nelson, 1984), 110–50; Heinrich Schlier, *Principalities and Powers in the New Testament* (QD 3; New York: Herder & Herder, 1961); Anthony J. Tambasco, "Principalities, Powers and Peace," in *Blessed Are the Peacemakers: Biblical Foundations on Peace and Its Social Foundations* (ed. A. Tambasco; New York and Mahwah, N.J.: Paulist Press, 1989), 116–33; Walter Wink, *Naming the Powers: The Language of Power in the New Testament* (Minneapolis: Fortress Press, 1984); Wink, *Unmasking the Powers*; and John Howard Yoder, *The Politics of Jesus* (rev. ed.; Grand Rapids, Mich.: Eerdmans, 1994), 135–214. An extended list of earlier contributions, 1920–1959, is cited by Morrison, *The Powers That Be*, 17, 40. For histories of research identifying the issues in interpretation, see O'Brien, "Principalities and Powers"; and for Ephesians especially, see Arnold, *Ephesians*, 42–51. See also chapter 10 of this volume, "Resistance and Nonresistance: When and How?"

27. O'Brien also sees no need to demythologize this view, for we confront the same reality today, and the faithful church is called to vigilance against these Powers through appropriating Christ's victory through prayer and the Word of God ("Principalities and Powers," 141–47).

28. Marva Dawn carefully analyzes Jacques Ellul on this matter. She points out that in his earlier writings (*The Ethics of Freedom* [Grand Rapids, Mich.: Eerdmans, 1976]) Ellul states that even after scrutinizing every dimension of political power, "we have still not apprehended its reality; [rather] *another power intervenes and indwells and uses political power, thus giving it a range and force that it does not have in itself.*" But she notes that later (in *The Subversion of Christianity* [Grand Rapids, Mich.: Eerdmans, 1986]) Ellul identifies six great evil Powers that the Bible speaks of: "Mammon, the prince of this world, the prince of lies, Satan, the devil, and death." They are characterized by "their functions: money, power, deception, accusation, division, and destruction. . . . There is no infernal world or hierarchy of fallen angels with superimposed eons. There is nothing behind it. We are told about powers that are concretely at work in the human world and have no other reality or mystery." Dawn observes that Ellul seems to have shifted his view. See her article "The Biblical Concept of 'the Principalities and Powers': John Yoder Points to Jacques Ellul," in *The Wisdom of the Cross: Essays in Honor of John Howard Yoder* (ed.

Stanley Hauerwas, Chris K. Huebner, Harry J. Huebner, and Mark Thiessen Nation; Grand Rapids, Mich.: Eerdmans, 1999), 168–86 (quotations from pp. 175, 184; italics in original). In my judgment, both his earlier and his later views need to be seen as one whole, with the earlier redefining the latter. Four of the six great Powers Ellul speaks of are spirit-beings and cannot be exhausted by "their functions," which he rightly identifies!

29. Two more issues are (4) whether Rom 13:1 assumes a double dimension, i.e., spiritual powers and human rulers (Cullmann, Morrison, Yoder), or whether one decides in each use which of the two levels of meaning is intended to the exclusion of the other (Von Campenhausen) (list on p. 40 of Morrison). See here J. R. W. Stott, *God's New Society: The Message of Ephesians* (Leicester: IntervVarsity Press, 1979), 267–75. And (5) whether Christ's victory over the Powers makes them subject to the lordship of the exalted Christ and thus effects a change in their status (Berkhof, Yoder) or whether the effectual benefits of Christ's victory are for its locus believers only, and therefore the scope of its effect extends only eschatologically to the Powers (Morrison).

30. Thomas Finger proposes that the second-century reflection on atonement as the "deception of the devil" was not actual deception. The "disguise" was none other than Jesus' true servant nature that the "powers" could not perceive—since it stands in opposition to their nature—and *thus* they were deceived: "Satan and the powers then were deceived by Jesus. But not because he tricked them by appearing in some deceitful disguise. In Jesus, God came to humankind as he truly was: gracious, forgiving, seeking to win people by love and not by force" (*Christian Theology* [vol. 1; Nashville: Thomas Nelson, 1985], 333; *Covenant of Peace*, 324–44).

31. Tambasco, "Principalities, Powers and Peace," 118–19. For treatment that develops continuity between the Synoptics and Paul, see Swartley and Finger, "Bondage and Deliverance," 10–38.

32. He was known as Paul Verghese in his Mennonite affiliation and student days at Associated Mennonite Biblical Seminaries.

33. Ernest D. Martin, *Colossians and Philemon* (The Believers' Church Bible Commentary; Scottdale, Pa.: Herald Press, 1993), 113. Martin points out that each of the three verses consists of participial clauses at beginning and end, with the declarative verb in the middle clause.

34. Philip D. Bender regards the middle form of the verb *apekdusamenos* as significant. He holds that the middle form indicates that Christ, rather than directly attacking the Powers, stripped himself off from their power, thus eluding their grasp and creating a new community of power independent of the Powers. He sums up his work on this text as follows: "In the context of *apekdusamenos* as 'stripping off from himself,' [this verse, Col 2:15,] suggests that Christ's warfare against the Powers consisted (1) of his obedience to God unto death, resulting (2) in the unmasking of those Powers as adversaries of God and humanity, leading (3) to their disarming through the stripping away of their power of illusion, which now (4) exhibits them as weak and humiliated captives. In Christ, the Powers have been 'deglorified,' through the exposure of their presumptuous and hostile claims. Relative to the power of God as evidenced by Christ in his rejection of their claims through obedience to God unto death, the power of the Powers now appears as 'weak and beggarly' (Gal. 4:9). For Paul, Christ's stripping away of the Powers was his instrument of divine warfare and victory." Bender, "The Holy War Trajectory in the Synoptic Gospels and the Pauline Writings" (MA thesis, Associated Mennonite Biblical Seminaries, 1987), 44.

35. David M. Hay, *Glory at the Right Hand: Psalm 110 in Early Christianity* (SBLMS 18; Nashville: Abingdon, 1973), 59ff.

36. For fuller description of issues involved in interpreting Revelation and the choices confronting the believers, see Willard M. Swartley, "War and Peace in the New Testament," in *Aufstieg und Niedergang der römischen Welt*, II.26.32 (1996): 2369–74; *Covenant of Peace*, 324–44

37. Yoder, *Politics of Jesus*, 148–49, 157–58.

38. Everett Ferguson, *Demonology of the Early Christian World* (New York/Toronto: Edwin Mellen Press, 1984), 129ff.

39. Ibid., 129. As far as I know, the most complete study of exorcism and healing in the early church is the most helpful work of Reginald Maxwell Woolley, *Exorcism and the Healing of the Sick* (London: Society for Promoting Christian Knowledge, 1932).

40. Alan Kreider, *The Change of Conversion and the Origin of Christendom* (Harrisburg, Pa.: Trinity Press, 1999), 17.

41. Ibid., 25.

42. Wink, *Unmasking the Powers*, 51. Compare his excellent discussion "Dying to the Powers," in *The Powers That Be*, 95–97.

43. Wink, *The Powers That Be*, 89. This is expressive of the Christus Victor view of the atonement, dominant in the early church.

44. C. J. Cadoux, *The Early Christian Attitude toward War* (New York: Scribner's, 1919 [reprint 1982]); J. M. Hornus, *It Is Not Lawful for Me to Fight* (trans. Alan Kreider; Scottdale, PA: Herald Press, 1980).

45. J. Helgeland, R. J. Daly, and J. P. Burns, *Christians and the Military: The Early Experience* (Philadephia: Fortress Press, 1985).

46. In Swartley, *Love of Enemy*, 126–36.

47. Justin Martyr, *First Apology*, 39; Irenaeus, *Against Heresies*, 4.34.4; Tertullian, *Against the Jews*, 3; Origen, *Against Celsus*, 5.33; 3.7–8; Hippolytus, *Apostolic Tradition*, 17b, 19. William Elster has shown that in many of the Fathers the "law of Christ" meant specifically beating swords into plowshares and loving the enemy. See his article "The New Law of Christ and Early Christian Pacifism," in *Essays on War and Peace: Bible and Early Church* (ed. Willard M. Swartley; Occasional Papers 9; Elkhart, Ind.: Institute of Mennonite Studies, 1986), 108–29. Elster has also written an unpublished complementary essay ("The Early Christian Doctrine of Pacifism," 1998) to this article, arguing the point in more detail.

48. Tertullian, *On Idolatry*, 19; *On the Crown*, 1; 11; Hippolytus, *Apostolic Tradition*, 17b, 19.

49. Tertullian, *Apology*, 32; Origen, *Against Celsus*, 8.68–75; Athanasius, *The Incarnation of the Word*, 52.4–6.

50. Tertullian, *Apology*, 30:4.

51. C. J. Cadoux, *The Early Church and the World* (Edinburgh: T & T Clark, 1925), 584.

52. Luise Schottroff, "Give to Caesar What Is Caesar's and to God What Is God's: The Theological Answer of the Early Church to Its Social and Political Situation," in Swartley, *Love of Enemy*, 223–57; quoting from 250.

53. Ibid., 242–43.

54. See here the excellent book by Klaus Wengst, *Pax Romana and the Peace of Jesus Christ* (trans. John Bowden; Philadelphia: Fortress Press, 1987).

55. Rodney Stark, *The Rise of Christianity: A Sociologist Reconsiders History* (Princeton: Princeton University Press, 1996). See the interview with Rodney Stark, "A Double Take on Early Christianity," in *Touchstone* 13, no. 1 (January–February 2000): 44–47, for quotations.

56. Stark interview, "A Double Take," 47.

57. *Building Communities of Compassion: Mennonite Mutual Aid in Theory and Practice* (ed. Willard M. Swartley and Donald B. Kraybill; Scottdale, Pa.: Herald Press, 1998), 32.

58. Robert E. Webber, *Celebrating Our Faith: Evangelism through Worship* (San Francisco: Harper & Row, 1986), 35–37.

59. Ibid., 82.

60. Alan Kreider, "Peacemaking in Worship in the Syrian Church Orders," *Studia Liturgica* 34 (2004): 177–90; and Taylor Burton-Edwards, "The Teaching of Peace in Early Christian Liturgies" (MA thesis, Associated Mennonite Biblical Seminaries, 1997). Eleanor Kreider, in *Communion Shapes Character* (Scottdale, Pa.: Herald Press, 1997), 44–50, documents that the Eucharist itself gave transformative power.

61. For background to this event, see Jürgen Moltmann, foreword to *Politics of Discipleship and Discipleship in Politics: Jürgen Moltmann Lectures in Dialogue with Mennonite Scholars*, ed. Willard Swartley (Eugene, Ore.: Cascade Books, 2006), xiii-xiv.

## CHAPTER 8. THE ECONOMICS AND POLITICS OF VIOLENCE

1. Walter Wink's trilogy on "the Powers" constitutes the theoretical backdrop and the primary metaethical interlocutor as regards the Powers in this essay. Wink's trilogy consists of *Naming the Powers: The Language of Power in the New Testament* (Minneapolis: Fortress Press, 1984); *Unmasking the Powers: The Invisible Forces That Determine Human Existence* (Minneapolis: Fortress Press, 1986); and *Engaging the Powers: Discernment and Resistance in a World of Domination* (Minneapolis: Augsburg Fortress, 1992).

2. Wink develops the Jesus-way of nonviolent engagement as *the* characteristic way for transforming the Domination System (*Engaging the Powers*, 175–93). But in spite of Jesus' many teachings about wealth and Jesus' placing the reference to the "year of Jubilee" at the center of the announcement of his ministry (Luke 4:18-19), Wink does not examine these economic *systems* undergirding greed and injustice. Wink does, however, list economics as one of the "societal modes" of power (*Engaging the Powers*, 47). "The gospel of Jesus champions economic equality, because economic inequalities are the basis of domination. Ranking, domination hierarchies, and classism are all built on accumulated power provided by excess wealth" (*Engaging the Powers*, 113–14). "Jesus counsels his hearers. . . . to lend without expecting interest" (*Engaging the Powers*, 183). The assumption seems to be that *transformation* will come about on a personal, inner, spiritual basis. This may help to explain Wink's relative lack of interest in economic *systems* or in pursuing economics itself as one of the Powers.

3. See Wink, *Engaging the Powers*, chs. 1–5.

4. In the message of Jesus, economics went well beyond the issue of *lifestyle* (cf. Matt 6:25-33). It was a God-issue—a central theological concern that reaches to the very core of the worshipping community's *being*: "You cannot serve God and wealth" (Matt 6:24).

5. "Functionalist" as opposed to substantivist—but not to be confused with functionalism.

6. My use of Kuhn focuses on his development of a metaepistemology, popularly called a worldview, and not on the debates with Karl Popper and Popperianism regarding Kuhn's history of science. The term "worldview" is often used nowadays to refer to little more than a "value orientation." My use of this term is as a near-synonym of "cosmology," or more literally, a cosmo-vision. When a Kuhnian paradigm shift occurs, it is a shift in worldview or in one's perception of cosmological reality. Thomas S. Kuhn, *The Structure of Scientific Revolutions* (2nd ed.; Chicago: University of Chicago Press, 1967, 1970).

7. *Die zwölf Artikel der Bauernschaft in Schwaben* (trans in full in Theodore G. Tappert, ed., *The Selected Writings of Martin Luther, 1523–1526* (vol. 3; Minneapolis: Fortress Press, 1967), 310–16 (hereafter Tappert, vol. 3). Precisely who authored the Twelve Articles is not known. See p. 306n7 for suggestions following a more "traditional religious" interpretation. These include Wilhelm Stolze, Balthasar Hubmaier, or Ulrich Schmid. Peter Blickle, maintaining that "the origins of the Articles are no longer controversial," sees them as coming from educated coworkers and sympathizers of the peasants and not with sympathizers of the Establishment Reformation (Peter Blickle, *The Revolution of 1525: The German Peasants' War from a New Perspective* [Baltimore: Johns Hopkins University Press, 1981], 208n1 and 18ff. See also H. S. Bender's comments disavowing any connection with Hubmaier or the Anabaptist movement because of the Articles' revolutionary nature in *The Mennonite Encyclopedia* (vol. 4; Scottdale, Pa.: Mennonite Publishing House, 1959), 1114.

8. Blickle, *Revolution of 1525*, 13.

9. Tappert, vol. 3, Article 1, p. 310.

10. Ibid., Article 3, p. 310.

11. Ibid., Article 4, p. 312.

12. Ibid., Article 5, p. 313, and Article 10, p. 315.

13. Ibid., Article 3, p. 312.

14. Ibid., Article 6, p. 313.

15. Ibid., Article 7, p. 314.

16. Ibid., end of Article 3, p. 312.

17. Ibid., Article 12, pp. 313–14.

18. Yet we should note that the Articles do not assume a classless society—a society in which the privileges and status of the peasants would be the same as, or bear the functional equivalency of, the feudal lords or the nobility. In this sense the Articles represent an economic system and a societal structure shared by the larger society—albeit the authority appealed to is the Scriptures and the norm is justice—equity, dignity, and participation. This is to say, the Articles were not revolutionary in what they demanded, nor is this an early sixteenth-century version of a "Communist Manifesto."

19. For a critique of Enlightenment thought, in which the "spiritual"/worldly ethical dualism expressed by Luther has become a dualistic worldview (cosmology), among the numerous ones available, Alasdair MacIntyre's *After Virtue* (Notre Dame, Ind.: University of Notre Dame Press, 1984) continues to be perhaps the most significant for theology.

20. Luther had developed his two-kingdom theory at least as early as 1523, and it is presented in his "Temporal Authority: To What Extent It Should Be Obeyed." See Theodore G. Tappert, ed., *The Selected Writings of Martin Luther, 1520–1523* (vol. 2; Philadelphia: Fortress Press, 1967), 271–319.

21. For a brief historical sketch of the background, see Tappert, vol. 3, 347–48. A more detailed picture emerges in Thomas A. Brady, "The Course of Events," Translators' Introduction, xiii–xx, in Blickle, *Revolution of 1525*. For a nonsocialist, religious perspective sympathetic to Luther's actions, see Robert N. Crossley, *Luther and the Peasants' War* (New York: Exposition Press, 1974). To review this event more favorably from the peasants' perspective and that of their principal leader (but written as history of ideas rather than as social history), see Abraham Friesen, *Thomas Muentzer, a Destroyer of the Godless: The Making of a Sixteenth-century Religious Revolutionary* (Berkeley: University of California Press, 1990).

22. Tappert, vol. 3, 350.

23. Immediately prior to the impending battle, Müntzer held before the peasants the image of Gideon's army and the victorious conquests of Moses (with the backdrop of Tauler's mystical piety): "Even if there are only three of you who stand yielded [*gelassen*] in God, seeking only to glorify His name and [vindicate] His honor, you will not fear a hundred thousand men. At them! At them! [*Dran, dran!*]." *Thomas Müntzer Schriften und Briefe* (Kritische Gesamtausgabe), *Quellen und Forschungen zur Reformationsgeschichte* (vol. 33; Gütersloh: Gerd Mohn Verlag, 1968), 454.

24. Müntzer came to May of 1525 with the firm "knowledge" that this was the apocalyptic struggle foretold in Matt 25 (Friesen, *Thomas Muentzer*, 260). And, as Müntzer reported shortly before the battle of Frankenhausen, "God was on the side of the peasants—this according to Hans Hut's confession some days later" (Friesen, *Thomas Muentzer*, 261).

25. According to Stayer, "The traditional historiography of the Peasants' War, noting the deaths of 100,000 peasants [in Frankenhausen and the surrounding areas] and the large fines following the movement's suppression, assumed that the peasantry of the Holy Roman Empire was finally crushed in 1525, and remained so until the nineteenth century. But on the contrary, . . . the outbreaks of German popular unrest continue more or less steadily from the beginning of the fourteenth century to the beginning of the nineteenth, even though no other uprising matched that of 1525." James Stayer, *The German Peasants' War and the Anabaptist Community of Goods* (Montreal: McGill-Queen's University Press, 1991), 42.

26. See James Stayer, "Numbers in Anabaptist Research," in *Commoners and Community: Essays in Honour of Werner O. Packull* (ed. C. Arnold Snyder; Kitchener, ON: Pandora, 2002).

27. See Clifford Geertz, "Religion as a Cultural System," in *The Interpretation of Cultures* (New York: Basic Books, 1973), 87–100, for a working definition of religion that I use in this chapter. See also Richard A. Horsley, "Religion and Other Products of Empire," *Journal of the American Academy of Religion* 71 (March 2003): 13–44.

28. Wink, *Engaging the Powers*, ch. 6ff.

29. Wink, *Naming the Powers*.

30. Wink, *Engaging the Powers*, ch. 3.

31. Other "societal modes" include "power," "relationships," "education," and "ecological stance" (Wink, *Engaging the Powers*, 46–47). One needs to raise the questions as to just *how* these societal modes, expressed here in noninstitutional terms, are embodiments of social realities, and *how* the various categories are related to each other—except through "invisible forces."

32. See ch. 1 of this volume, "The New Worldview: Spirit at the Core of Everything." See also Wink, *Engaging the Powers*, 5.

33. Wink, *Engaging the Powers*, 5.

34. Terms and phrases in quotation marks are from Geertz, *Interpretation of Cultures*, 90. Emphasis added.

35. Wink, *Engaging the Powers*, 5–9. In defining "spirituality" and "the spiritual," Wink comments as follows: "The psychologist Carl Jung spoke of this inner dimension as the collective consciousness, meaning by that a realm of largely unexplored spiritual reality linking everyone to everything. . . The spiritual aspect of the Powers is not merely a 'personification' of institutional qualities that would exist whether they were personified or not. On the contrary, the spirituality of an institution exists as a real aspect of the

institution even when it is not perceived as such. *Institutions have an actual spiritual ethos.*" What in the ancient worldview were demons and angels, thought of today as separate beings residing in the sky somewhere, are the spirituality of institutions and systems—i.e., the Powers. Wink, *Engaging the Powers*, 6–7 (emphasis added).

36. Geertz, *The Interpretations of Cultures*, 109.

37. Cf. Wink, *Unmasking the Powers*. This is a functional descriptor of the Powers. The Powers are further elaborated on at chapter-length as "Satan," "demons," "angels," and "the elements of the universe."

38. Borrowing from Peter L. Berger, this *intra-social ethos* may also be defined as the *institutions* that we create (which can be defined in terms of neither materiality nor spirituality), and after we have created them, they in turn create us. "Forgetting" their origins, they become clothed with an aura of facticity, creating an ethos that enshrouds us, making us and molding us into who we are. *The Sacred Canopy: Elements of a Sociological Theory of Religion* (New York: Anchor Doubleday, 1969), ch. 1, "Religion and World-Construction."

39. Traditional religion in our contemporary North American society functions primarily as a smoke screen, a camouflage, a distracter for the far more powerful, persuasive, and dominating religion of free-market capitalism. David R. Loy has written a groundbreaking essay demolishing the narrowly sacred and traditional categories in which religion is yet all-too-frequently defined ("The Religion of the Market," *Journal of the American Academy of Religion* 65, no. 2 [Summer 1997]: 275). I am indebted to Loy, particularly at points of application, throughout this essay.

40. Already in 1967 (German edition in 1963), well before the day when we were running everything through a postmodern grid, Thomas Luckmann published his work *Invisible Religion* (London: Macmillan, 1967). This is an expansion of a paper titled "Notes on the Case of the Missing Religion" (see Luckmann's foreword). Here Luckmann began to ask, if religion is today expressed less in the traditional visible "church," where and how is it being practiced? He wanted to determine whether people were actually becoming less religious (which he doubted), or whether something in our perceptions of reality keeps us from recognizing the new form religious expression takes.

41. Luther, most likely in good faith, presumed to present an integrated theology. But it is precisely Luther's mode of thinking, in which he separates the sacred from the secular and the private from the public, that has contributed to the Christian religion's becoming a tool of violent oppression. See n. 19 above.

42. See above, the story of the peasants' rebellion.

43. Wink, *Engaging the Powers*, 6ff.

44. "Ethos" is one of the near-synonyms for Wink's understanding of the Powers. Note how Wink describes the "angels" of the churches in the book of Revelation: "Through the angel the community seems to step forth as a single collective entity or Gestalt. But the fact that the angel is addressed [Revelation 2 and 3] suggests that it is more than a mere personification of the church, but the actual spirituality of the congregation as a single entity. The angel [i.e., one of the Powers] would then exist in, with, and under the material expression of the church's life as its interiority. . . . Angel and people are the inner and outer aspects of one and the same reality." Wink, *Unmasking the Powers*, 70.

45. Geertz, "Religion as a Cultural System," 87–100.

46. David Loy notes that "in order for market forces to interact freely and productively, the natural world had to become commodified into [marketable] land, life commodified

into labor, and patrimony commodified into capital." This critical stage in the development of capitalism, which Loy avers occurred in the late eighteenth century, was already pushing its rhizomes in early sixteenth-century Germany. Loy, "Religion of the Market," 281. See also Blickle, *Revolution of 1525*, ch. 4.

47. Succinctly stated, "God is the source of our values and the center of our loyalties." To the degree that we can identify the source of our values and locate the center of our loyalties, we have found the "God" whom we de facto serve. Functionally, i.e., in everyday life, this is the case, regardless of any confessional statements we may put forth indicating otherwise.

48. "Market capitalism," asserts Loy, not only plays a role functionally equivalent to traditional religion, but in terms of both numbers of adherents won and cultural influence wielded, it has become the most successful religion of all time. Loy, "Religion of the Market," 276.

49. Wink includes among the Powers "the angels of the seven churches" in Asia Minor. It is to the "angels" of the churches, not the churches themselves or to their pastor-leader, that the letters are addressed. But not merely angels but also "Satan" and the "demons" are among the Powers. Angels, demons, and Satan are differing forms of a permeating, enveloping ethos that is personified and in some measure controls the entire community. Wink, *Unmasking the Powers*, chs. 1–5, 7. What seems less applicable to this particular chapter are the Powers of the "elements of the universe" (*stoicheia tou kosmou*) developed in *Unmasking the Powers*, ch. 6—one of Wink's most daring and creative pieces, and perhaps also one of the more unfinished ones.

50. I am using the term "commoners" as a quasi-synonym for peasants. But under "commoners" I include miners and villagers (*Dorfleute*), thus making it more inclusive of the lower working class and more reflective of a society in its earliest stages of industrialism.

51. Stayer, *German Peasants' War and the Anabaptist Community of Goods*, 108.

52. What is at stake here is more than the threat of tax resistance exacerbated by the princes' need for resources to oppose the Turks. Loy has noted that communism is "best understood as a capitalist heresy." Likewise, the threat presented by the communalism of the peasants, in their resistance to the commodification of common property, is best understood not simply as politico-economic resistance, but as a religious heresy. Loy, "Religion of the Market," 275.

53. "Against the Robbing and Murdering Hordes," Tappert, vol. 3, 350.

54. Wealth as an ultimate end is a "god that is not God." It is one of the "great deceivers," unable to deliver what it promises.

55. Wink, *Engaging the Powers*, 82. The theo-political profundity of this claim should not be overlooked. It serves as a window into much of Wink's work, especially *Engaging the Powers*. So much so is this the case that one hopes he will add yet a fourth treatise— *Transforming the Powers*—to his current trilogy. Such a work on transformational engagement of the Powers could offer some of the theological underpinnings currently lacking in the system of conflict transformation skills.

Donald W. Shriver Jr., in *An Ethic for Enemies: Forgiveness in Politics* (New York: Oxford University Press, 1995), although not focusing directly on Jesus' death and the language of atonement, has written one of the most insightful and well-researched essays of the past half century on the "redemption of the Powers," integrating the categories of Judeo-Christian theology with the political Powers of the contemporary world. See, for example, his response to the question, "Can Nations Remember, Repent, and Forgive?" 71ff.

56. We should recognize, however, that not all those who were not felled in the slaughter or smothered in the societal structures became Anabaptists: (1) There were those who returned to the establishment—either the papal establishment known as the Roman Catholic Church or Luther and Zwingli's new establishment later known as Protestantism. (2) Others, perhaps a lesser number but even more cynical and alienated, maintained no organized allegiance—the disenfranchised societal sediment providing the bedrock residual resistance for future uprisings. And, finally, (3) there were the communally oriented, pacifist Anabaptists whom I am here identifying as a segment of the population that underwent a "paradigmatic change" in its perceptions of the meaning and purpose of life—specifically in its orientation toward the Powers of religious authority, violence, and economics. For the first two groups of peasants, the understanding of reality at a cosmic or ontic level remained fundamentally the same as before the catastrophic slaughter.

57. Stayer, *German Peasants' War and the Anabaptist Community of Goods*, 92.

58. This is a term that Thomas Kuhn has codified with special meaning: an event that changes our perception of reality, that enables us individually and/or collectively to see what we were previously unable to see, and to see from a different angle what we had previously seen. See Kuhn, *Structure of Scientific Revolutions*, ch. 2, "The Route to Normal Science," and throughout all the later chapters of the book. But Kuhn himself does not use the term univocally, applying it usually to the epistemology of a culture (hence a cosmology) but at times to a very limited segment of society (hence a psychosocial structure).

59. Ibid., 111.

60. Ibid.

61. Kuhn takes approximately nine chapters to outline and illustrate what I have tried to state in a few sentences. His laborious arguments, in my estimation, still provide one of the best exercises to help us understand the inadequacies and deceptions of modernity (a theme that runs through all of Wink's works) and give us the tools for constructing a bridge between the "worldviews" (i.e., the metaepistemology) of the first century and the twenty-first.

62. The classic illustration on which Kuhn elaborates is the Copernican revolution—the paradigm shift from a geocentric universe to a heliocentric one. See Thomas S. Kuhn, *The Copernican Revolution: Planetary Astronomy in the Development of Western Thought* (Cambridge, MA: Harvard University Press, 1957).

63. Hans Hut, a follower of Müntzer, later turned Anabaptist and baptized thousands. Hut said that Müntzer had told the peasants that "God almighty was about to cleanse the world and had taken power away from the rulers and given it to their subjects. . . . God was on the side of the peasants." Friesen, *Thomas Muentzer*, 260.

64. War for the peasants can be seen as much less naïve when we realize that their weapons were, at one level, only symbolic of the weapons they believed Christ would wield upon his triumphal return. They held Christ to be the warrior on the white horse. "It was Muentzer who entered with the conviction that this was the apocalyptic struggle foretold in Matthew 24. He was the one who talked about uprooting the tares in the time of harvest. He was the one who preached to the peasant forces about the covenant made with God" (Friesen, *Thomas Muentzer*, 261). The wicked with their wealth were to be destroyed. Within the classic apocalyptic worldview (i.e., paradigm) of their times, they saw themselves as the midwives of God's new rule through Christ, to be accomplished through their own violent struggle in battle. But they did not believe the size of the cannon

to be a decisive factor. "According to Ruehel [the brother-in-law of Martin Luther], the first shots of the enemy fell short, and Muentzer is supposed to have shouted, 'Did I not tell you no bullet would harm you?'" (Friesen, *Thomas Muentzer*, 261).

65. As Hannah Arendt so eloquently summarizes the case in philosophical terms: "Power and violence are opposites; where one rules absolutely, the other is absent. Violence appears where power is in jeopardy, but left to its own course it ends in power's disappearance." Hannah Arendt, *On Violence* (New York: Harcourt, Brace & World, 1970), 56. Yet, for the followers of Jesus, solidarity with him is seldom strong enough to enable us to make this claim an experiential reality.

66. Luther's response regarding the soteriological status of soldiers, with its long shadow extending throughout the twentieth century and into the present one, is a near-reification in the name of God for the use of the sword. Luther discusses how a soldier must execute his God-given office: "I myself," he notes, "have heard some of them [i.e., soldiers] say that if they thought too much about these problems, they would never be able to go to war again. . . . I promised . . . to give the best advice to these weak, timid and doubting consciences. . . . For whoever fights with a good and well-instructed conscience will also fight well." The gist of the argument was not the matter of weighing the morality of killing but rather that of having courage so that they could be better soldiers ("Whether Soldiers, Too, Can be Saved, 1526," in Tappert, vol. 3, 433; see also pp. 434–77).

67. For an extensive treatment of this subject, see Ray C. Gingerich, "The Mission Impulse of Early Swiss and South German–Austrian Anabaptism" (Ph.D. diss., Vanderbilt University, 1980), especially the segments on the legacy of Hans Hut, 129–39, 171–75, 256–57, and the entire last chapter, 268–335.

The best popular theological exposition of this theme, clearly influenced by his studies in Anabaptism, is Donald Kraybill, *The Upside Down Kingdom* (3rd ed.; Scottdale, Pa.: Herald Press, 2003).

68. Wink, *Engaging the Powers*, 47.

69. Ibid., 88.

70. Kuhn, *The Structure of Scientific Revolutions*, 111.

71. Wink, *Engaging the Powers*, 82.

72. The shift from the predicate adjective to the nominative is intended as a way to enable the reader to follow the logic of thought, even though the longer and more substantive argument cannot be presented in this chapter.

73. "Market capitalism . . . has already become the most successful religion of all time winning more converts more quickly than any previous belief-system or value-system in human history." Loy, "Religion of the Market," 276. This is what, at a much earlier date (1967), Thomas Luckmann alluded to as an "invisible religion"—invisible not because it had no external form but because we are looking through the wrong "windows"—we are blind to it because our worldview hides it from us. Cf. Luckmann, *Invisible Religion*, ch. 2, "Church-Oriented Religion on the Periphery of Modern Society."

74. A month prior to the war, Luther, in his letter "Against the Robbing and Murdering Hordes," wrote: "For baptism does not make men free in body and property, but in soul; and the gospel does not make goods common, except in the case of those who, of their own free will do what the Apostles and the disciples did in Acts 4[:32–37]. *They did not demand, as do our insane peasants in their raging, that the goods of others—Pilate and Herod—should be in common.* . . . Fine Christians they are! I think there is not a devil left in hell; they have all gone into the peasants." Tappert, vol. 3, 351–52; emphasis added.

75. "Just as they wanted to practice baptism and the Lord's Supper in the manner of the apostles, so did they wish to replicate the apostolic practices described in Acts 2 and 4. By community of goods, they meant literal imitation of Acts 2 and 4; they could not possibly have meant anything else." Stayer, *German Peasants' War and the Anabaptist Community of Goods*, 105.

Mennonite historians of the past century have treated the many accounts of the Anabaptist community of goods with skepticism, or they have ignored them. Might a contributing factor be that the Powers (both visible and invisible) of free-market capitalism, whether on the Continent or in North America, determined Mennonite existence far more than did Acts 2 and 4?

76. Zwingli, like Erasmus, who served as an unofficial mentor to Zwingli, recognized the community of goods as a Christian ideal. Quotation taken from Zwingli's *Apologeticus Archeteles* in *The Latin Works and the Correspondence of Huldreich Zwingli*, ed. Samuel Macauley Jackson and Clarence Nevin Heller (3 vols.; New York: Putnam, 1912–1929), 1:267, as quoted by Stayer, in *German Peasants' War and the Anabaptist Community of Goods*, 99.

77. Ulrich Zwingli, *The Sources of Swiss Anabaptism: The Grebel Letters and Related Documents* (Classics of the Radical Reformation, vol. 4; ed. Leland Harder; Scottdale, Pa.: Herald Press, 1985), 409.

78. The reference here is specifically to the Swiss Brethren. Several of their leaders (e.g., Conrad Grebel and Felix Mantz) were significantly influenced by the great pacifist-humanist scholar Erasmus and associations with humanism in Vienna. This group, later called Anabaptists, was less directly associated with the Peasants' War but nevertheless also struggled with the issues of violent revolution and unjust economic practices. Gingerich, "Mission Impulse," ch. 3, "The Counter-Community: The Church in Relation to the State"; see also ch. 1 "Proto-Anabaptism," in which I give background on Grebel and Mantz.

79. Kuhn, *Structure of Scientific Revolutions*, 175; emphasis added. The "Ascension" and the instructions of Jesus immediately preceding (Acts 1:6-11) might well be understood as a theological account of a Kuhnian paradigm shift.

80. Ibid., 121. But see also Kuhn's entire ch. 3, "Revolutions as Changes of World View."

81. Ibid., 109–10.

82. Gingerich, "Mission Impulse," 256–58, 221–28, 291–305, respectively.

83. For extensive documentation of Hut's movements away from Müntzer to become a leader in communal Anabaptism, see my dissertation, "Mission Impulse," ch. 4, "The Eschatological Movement: Incarnational Presence of the Future." This entire chapter is devoted to Hut.

84. Kuhn, *Structure of Scientific Revolutions*, 111.

85. Even the earlier, oft-cited "Here I am, I can do no other" is a myth, if by that we mean that Luther broke with the ethos of his time. Luther had the security of his protector, the Elector Frederick the Wise, and the ethos of German nationalism that, while freeing him from the pope and emperor, nevertheless enshrouded him within the larger ethos of power through violence and kept him firmly bound to his death.

86. Culture-religion consists of the dominant *invisible* religion (economic systems sustained by militaristic nationalism), sheltered beneath the sacred canopy of *visible* traditional religion—i.e., entire congregations, parishes, mosques, and synagogues, and even Christian denominations that maintain social solidarity through religiously/nationally

correct doctrine and loyalty. Both peasants and the Establishment were driven by death-dealing, destructive ideologies under the sacred canopy of traditional religion.

87. In my own life span, I can think of only two such models, Mahatma Gandhi and Martin Luther King Jr., in whose wake a transformative ethos of culturally life-giving proportions emerged. For the Christian faith, Jesus the Messiah and his resurrected body of followers (wherever these may be found) constitute such a transformative power. For the postwar peasants, this was the paramount understanding of what it meant to be "Anabaptist," regardless of the particular verbal and cultural symbols that were attached.

## CHAPTER 9. JESUS' WAY OF TRANSFORMING INITIATIVES AND JUST PEACEMAKING THEORY

1. Walter Wink, "Beyond Just War and Pacifism; Jesus' Nonviolent Way," *Review and Expositor* 89, no. 2 (Spring 1992): 199. See also his *Engaging the Powers: Discernment and Resistance in a World of Domination* (Minneapolis: Fortress Press, 1992).

2. Walter Wink, "Neither Passivity nor Violence: Jesus' Third Way," in *The Love of Enemy and Nonretaliation in the New Testament* (ed. Willard Swartley; Louisville: Westminster John Knox: 1992), 114–15; N. T. Wright, *Jesus and the Victory of God* (Minneapolis: Fortress Press: 1996), 290–91.

3. Clarence Jordan, *The Substance of Faith and Other Cotton Patch Sermons* (ed. Dallas Lee; New York: Association Press, 1972), 69.

4. Donald Hagner, *Matthew 1–13* (Dallas: Word Publishing, 1993), 130–31.

5. Glen Stassen, "The Time Machine" (Sermon of the Month), *Pulpit Digest* (August 1980), reprinted in *Twentieth-Century Pulpit* (vol. 2; ed. James W. Cox, Nashville: Abingdon, 1981); "Beginning Recovery of the Biblical Meaning of Peacemaking," *Campus Minister*, Winter 1981, 43–55; *Journey into Peacemaking* (2nd ed.; Memphis: Brotherhood Commission of the Southern Baptist Convention, 1987). A much more thorough exposition of my approach is now available in Glen H. Stassen and David P. Gushee, *Kingdom Ethics: Following Jesus in Contemporary Context* (Downers Grove, Ill.: InterVarsity Press, 2003).

6. See Glen H. Stassen, *Just Peacemaking: Transforming Initiatives for Justice and Peace* (Louisville: Westminster John Knox Press, 1992), chs. 2 and 3. There I explain that the teaching on divorce is an exception, but the missing transforming initiative is reported by Paul in 1 Cor 7:11. I demonstrate the structure in more detail in my article "The 14 Triads of the Sermon on the Mount," *JBL* 122, no. 2 (2003): 267–308.

7. See Stassen, *Just Peacemaking: Transforming Initiatives*, ch. 3, for a fuller explanation.

8. John Howard Yoder, *The Politics of Jesus* (Grand Rapids, Mich.: Eerdmans, 1994), ch. 5.

9. John Dominic Crossan, *The Historical Jesus* (San Francisco: HarperSanFrancisco: 1991), 135–36.

10. See Daniel Buttry, *Christian Peacemaking* (Valley Forge, Pa.: Judson Press, 1994).

11. Glen Stassen, ed., *Just Peacemaking: Ten Practices to Abolish War* (Cleveland: Pilgrim Press, 1998).

12. See John Howard Yoder, *Body Politics: Five Practices of the Christian Community before the Watching World* (Scottdale, Pa.: Herald Press, 1992), ch. 1.

13. I do not claim that conflict resolution is a wooden, detail-by-detail application of Jesus' teaching in our time. That is not how we are to follow Jesus' practices in a different

historical period, and it is not, for example, how Paul followed them in 1 Cor 7:11, where he explicitly quoted a teaching of Jesus against divorce and taught that a Christian should seek reconciliation rather than divorce, akin to Jesus' teaching in Matt 5:23ff., but then went on to teach what people should do if they did divorce, and to allow divorce if an unbelieving spouse divorced. Rather, we are to seek to understand as fully as possible the way Jesus' practice functioned in his social context and how the analogous practice would function in our social context, always paying attention to how it witnesses to Jesus and gives glory to God (Matt 5:13-17). John Yoder spells out the method in *Body Politics* and in *The Royal Priesthood: Essays Ecclesiological and Ecumenical* (ed. Michael G. Cartwright; Grand Rapids, Mich.: Eerdmans, 1994) in the final chapter, "Sacrament as Social Practice"; and I do in *Authentic Transformation: A New Vision of Christ and Culture* (Nashville: Abingdon, 1996). I will follow this *via analogia* in the subsequent practices as well.

14. Glen Stassen, "Nonviolence in Time of War," *Sojourners*, July–August 1999, 18–21.

15. Donald Shriver, *An Ethic for Enemies: Forgiveness in Politics* (New York: Oxford University Press: 1995), 38–44.

16. Miroslav Volf, *Exclusion and Embrace: A Theological Exploration of Identity, Otherness, and Reconciliation* (Nashville: Abingdon, 1996). L. Gregory Jones, *Embodying Forgiveness: A Theological Analysis* (Grand Rapids, Mich.: Eerdmans, 1995), also develops the theme. And see its application to nations that make the transition from dictatorship or oppression to democracy and human rights, and that then need to act on amnesty, punishment, or truth and reconciliation, for their past rulers who so viciously oppressed them, in Walter Wink, *When the Powers Fall* (Minneapolis: Fortress Press, 1998).

17. See *Just Peacemaking: Ten Practices for Abolishing War*, ch. 9.

18. Joseph Nye and Robert Keohane, *Power and Independence* (2nd ed.; New York: HarperCollins, 1989).

19. Stassen, *Just Peacemaking: Ten Practices for Abolishing War*, 103.

20. Wright, *Jesus and the Victory of God*, 317.

21. See Yoder, *Body Politics*.

## CHAPTER 10. RESISTANCE AND NONRESISTANCE

1. Leo Driedger and Donald B. Kraybill, *Mennonite Peacemaking: From Quietism to Activism* (Scottdale, Pa.: Herald Press, 1994), 62.

2. Ibid., 222–24.

3. *Confession of Faith in a Mennonite Perspective* (adopted 1995; Scottdale, Pa.: Herald Press, 1995), Article 22, "Peace, Justice, and Nonresistance," 81–85.

4. Driedger and Kraybill, *Mennonite Peacemaking*, 214.

5. Ibid., 215.

6. One can imagine why the phrase was dropped. Further discussion led to the observance that nonresistance does not promise justice, nor does nonviolence guarantee it. Which concept of justice is operative in the statement? Is justice God's business, not ours, to decide or settle?

7. *Confession of Faith in a Mennonite Perspective*, 83.

8. Ibid., 81.

9. Ibid., 83.

10. Ibid.

11. Walter Wink, *Unmasking the Powers: The Invisible Forces That Determine Human Existence* (Minneapolis: Fortress Press, 1986).

12. Walter Wink, *Naming the Powers: The Language of Power in the New Testament* (Minneapolis: Fortress Press, 1984), 52.

13. This text echoes Ps 18:1-3, in that God provides the resources for security and victory. For fuller exposition of this section see Willard M. Swartley, *Covenant of Peace: The Missing Peace in New Testament and Ethics* (Grand Rapids, Mich.: Eerdmans, 2006), 213–16, 240–45.

14. Clinton E. Arnold, *Powers of Darkness: Principalities and Powers in Paul's Letters* (Downers Grove, Ill.: InterVarsity Press, 1992), 154–58.

15. Adolf von Harnack, *Militia Christi: The Christian Religion and the Military in the First Three Centuries* (trans. D. M. Gracie; Philadelphia: Fortress Press, 1981), 35–36.

16. Miroslav Volf, *Exclusion and Embrace: A Theological Explanation of Identity, Otherness, and Reconciliation* (Nashville: Abingdon, 1996), 293.

17. On this point, see Millard C. Lind, *God Is a Warrior* (Scottdale, Pa.: Herald Press, 1980). Note also the helpful study by Gregory A. Boyd, *God at War: The Bible and Spiritual Conflict* (Downers Grove, Ill.: InterVarsity Press, 1997).

18. Thomas R. Yoder Neufeld, *"Put on the Armour of God": The Divine Warrior from Isaiah to Ephesians* (Sheffield, UK: Sheffield Academic Press, 1997); Clinton Arnold, *Ephesians: Power and Magic: The Concept of Power in Ephesians in Light of Its Historical Setting* (SNTSMS 63; New York: Cambridge University Press, 1989), 121.

19. Ragnar Leivestad, *Christ the Conqueror: Ideas of Conflict and Victory in the New Testament* (London: SPCK, 1954).

20. 1 Cor 4:12b-13a is especially important here: "When reviled, we bless; when persecuted, we endure; when slandered, we speak kindly."

Gordon Zerbe sums up the list. He identifies as passive responses: (1) "not repaying evil for evil" (1 Thess 5:15a; Rom 12:17a); (2) "not taking vengeance for oneself" (Rom 12:19a); (3) "not cursing" (Rom 12:14); (4) "forbearance" (Phil 4:5; 1 Thess 5:14; 1 Cor 13:4; Gal 5:22; 2 Cor 6:6); (5) "endurance" (1 Cor 4:12; 2 Cor 11:20; cf. Col 3:13; 2 Thess 1:4; Rom 12:12; 2 Cor 6:4; 1 Cor 13:7; cf. Rom 5:3-4; 2 Cor 1:6); (6) not litigating (1 Cor 6:1-8); (7) "not reckoning evil" (1 Cor 13:5).

Active responses include: (8) responding with good/kind deeds (1 Thess 5:15b; Rom 12:17b, 20-21); (9) "blessing" (Rom 12:14; 1 Cor 4:12); (10) "conciliating" (1 Cor 4:13); (11) "being at peace" (1 Thess 5:13; Rom 12:18; cf. Gal 5:20, 22); (12) "forgiving" (2 Cor 2:7-10; Col 3:13); (13) "loving" (1 Cor 13:4-7; cf. 2 Cor 6:6; Rom 12:9; 1 Thess 3:13). From Gordon Zerbe, "Paul's Ethic of Nonretaliation and Peace," in *The Love of Enemy and Nonretaliation in the New Testament* (ed. Willard M. Swartley; Louisville: Westminster John Knox, 1992), 179–80.

21. See Willard M. Swartley, "Politics and Peace (Eirene) in Luke's Gospel," in *Political Issues in Luke-Acts* (ed. Richard J. Cassidy and Philip J. Scharper; Maryknoll, N.Y.: Orbis Books, 1983), 33–35.

22. Arranged as twelve study lessons for congregational teaching, this was authorized by the Churchwide Peace Problems Committee and released in 1948. Both publications were motivated by World War II and the need for Mennonites to know what they believed in order to refuse enlistment in the military. The emphasis on nonresistance has given way to justice emphases, and more recently to active nonviolent resistance, along with mediation, conflict transformation, and reconciliation. Conference and church-wide organizations are Peace and Justice organizations, with little reference to the nonresistance tradition. This tradition, however, comes into focus when stories of the past are told, such as that of the Jacob Hochstetler refusal to defend himself and refusal to allow his sons to defend the family during an Indian raid.

The nonresistance teaching regularly begins with a good creation story, followed by the fall and the first murder (by Cain) as the basis for the warfaring society. Care is taken to point out the nonresistant acts of Abraham, Moses, etc., to show unity between the Testaments. The teaching includes, of course, the Anabaptist history and the Mennonite history of the eighteenth and nineteenth centuries. Earlier twentieth-century articulation of the position came from John Horsch and George R. Brunk.

23. Significant echoes of the earlier tradition continue, mostly in story form. In 1954 (reprinted 1994), Elizabeth Bauman published *Coals of Fire*, a collection of stories for children in which defenselessness and nonresistance are dominant themes (Scottdale, Pa.: Herald Press). In 1980, Cornelia Lehn published an even wider historical collection of peace stories with much the same themes but with clear accent on peacemaking in the interpretive grid of the stories (*Peace Be with You* [Newton, KS: Faith and Life Press]). In Swaziland, in 1982, when I taught a peacemaking course to fifty southern African leaders in the struggle against apartheid, and against oppression more broadly, Lehn's book was the most in demand in order for these leaders to teach the peacemaking way to their communities in six countries seeking freedom and a new order. None of these stories is oriented, however, to seeking justice as such, but instead to faithfulness and nonviolent resistance amid an evil social order.

24. Stanley Hauerwas, *Unleashing the Scriptures: Freeing the Bible from the Captivity to America* (Nashville: Abingdon, 1993), 64. See similar emphases in Gerhard Lohfink, *Jesus and Community: The Social Dimension of the Christian Faith* (trans. John P. Galvin; Philadephia: Fortress Press; New York: Paulist Press, 1984), esp. 70–73; and Richard B. Hays, *The Moral Vision of the New Testament* (San Francisco: Harper Collins, 1996), 304–6, 310 (point 10).

25. "What I Believe," in *The Illustrated Book of Christian Literature: The First Two Millennia* (ed. Robert van de Weyer; Nashville: Abingdon, 1998), 11–13.

26. Willard M. Swartley and C. J. Dyck, eds., *Annotated Bibliography of Mennonites on War and Peace: 1930–1980* (Scottdale, Pa.: Herald Press, 1987), ch. 4, "The Bible, Peace and War," 96–127. Some of the entries are from as late as 1985, but effort to find all published articles focused on 1930–1980, and only prominent ones from 1981–1985 were included.

27. See my paper "The Christian and the Payment of Taxes Used for War" (the first draft from the late 1970s; the second draft from 1980; revised in 1981). A shortened and adapted version was published in *Sojourners* (February 1979), and another version, coauthored with Lois Barrett, appeared in the Mennonite Central Committee *Peace Section Newsletter* (January 1981).

28. Klaus Wengst, *Pax Romana and the Peace of Jesus Christ* (Philadelphia: Fortress Press, 1987), 84.

29. "Give to Caesar What Belongs to Caesar and to God What Belongs to God": A Theological Response of the Early Christian Church to Its Social and Political Environment," in Swartley, *Love of Enemy and Nonretaliation in the New Testament*, 223–57.

30. Luise Schottroff, "Give," in Swartley, *Love of Enemy and Nonretaliation in the New Testament*, 232.

31. Ibid., 235. For exposition on Schottroff in the context of other scholarly efforts to resolve this issue, see Swartley, *Covenant of Peace*, 60–65.

32. Ibid., 236.

33. It may be that this entire instruction of Rom 12:14–13:10 was occasioned by a tax revolt brewing at the time Paul wrote his letter. Possibly the believers thought they should join the revolt and help crush the evil unjust system. But Paul's word, and the gospel word,

is: God can well handle the evil in the world. What is necessary for you is to not repay evil with evil, but rather to overcome evil with good. Be subject to the authorities and pay your taxes. Let love only rule your lives, and let other people, those in God's wrath department, care for the necessary restraint of evil. Yours is a different vocation. This is your freedom from the Powers; it is a freedom to respond to evil that is of a completely different type. You follow the Christ who has subjugated the Powers, and thus frees you to be free from them in your subjection to them. Thus you participate in my victory, says the God of our Lord Jesus Christ.

34. Schottroff, "Give," 242–43.

35. Ibid., 244.

36. This section is drawn from Willard M. Swartley, "Method and Understanding for Texts and Disciples," in *Perspectives on Feminist Hermeneutics* (ed. Gayle Gerber Koontz and Willard M. Swartley; Occasional Papers No. 10; Elkhart, Ind.: Institute of Mennonite Studies, 1987), 115–16.

37. Mary Schertz, "'Likewise You Wives . . .' : Another Look at 1 Peter 2:11–5:11," in Koontz and Swartley, *Perspectives on Feminist Hermeneutics*, 78.

38. Glen H. Stassen has helpfully shown that the Sermon on the Mount contains a triadic structure, so that the third component of each injunction consists of some transformative initiative. See *Just Peacemaking: Transforming Initiatives for Justice and Peace* (Louisville: Westminster John Knox, 1992), 33–88, and ch. 9 above.

## CHAPTER 11. THE KIND OF JUSTICE JESUS CARES ABOUT

1. Willard M. Swartley, ed., *The Love of Enemy and Nonretaliation in the New Testament* (Louisville: Westminster John Knox, 1992).

2. Richard Horsley, *Jesus and the Spiral of Violence* (San Francisco: Harper & Row, 1987), 77, sets up the German Lutheran Martin Hengel as the error to be attacked. He is reacting against Hengel's interpretation of Jesus as a passive quietist and against other German Lutherans represented by Hengel (347n21). Hengel and others use the Zealots as a foil to advocate an apolitical Jesus. They say Jesus rejected the Zealot strategy, which was a political strategy. Instead, Jesus avoided politics and advocated merely an individualistic, quietistic, passive strategy. See Horsley's summary of this foil on pp. 149–50.

And notice Horsley's comment that he agrees with John Howard Yoder—agrees that Jesus advocated a nonviolent strategy and with Yoder's criticism of those who think that that means Jesus was apolitical (164). Although Horsley has written at least a dozen articles arguing that the Zealots had not yet arrived on the scene by the time of Jesus, here he does not criticize Yoder and his Zealot thesis but at the same time does argue strenuously against Wink. The difference, I suggest, is that Yoder used the Zealot option to argue not that Jesus was apolitical but that he was indeed political, advocating an alternative political strategy. And Yoder's understanding of Jesus' political strategy has a clear emphasis on restoring economic justice, the Jubilee. See Yoder's footnote reference to Richard Horsley, in *The Politics of Jesus* (Grand Rapids, Mich.: Eerdmans, 1994), 55, 57. William Klassen has refuted Horsley on the Zealots in *The Wisdom of the Cross* (Grand Rapids, Mich.: Eerdmans, 2000), the Festschrift for Yoder.

3. Hengel writes that Jesus' alternative to the Zealot strategy was alleviating need, avoiding making a "social-ethical" appeal, and instead making a personal appeal directed to the individual conscience for living with inner freedom and joyous abandon. Martin

Hengel, *Was Jesus a Revolutionist?* (Philadelphia: Fortress Press, 1971), 20, 24–25, 27, 34.

4. See Swartley, *Love of Enemy and Nonretaliation in the New Testament*, 91; and Horsley, *Jesus and the Spiral of Violence*, passim.

5. Shortly after the publication of *The Politics of Jesus*, the Mennonite Central Committee organized a stimulating conference in Kansas City of scholars responding to the book. I was privileged to be invited to give one of the papers. I argued that Yoder would symbolize Jesus' concern about justice more effectively, and set it on a broader base, if he would base it not only on the Jubilee thesis but also on Jesus' repeated references to Isaiah and other prophets. I argued that many scholars would not agree with the Jubilee thesis but would agree with an Isaiah thesis or a prophetic thesis. I also assessed Yoder's criticisms of H. Richard Niebuhr. Yoder proposed that we do a series of dialogue lectures in three different locations and coauthor the book, *Authentic Transformation: A New Vision of Christ and Culture* (Nashville: Abingdon, 1996).

6. See pp. 104, 116, 125, in Swartley, *Love of Enemy and Nonretaliation in the New Testament*, for examples.

7. Wink, in Swartley, *Love of Enemy and Nonretaliation in the New Testament*, 133–34.

8. N. T. Wright, in Swartley, *Love of Enemy and Nonretaliation in the New Testament*, 156ff.

9. John Dominic Crossan, *The Historical Jesus* (San Francisco: HarperSanFrancisco: 1991), 218–20.

10. Ibid., 171–223 and 304.

11. Walter Wink, *Engaging the Powers: Discernment and Resistance in a World of Domination* (Minneapolis: Fortress Press, 1992), 113ff.

12. Gerd Theissen, *Social Reality and the Early Christians* (Minneapolis: Fortress Press, 1992), 10–13.

13. N. T. Wright, *Jesus and the Victory of God* (Minneapolis: Fortress Press, 1996), especially chs. 3, 5, and 9. See also E. P. Sanders, *Jesus and Judaism* (Philadelphia: Fortress Press, 1985), introduction and passim.

14. See especially Sanders, *Jesus and Judaism*, ch. 1.

15. Wright, *Jesus and the Victory of God*, 335, 61.

16. David Garland, *Mark: The NIV Application Commentary* (Grand Rapids, Mich.: Zondervan, 1996), 433–39.

17. Ibid., 438.

18. Ibid., 439.

19. Wright, *Jesus and the Victory of God*, 11. Some examples of pages where Wright shows the biblical witness to Jesus' acting in the tradition of the prophets are 93, 97, and 116, but the evidence is amassed throughout the book. Some pages where he discusses Jesus' announcement of the kingdom of God are 20–21, 40, 50, 72, 101–2.

20. Ibid., 164–65.

21. Ibid., 166–67.

22. Ibid., 167–68.

23. See Glen Stassen, *Just Peacemaking: Transforming Initiatives for Justice and Peace* (Louisville: Westminster John Knox, 1992), 71ff.

24. Based on his historical analysis of the most authentic sayings of Jesus, and focusing on the question of the timing of the kingdom, E. P. Sanders (*Jesus and Judaism*, ch. 4) presents six diverse but likely meanings of the timing of the kingdom of God. His

argument is that we cannot answer the question of timing with any certainty. "We cannot say clearly what is present—nor even precisely what he thought of as future, whether a new order or a cosmic cataclysm. . . . He may well have thought that 'the kingdom' in the sense of 'the power of God' was at work in the world, but that the time would come when all opposing power would be eliminated, and the kingdom of God in a somewhat different sense would 'come'—be ushered in." This "seems the most probable supposition" (152).

25. In his summary of his understanding of the historical Jesus, Richard Hays, *The Moral Vision of the New Testament* (San Francisco: HarperSanFrancisco, 1996), 163–64 and 166–67, emphasizes continuity with Israel, especially the prophets, and God's care for justice and judgment of injustice, especially care for justice in the sense of reversal for the poor and powerless, inclusion for the outcasts, and opposition to violence. This seems to me to be exactly right.

26. Wright, *Jesus and the Victory of God*, 221.

27. Ibid., 104.

28. Ibid., 128, 130.

29. Ibid., 128–33, 203–4, 207, 214, 221–24. See also See W. D. Davies, *The Territorial Dimension of Judaism* (Berkeley: University of California Press, 1982).

30. Ibid., 57. Wright's reference is to N. T. Wright, *The New Testament and the People of God* (Minneapolis: Fortress Press, 1992), 10.

31. You can see some of what I would say in *Just Peacemaking: Transforming Initiatives for Justice and Peace*, 38–42 and 71–77.

32. Wright, *Jesus and the Victory of God*, 214.

33. Hays, *Moral Vision of the New Testament*, 159–60.

34. See Sanders, *Jesus and Judaism*, 309ff., who argues that the chief priests had the leading political/religious role, presents evidence for the role of other powerful persons in Jerusalem, and shows conflicting evidence about the Pharisees while downplaying their role in the inner ruling hierarchy. Sanders also warns against taking polemical sources as accurate historical descriptions of the motives of those criticized. I am, rather, taking these passages as witnesses to the standards of justice the Jesus of the Gospels employed. They do fit Sanders's emphasis on covenant and restoration of Israel in continuity with the Hebrew Scriptures, plus Jesus' welcoming of sinners and outcasts.

35. Other passages are Matt 2:7ff., 13; 5:5-6; 12:17ff.; 13:24ff.; 15:18ff.; 21:37ff.; 23:34; Luke 3:10ff.; 4:28; 12:45ff.; 19:41. The temptation to worship and serve Satan surely entails some unjust way to get power, and in Jesus' context, it probably is the temptation of insurrection, as Yoder argues. Jesus' entering Jerusalem on a colt is symbolic fulfillment of the prophecy of the King of peace in Zech 9:9ff. His rejection of the sword in the garden and his going through his trial and crucifixion nonviolently are further evidence.

36. Wright, *Jesus and the Victory of God*, 195–96, 317, 321–36, and others.

37. Yoder, *The Politics of Jesus*; John Howard Yoder, *Body Politics: Five Practices of the Christian Community before the Watching World* (Scottdale, Pa.: Herald Press, 1997), 11ff.

38. In addition, we might count the following passages: Matt 5:42; 6:2, 19ff., 33; 12:7; Luke 1:52; 3:10ff.; 4:18; 6:20-21; 7:41ff.

39. Yoder, *Body Politics*, ch. 2.

40. Crossan, *Historical Jesus* (223 et passim), gives evidence that large numbers of the peasant class were being pushed down among the unclean, degraded, and expendable classes because of increasing indebtedness, because the wealthy needed ways to invest.

Wealth was being concentrated in Jerusalem, where the wealthy gathered excessive wealth by their dealings with the Pax Romana and their exploiting of the poor. Jesus contrasted with this by practicing meal-sharing on an egalitarian basis and a society of brotherhood with no rich or poor, distinctions of rank or status, or religious hierarchy, but instead communities of equal believers in a radically egalitarian way (262–64 and 298).

41. Other passages include Matt 13:24; 15:1ff.; 21:13; 23:23-25, 34; Mark 6:18; 8:15; 10:35ff.; 12:40; Luke 1:52; 3:5; 4:18; 13:10ff. And, finally, Jesus' trial and crucifixion were his confrontation of massive injustice in the form of domination by religious and political authority, Jewish and Roman.

42. Yoder, *Body Politics*, chs. 4 and 5.

43. Crossan, *Historical Jesus*, 320–32.

44. Wright, *Jesus and the Victory of God*, 191–92.

45. Ibid., 246.

46. Yoder, *Body Politics*, chs. 3 and 4.

47. Michael Walzer, "A Particularism of My Own," *RelSRev* 16, no. 3 (1990): 193–97.

48. John Howard Yoder, "Meaning after Babel: With Jeffrey Stout beyond Relativism," *JRE* (Spring 1996): 135n.

49. Michael Walzer, *Spheres of Justice: A Defense of Pluralism and Equality* (Cambridge, MA: Harvard University Press, 1984).

50. I have told a key part of the story of the free-church, Anabaptist-Baptist grounding of human rights prior to the Enlightenment in "Christian Origin of Human Rights," in *Just Peacemaking: Transforming Initiatives for Justice and Peace*. See Michael Walzer, *Revolution of the Saints* (Cambridge, MA: Harvard University Press, 1965). Some have misunderstood Walzer's understanding of justice to be merely conventional because of its grounding in particular narratives and have missed the transcultural dimension of human rights. I correct that misinterpretation in "Michael Walzer's Situated Justice," *JRE* (Fall 1994): 375–99. See also my "Narrative Justice as Reiteration," in *Ethics without Foundations* (ed. Mark Nation, Nancey Murphy, and Stanley Hauerwas; Nashville: Abingdon, 1995), 201-25.

51. Michael Walzer, *Obligations: Essays on Disobedience, War, and Citizenship* (New York: Simon & Schuster, 1970).

52. Wink, *Engaging the Powers*, 212–24.

# Index of Subjects

Anabaptists, 123, 124, 125, 174, 203n56, 215n78. *See also* Radical Reformation
apocalyptic, 116, 122, 126, 132, 161, 166–67, 168, 178, 194n22, 200n24, 203n64
baptism, baptismal, 78, 106, 107, 110, 125, 169, 170, 172, 205n75
Bell's Theorem, 24, 25, 27
capitalism, 7, 11, 37, 69, 113, 114ff., 119, 120, 123, 125, 189, 201n39, 202n46, 204n73, 205n75
charity and mutual aid, 109–10, 198n57
Christian epistemic practice, 91–93, 169
Christianity, early 10, 68, 97, 106–11, 197n35, 198n55
coercion, 12, 34–35, 55
community, 13, 26, 37, 40, 46, 56, 57, 61, 62, 90, 91–96, 102, 105, 106, 107, 110, 114, 119, 120, 121, 123–26, 133–35, 138, 140, 150, 151, 164–66, 168–74, 175, 192n22, 195n75, 196n34, 201n44, 206, 209, 212n38
    alternative, 140, 170
    church as, 124
    counter-community, 205n75
    covenant community, 123, 164, 166
    of goods, 123, 200n25, 202n49, 203n57, 205n75
    integrative, 174
    of love, 170
    redemptive, 90
    worshipping, 198n4
concealment, 8, 53–54, 56, 58, 113, 122
conflict resolution, 133–35, 144, 168, 206n14
creation, 1, 2, 5, 6, 9, 24–25, 26, 34, 35, 40, 44, 50, 53, 54, 56, 57, 58, 62, 64, 75, 98, 103, 198, 104, 107, 110, 149, 150, 209n22
crucifixion of Jesus, crucified, 10, 70–73, 90, 97, 100, 103, 104, 111, 121, 157, 161, 162, 165, 190, 212n36, 213n42
demonic, 51, 73, 80, 96–112, 193n9, 197n36

oppression, 99
power, forces, 12, 39, 51, 90, 98, 101, 102, 107, 148, 150
Powers, 104, 195n26
spell, 112
spirits, 98
structures, 69
Divine Warrior, 10, 96–97, 101, 105, 150, 194n15, 208n18
domination of nature, 57, 60–62
Domination System, 5, 35, 40, 47, 48, 50, 69, 72, 98, 101, 113, 116, 117, 122, 158, 160, 161, 173, 179, 198n2
economics, 7, 9–11, 29, 34, 40, 43, 56, 113–19, 121, 123–26, 134, 137, 158, 159, 169, 198, 202
epistemology, 9–10, 30, 84, 85, 87, 88, 91–92, 94
evil, 4, 7, 8, 9, 10, 11, 12, 19, 20, 26, 30, 46–49, 50–52, 70, 73–75, 80–83, 96–104, 97, 98, 106–12, 120, 122, 129, 130, 131, 133, 147–52, 154–56, 169, 184–86, 188, 193n9, 196n30, 204n74, 209n23
    absolute, 47
    God does not cause, 80
    human caused, 7
    powers of, 112, 150
    response to, 153–55
    retaliatory, 153, 208n20, 210n33
    spiral of, 8
    ultimate, 47
exorcism, 10, 25, 96–99, 106–7, 110–12, 161, 168, 192n3, 194n17, 197n39
fetishes, 45–48
forgive, forgiveness, 12, 100, 101, 102, 111–12, 134–36, 140, 163, 169, 202n55, 207n16
free church polity, 91–93, 160, 174
generative death anxiety, 7, 41–46, 160, 184
gospel, 4, 6, 7, 10, 11, 24, 27, 30, 70, 71, 90, 92, 98–101, 103, 110, 114, 118, 119, 141, 144, 148, 149, 163, 167, 178, 181, 192–96, 198n2, 204n75, 208n21, 210n33, 212n35

215

# Index of Names

# Index of Scripture